Multiculturalism, Educational Inclusion, and Connectedness

This book offers a unique focus on the well-being of Chinese and South/Southeast Asian students in the context of Hong Kong and in particular the experience of integrating these young people into its schooling system. Yuen uses a narrative method that captures and offers a vivid insight into the actual experience of students from disadvantaged backgrounds, whilst providing fascinating comparisons between students coming from Mainland China and those whose parents are South/Southeast Asian immigrants. Readers will be particularly interested in the attention given to spiritual well-being and how religious participation and affiliation make a difference in giving meaning to life and in creating a positive mindset, as viewed and explained by the students themselves.

This well-organised volume begins by laying out the major themes relating to the United Nations Convention on the Rights of the Child, followed by a richly elaborated theoretical chapter which defines core concepts and their interconnection. This is followed by substantive chapters where the voices of each of the different diverse groupings of students, Chinese Mainland immigrants, Chinese Cross-boundary youth, South/Southeast Asian ethnic youth and mainstream HK youth from underprivileged backgrounds, are heard and interpreted in relation to themes of inclusion and well-being. It then builds upon the narratives to provide bottom-up solutions and pathways towards the inclusion and well-being of all students, as well as the professional development of teachers who can take up the challenge of ensuring that all young people are nurtured to fulfil their potential.

Providing readers with practical implications and takeaways for education practice, this must-read work will appeal to a wide range of education practitioners and students involved in providing or researching inclusive education relating to mainstream and non-mainstream Chinese, South Asian, and other ethnic minority students.

Celeste Y.M. Yuen, PhD, is an Associate Professor of the Faculty of Education, and Associate Director of the Leadership Centre, the Hong Kong Institute of Educational Research at the Chinese University of Hong Kong. Celeste is also the President-elect of the Hong Kong Educational Research Association (2021). Celeste earned her doctorate from the UCL-IOC, University of London, UK.

Currently, she lectures in intercultural teacher education, school leadership, foundations of education and life and death education. Her research employs a mixed-method empirical approach to study interculturalism, Chinese immigrant and South Asian minority education, youth studies, well-being, religiosity and spirituality, and student engagement. Her scholarship in minority studies has been recognised locally and internationally, and has enabled her to win 20 projects funded by, for example, the Research Grants Council of Hong Kong, Education Bureau, Oxfam Hong Kong and HSBC, in each case as principal investigator. Celeste has authored multiple articles and books in these fields.

Routledge Research in Educational Equality and Diversity

Books in the series include:

The Hidden Academic Curriculum and Inequality in Early Education
How Class, Race, Teacher Interactions, and Friendship Influence Student Success
Karen Phelan Kozlowski

Applying Anzalduan Frameworks to Understand Transnational Youth Identities
Bridging Culture, Language, and Schooling at the US-Mexican Border
Edited by G. Sue Kasun and Irasema Mora-Pablo

Advancing Educational Equity for Students of Mexican Descent
Creating an Asset-based Bicultural Continuum Model
Edited by Andrea Romero and Iliana Reyes

The Lived Experiences of Filipinx American Teachers in the U.S.
A Hermeneutic Phenomenological Study
Eleonor G. Castillo

Multiculturalism, Educational Inclusion, and Connectedness
Well-Being, Ethnicity, and Identity among Chinese, South, and Southeast Asian Students
Celeste Y.M. Yuen

Counternarratives of Pain and Suffering as Critical Pedagogy
Disrupting Oppression in Educational Contexts
Edited by Ardavan Eizadirad, Andrew B. Campbell, and Steve Sider

Global Perspectives on Microaggressions in Higher Education
Understanding and Combating Covert Violence in Universities
Edited by Christine L. Cho and Julie K. Corkett

For more information about this series, please visit: www.routledge.com/Routledge-Research-in-Educational-Equality-and-Diversity/book-series/RREED

Multiculturalism, Educational Inclusion, and Connectedness
Well-Being, Ethnicity, and Identity among Chinese, South, and Southeast Asian Students

Celeste Y.M. Yuen

LONDON AND NEW YORK

First published 2022
by Routledge
4 Park Square, Milton Park, Abingdon, Oxon OX14 4RN

and by Routledge
605 Third Avenue, New York, NY 10158

*Routledge is an imprint of the Taylor & Francis Group,
an informa business*

© 2022 Celeste Y.M. Yuen

The right of Celeste Y.M. Yuen to be identified as author of this work has been asserted in accordance with sections 77 and 78 of the Copyright, Designs and Patents Act 1988.

All rights reserved. No part of this book may be reprinted or reproduced or utilised in any form or by any electronic, mechanical, or other means, now known or hereafter invented, including photocopying and recording, or in any information storage or retrieval system, without permission in writing from the publishers.

Trademark notice: Product or corporate names may be trademarks or registered trademarks, and are used only for identification and explanation without intent to infringe.

British Library Cataloguing-in-Publication Data
A catalogue record for this book is available from the British Library

Library of Congress Cataloging-in-Publication Data
A catalog record has been requested for this book

ISBN: 9781138343160 (hbk)
ISBN: 9781032271545 (pbk)
ISBN: 9780429439315 (ebk)

DOI: 10.4324/9780429439315

Typeset in Galliard
by KnowledgeWorks Global Ltd.

Contents

List of Illustrations ix
Foreword x
Preface xii
Acknowledgements xv

1. Equity, Access, and Obstacles in Education across the Globe 1
2. The Changing Student Demographics 19
3. Well-Being and Connectedness 36
4. Young People's Notion of Spirituality and Life Satisfaction 53
5. Teachers' Perspectives on the Civic Engagement of Chinese Immigrant and Non-Chinese Speaking (NCS) Students in Hong Kong 69
6. Inclusion and Rejection of Chinese Immigrant Students (CIS) 86
7. Belonging and (Dis)Connectedness of Chinese Cross-Boundary Students (CBS) in Hong Kong 101
8. Educational Assimilation and Inclusion of South/Southeast Asian Students 118
9. Aspirations of Mainstream Youth from Underprivileged Backgrounds in Post-Secondary Education 137

10 Wellness of Underprivileged Youth Approaching
   Post-Secondary Education and Career in Hong Kong   151

11 Connecting Youth, Promoting Well-Being, and
   Facilitating Productive Engagement for Equitable
   Schooling   167

12 Educating Teaching Professionals for Cultural
   Inclusion and Connectedness   185

13 Conclusion   202

   Index   205

List of Illustrations

Figure

3.1	Path Analysis on Factors Affecting Transcendental Well-Being	40

Tables

2.1	Population of Chinese immigrants and ethnic minority in Hong Kong in 2006, 2011, and 2016	20
2.2	Number of immigrant and minority students in Hong Kong between 2013 and 2020	20
2.3	Household income distribution by the selected ethnic household groups in 2016	24
3.1	Regression coefficients on Transcendental Well-Being	41
3.2	Probit regression coefficients on prayer frequency	41
3.3	Probit regression coefficients on religious activities frequency	42
3.4	Indirect effects to Transcendental Well-Being through prayer frequency	42
7.1	Profile of the cross-boundary students (CBS)	104
8.1	Profile of the non-Chinese speaking (NCS) students	122
12.1	Aspiring intercultural teacher education for a diverse Hong Kong society	194

Foreword

This volume focuses on Hong Kong and provides a unique example of an exploration of many aspects of well-being from spiritual to psychological to academic dimensions in a city whose multiculturalism is rooted in its history as a part of China that developed a unique identity under British colonial rule for 152 years and has attracted a considerable immigrant population from South Asia. The voices of four distinctive groups of students are heard throughout the book, local students who grew up with Cantonese as their mother tongue, students who immigrated to Hong Kong from Mainland China with Putonghua (Mandarin) as their mother tongue, students whose families live on both sides of the border, and students whose families had immigrated to Hong Kong from India, Pakistan, and other South Asian countries, for whom the learning of Chinese is a special challenge. The book draws upon the findings of three major research projects, from 2013 up to the present, which gave priority to hearing the voices of young people who found themselves marginalised and silenced in an education system tending to be somewhat regimented and oriented towards the needs of the mainstream Hong Kong population.

One of the striking features of the book is the dynamic way in which extensive quotations from individuals in each of these minority groups enable the reader to connect with their thinking and experience. Of particular significance is the recognition of the importance of spirituality in enabling these disadvantaged young people to find a degree of well-being as they seek to overcome the many obstacles they face. The differential degree to which this was evident in each of the demographic groups is also a fascinating finding. This is a study that looks at well-being in a holistic way with a core concern for educational reform that promotes equity, recognises the value of diversity, and makes possible genuine inclusion, such that each child and young person is enabled to become a well-rounded and responsible citizen of Hong Kong, of China, and of the global community. It also provides valuable insights for many aspects of teacher education and the nurturing of teachers who are able to support the fullest possible development of the rich potential in the identity of every student in ways that value diversity and foster intercultural understanding.

Given the ongoing stress of the pandemic and the strain this has imposed on the mental health of students at all levels, the focus of the book on a holistic understanding of well-being is particularly valuable and will be relevant to research on current educational challenges in multicultural communities around the world. The longitudinal character of the research, its clearly articulated conceptual frames, its rich empirical roots in extensive interviews with students themselves, and its detailed documentation and analysis of changing contexts are all exemplary.

Professor Ruth Hayhoe
Department of Leadership,
Higher & Adult Education (LHAE)
OISE, University of Toronto

Preface

Immigration and crossing borders for educational reasons are global social phenomena. Hong Kong is a dynamic Asian immigrant city and has been for more than a century. Yet, its ability to address and nurture immigrant and ethnic minority students for the future betterment of Hong Kong has been questioned. Hong Kong's future is inseparable from its vision for building an inclusive, connected, and sustainable society for people from all walks of life across ethnicities and races. The school remains the most critical organisation for preparing future citizens for a productive and meaningful engagement with life. In developing appropriate and comprehensive policies and practices, schools and educators need to understand the diverse nature of the school and civic engagement of both mainstream and non-mainstream students, especially those from underprivileged socio-economic backgrounds.

The non-mainstream students broadly fall into the following categories: Chinese immigrant students (CIS) from Mainland China, non-Chinese speaking (NCS) South/Southeast Asian students, and cross-boundary students (CBS) mostly coming from low socio-economic backgrounds. These student groups face a myriad of social, economic, linguistic, and cultural adjustments in mainstream schooling. Their educational outcomes are mixed and varied from group to group. Educators need to be informed on how individual and contextual factors contribute to the varied impacts on mainstream students, especially those from underprivileged backgrounds. The empirical findings of previous studies, namely the "Educational Experiences, Self Identity and Spirituality: A Study on the Well-Being among Students from Diverse Cultures in Hong Kong" (RGC Ref. No. 844812), "Engagement of Immigrant and Minority Students with Schools and Civil Society" (RGC Ref. No. HKIEd 8005-PPR-12), and "Transition from Secondary to Post-secondary Education: Access, Obstacles, and Success Factors of Immigrant, Minority and Low Income Youth in Hong Kong" (RGC Ref. No. 18606717) have confirmed that engagement with school and society is segmented across the immigrant and mainstream student groups.

These studies yielded some surprising and unforeseen results. They showed that contrary to conventional understanding and intuition, underprivileged South/Southeast Asian immigrants scored higher life satisfaction, spiritual well-being, and engagement with school and society than their Chinese mainstream and immigrant counterparts. Conversely, mainstream students scored lower levels of life satisfaction and wellness than expected across the board. The case for the Chinese immigrants was even more worrying. They scored the lowest in most areas and their life satisfaction turned out to be particularly low. These wide-ranging results concerning wellness are linked with cultural values (e.g., South Asians are naturally optimistic and Chinese are self-critical) and are related to spiritual well-being (e.g., self-perceived purpose and meaning of life, which goes beyond one's religious affiliation). Religious, ethnic minority students reported higher life satisfaction and well-being scores, and yet they also perceived more cultural and financial barriers in accessing post-secondary education (PSE) compared with their mainstream peers.

Hong Kong mainstream students (HKMS) have gone through a period of sociopolitical transition leading many to a negative and unproductive mindset such as losing hope, especially after the social unrest of 2019. Thousands of students have been arrested, and many have suffered from an array of post-traumatic stress disorders triggered by intensive conflict and confrontation. During the preparation of this manuscript, Hong Kong society has recorded a peak of emigration directly linked to the troubles and their aftermath. The anti-government protests of 2014 and 2019 have consistently led HKMS to a sense of disillusionment and vulnerability about the future. At the time of concluding the book, Hong Kong is at full stretch to battle with the unprecedented surge of the fifth wave of the COVID-19 epidemic. The support from Mainland China is both critical and timely. Looking ahead, with the implementation of the National Security Law (Hong Kong) in July 2020, the subsequent electoral system change, and merge with the Greater Bay Area, Hong Kong society is entering the second stage of sociopolitical transition. Such significant societal changes and development concern the HKMS and their immigrant and ethnic minority peers. Hence addressing youth's wellness and instilling hope for desirable futures is paramount to preparing them for a positive and productive engagement in the new society.

The book's contents

The organisation of this book is centred around several key aspects of the global well-being and engagement of Hong Kong youth, namely spiritual wellness, academic wellness, school engagement, civic engagement, sense of belongingness and inclusiveness, and post-secondary education (PSE) aspirations. The book begins by introducing why youth matters in today's Hong Kong society. Chapter two provides an overview of the multicultural student groups in mainstream schooling and their associated wellness and engagement issues. Chapters 3 and 4 underline the theoretical groundings of spiritual health and life satisfaction and the assessment of students on their spiritual wellness. Chapter 5 discusses youth civic engagement from a teacher's perspective. Chapters 6–10 interrogate the lived experiences of each of the student groups with a specific focus. Chapter 6 probes the educational inclusion and self-identity of CIS.

Chapter 7 investigates the sense of belongingness and connectedness of CBS. Chapter 8 appraises the educational assimilation of NCS South and Southeast Asian students. Chapter 9 discusses the aspirations of HKMS for PSE. And Chapter 10 examines the wellness of Hong Kong Diploma of Secondary Education (HKDSE) students. Drawing upon the insights from previous chapters, Chapter 11 summarises the essential wellness and engagement issues and discusses implications for the senior secondary education curriculum. Chapter 12 discusses youth wellness and engagement issues with reference to teacher preparation by highlighting the role of intercultural competence. Finally, Chapter 13 concludes the book by underlining the changing society and perspectives on youth development.

Acknowledgements

This book is one of the consequences of the qualitative findings generated from four government-funded projects (GRF 18606717, GRF 18406214, GRF 844812, and HKIEd 8005-PPR-12). Hence, I wish to express gratitude for the generous funding support of the Research Grants Council of the University Grants Committee of Hong Kong. The rich interview data were collated from several hundred youth from both mainstream and non-mainstream cultures and diverse socio-economic backgrounds between 2013 and 2021. My deepest thanks, therefore, go to the youth who have readily talked to me about how they coped with aversive circumstances in a high-stake education system whilst struggling with self-identity, connectedness, and aspirations for the future within an uncertain context. I am also indebted to the long-term professional friends, principals, teachers, collaborators, and colleagues from all the participating secondary schools, research units, and higher education institutions. Without their partnership, thoughtful coordination, and professional dialogues, it would not be possible for me to have gained a deep understanding of their students.

My deep appreciation goes to my research team, Professors Alan C.K. Cheung, Moosung Lee, Sam C.S. Leung, Timothy W.W. Yuen, and Hayes H.H. Tang, for their long-term professional partnership and friendship. I must also express my gratitude to my wonderful colleagues for their reliable assistance in various research projects, especially Sit Yeung, Chunlan Gao, Lynn Yuan, Alex Zhuang, and William Leung. In addition, my heartfelt thanks go to Professor Ruth Hayhoe for her insightful comments on the earlier draft and for the spiritual partnership she has provided. Last but not least, I wish to thank Mr. David John Eason for checking the manuscripts and for his inspiration, prayer support, and encouragement throughout the book project.

1 Equity, Access, and Obstacles in Education across the Globe

Introduction

The inception of this book began with a vision and mission to promote a productive and meaningful life for youth in Hong Kong from diverse cultural backgrounds. As the society is undergoing an era of rapid change and facing multiple unprecedented challenges since the post-1997 handover, and under the rule of "One Country, Two Systems", youth engagement in schools and society reflects the level of inclusion and connectedness of each youth in the society. I consider myself privileged to have had the opportunity to interact personally and intensively with hundreds of youth from both mainstream and non-mainstream cultures during the past decade. Our conversations were held during their free school time and participation was voluntary. Since 2013, I have engaged in numerous person–person interviews with youth as part of my data collection for several public and government-funded projects. A large proportion of narratives were generated through a project entitled, Educational experiences, self-identity and spirituality: A study on the well-being among students from diverse cultures in Hong Kong (RGC 18406214, 2015–2017). Another batch of interview data was generated from my recent conversations with senior secondary students participating in my project entitled, Transition from secondary to post-secondary education: Obstacles, and success factors of immigrant, minority and low-income youth in Hong Kong (RGC 18606717, 2018–2021). Aiming to examine students' self-appraised educational experiences, ethnic identities, spiritual lifestyles, and global well-being, these interviews revolved around several personal issues, ranging from personal to societal issues.

    Students shared their profound thoughts on life issues and deep emotions about family, friendships, academic stress, intercultural learning, and interethnic group conflicts and future aspirations in many dialogues. With a sense of trust, they often poured out their hearts to this "stranger listener" (me) in the belief that our paths would never cross again, and hence their identities would be protected (pseudonyms were used). Throughout these face-to-face or small group interviews or conversations, I was truly humbled, thankful, and inspired by their

DOI: 10.4324/9780429439315-1

deep thoughts about life, dedication to learning, commitment to family welfare, aspirations for serving the community, and resilience in overcoming negative life experiences. Of course, in some cases, I was also concerned with their academic disengagement, struggles with parental issues (especially for students born from HK-Mainland Chinese families), financial needs, lack of direction, and a sense of despair at approaching adulthood. Gradually, I connected with some of them as a friend by just being someone who listened. To me, these youth have multiple roles in our contemporary and interconnected society. As Hong Kong citizens, they are the backbone of Hong Kong's future. As Chinese citizens, they are pillars of the wider nation. As global citizens, they have the potential to become cultural bridges for global development. In a sense, they represent all societies' talents, and, hence, it is imperative to equalise the educational conditions for all students, especially youth from an immigrant or ethnic minority background.

Youth matters

Youth in family, society building, and global development have gained renewed attention on all fronts. Traditionally, scholars (e.g., Knight, 2017) focus on stage development and associated characteristics and responsibilities, while sociologists (e.g., Apple, 1996) devote their attention to youth identity and roles in society as individuals and members of that society. Today, international attention is directed towards creating conditions for empowering youth for their present and future development (UNESCO, 2015, 2016, 2017). With the advancement of information technology and the influence of social media, societies are increasingly interconnected and inter-dependent. What happens in one society will have an impact on others, no matter what the distance is. Under the influence of globalisation, western ideologies of liberalism, democracy, equity, cultures, and norms have also travelled worldwide and are gradually being disseminated as universal values, as can be seen, for example, in growing demands for democracy and human rights worldwide.

By virtue of having one foot in adolescence and the other in adulthood, youth are agentive in co-constructing universal values and serving as ambassadors for such values in their societies. To a large extent, we cannot fully comprehend their aspirations, identity, and roles in society by following stereotypical portrayals of youth. For example, they may fall into rigid social categories such as being academically focused vs. disengaged, innovative and open-minded vs. self-centred and self-focused, productive vs. disillusioned, civic-minded vs. rebellious, and so on. But in today's world, youth are also treading new ground and exploring new opportunities, which in turn generate new risks and anxieties. More importantly, they express a deep desire to be understood and supported and to be able to contribute to the broader society. The world has recently witnessed a series of youth movements in different forms involving social concerns such as climate change, civic engagement, and political advocacy, with influences moving around the world and, to some degree, observed in every connected society. Parallel to this global phenomenon is the generation of heated debates on maximising the talent and worth of the youth for the best interest of each society and the world.

Global popularisation of equity in education

Youth research is gaining global attention (Ball et al., 2000; Eglinton, 2013; Shek, 2020; Spratt, 2017; Yuen, 2019). Today's youth are tomorrow's leaders of all nations. To make any society sustainable, young people must be prepared for tomorrow's world. All civil societies have moral obligations to provide youth with conditions conducive to nurturing their potentialities and value their participation. Under a culture of marketisation in education, it requires more deliberated government efforts to raise the academic standards of public schooling to address equity education for all. The United Nations Convention on the Rights of the Child (United Nations, 1989) has drawn worldwide attention to the importance of addressing the rights and entitlements and equal access of every child regardless of their socio-economic background, religion, language, sex, or ethnic background. Equity and equal opportunity in education have been recognised as essential children's rights under the Convention.

Education as a public good and its outcomes directly bear civil society (Levin, 1987). Education and equity are two sides of the same coin. On the one hand, education must be made universal for all school-age children, especially those from disadvantaged families who often cannot afford school fees and with multiple challenges in life. On the other hand, to equalise the conditions of all people, equity must be ensured to make education as fair, just, and impartial as possible and with access to all (Jacob & Holsinger, 2008). Equity addresses the "normative-ethical issue of the fair attribution/acquisition of resources" (Hutmacher, 2001; p. 10) and is a global agenda advocating for providing inclusive and equitable quality education to help realise the rights and capacities of all people, without leaving anyone behind (United Nations, 2015a).

Despite numerous global policy initiatives enabling equal access of all students to the education system, high exclusion rates of primary and lower secondary education remain a prominent issue to be tackled in regions like sub-Saharan Africa and southern Asia (UNESCO, 2016). The Education 2030 Framework for Action calls for 12 years of free and equitable quality primary and secondary education for children and adolescents, with at least 9 years of compulsory education (United Nations, 2015b). Currently, in many countries in Africa and Asia, senior secondary education is still not compulsory. Huge funds are needed annually to enrol all youth in secondary education globally (UNESCO, 2016).

The above data concerning education access and outcomes reveal immense challenges in ensuring equity education at the global level. A large portion of children and youth are battling with social, economic, and political adversities and encountering tremendous obstacles in schooling due to interruptions and/or poor education (UNESCO, 2016). There is ample evidence to suggest that school attendance rates, participation levels, and academic performance of disadvantaged children are severely affected by the need to divert time and energy towards earning, consequently impacting their academic success (e.g., Holgado et al., 2014). For example, child labour is still common in Tanzania and vulnerable populations with poor living conditions (Levison et al., 2018).

Equity and equality in educational practice

Equity in education stands at the intersection of two issues: (1) enabling equal access of all learners to receive a quality education and (2) ensuring equal learning outcomes. In the equality of enrolment, quality is also a necessary condition for making education a driving force in achieving Sustainable Development Goals (SDGs). Fairness and inclusion are two dimensions of equity in education (Simon et al., 2007). Inclusion at its lowest level means the opportunity for all to obtain basic literacy and numeracy skills (Simon et al., 2007), yet this would merely be the beginning of the process towards equal access at all levels in the SDG4 agenda (United Nations, 2015b). Fairness and justice, regardless of individual social status, are the foundations of equitable access and outcomes for all. Equity in access is measured by the extent to which resources have been distributed and how they are used, and how opportunities are offered and administered to students. From a cultural relativist perspective and/or a pluralist sociological perspective, a major issue here is that schools can both uphold existing inequalities and produce new inequalities in the educational process (Benadusi, 2001) for resource redistribution.

Worldwide, disproportions in educational outcomes are associated with inequalities in social status, gender, ethnic status, race, inborn capabilities, and other social conditions. Students from affluent families are better nurtured in physical health, educational opportunities, and holistic development than their underprivileged counterparts. Social inequality involves multiple layers of social structural problems, and it is unrealistic to expect education to reverse the entire disadvantaged conditions of the under-served families. Despite the fact that education alone cannot alleviate structural social inequality, nevertheless, education is a vital instrument in making a significant impact on reversing the disadvantaged communities by working with different agencies (Mortimore & Whitty, 1999). Education is value-laden and has a function for social reproduction, which contributes to strengthening the status quo. Studies (Bourdieu, 1973; Harris & Halpin, 2002) have consistently confirmed that both social class and race/ethnicity are key factors contributing to the social and educational inequalities facing socially disadvantaged student groups. A disadvantaged group may be characterised by various identities or intersectionality, which prevents them from upward social mobility due to the mediation effect of a glass ceiling. Immigrant, ethnic minority, and low-income mainstream students are typical examples facing multiple disadvantages and suffering from a greater intersectionality effect (Guittar & Guittar, 2015; Stockfelt, 2018). Home factors (Lareau, 2000) are a primary source of inequality in educational outcomes, creating either advantaged or disadvantaged learning and development conditions. Students from low-income families do not have much prior knowledge of higher education and feel alienated from the culture of HEIs, which may defeat their aspiration for post-secondary education (PSE).

Education, belongingness, and well-being

School is second to home for students. The Hong Kong education system consists of 3-year kindergarten, 6-year primary (P1–P6), and 6-year secondary education. This book concentrates on discussing the wellness and engagement of the senior secondary students, from secondary four (S4) to secondary six (S6), and the first-year college students. Student engagement is a vibrant topic in educational studies because academic success gives an impetus to social and economic advancement. Researchers are keen to understand the mechanism of enhancing motivation and learning effectiveness (Christenson et al., 2012). Viewed from a psychological approach, Voelkl (2012) argues that appreciation and recognition from teachers can greatly enhance students' sense of belonging and connectedness with the school. Granted with such intrinsic gratification, they will value learning more and invest more in coursework.

Belongingness is defined as "feelings that one is a significant member of the school community, is accepted and respected in school, has a sense of inclusion in school, and includes school as part of one's self-identification" (Voelkl, 1996, as cited in Voelkl, 2012; p. 195). Promoting a sense of belonging is crucial to unlocking disengagement at school and allowing learning to flourish. Students who have developed a strong sense of belonging take pride in the school, engage in self-directed learning, and demonstrate a greater sense of positive development in their academic success. Identification with school raises students' sense of belonging, gives them pleasure in academic work, and develops academic competence and self-gratification.

Education and life chances are integrated components. Hence, publicly funded education, significantly higher education, is seen as an arena for reducing inequality and accelerating the vertical social mobility of young people (Hazelkorn & Gibson, 2019). Higher education institutions are accountable for the equality in educational outcomes of their diversified student population. Following a growing demand for the internationalisation of higher education, there is a corresponding responsibility incumbent upon higher education to equip students for the interconnected and complex global world. Certain aspects of the discussion and investigation are inevitably coloured by political interests and considerations (Cameron & Daga, 2018).

First-year college students are in a crucial transition phase interwoven with identity reconstruction changes and adjustment to their new role in higher education (O'Donnell et al., 2016). This makes them prone to emotional problems (Amirkhan & Velasco, 2019). There is a growing concern about the discrepancy in first-year student success in higher education, with educational success typically indicating achievement (Van der Zanden et al., 2018). Viewed from the transition theory, Kahu and Nelson (2018) analyse the factors behind the failure of higher education to provide remedial measures for first-year college students in the beginning year to improve the retention rate.

From global to local policy enactment

Hong Kong has undergone a unique historical and sociopolitical development, from being a former British colony to becoming a Special Administrative Region (SAR) of China in 1997. Under the "One Country, Two Systems" rule introduced by the Chinese government following the merger, the socio-economic fabric of the SAR has been kept intact for the last two decades. Under this system, the capitalist SAR remains very sensitive and greatly affects global and Mainland Chinese sociopolitical developments. The colonial past facilitated close ties between the SAR and the English-speaking world and increased the impact of global values on its development, especially in education. For instance, to align with the international drive for inclusive and equitable education, a series of education reforms have been launched to address the rights-based educational goals with the No Child Left Behind principle as emphasised by the SDG4 (United Nations, 2015b). The enactment of the Hong Kong Racial Discrimination Ordinance in 2008 was a milestone in addressing equity issues in education. It was the first document highlighting equal opportunities for the enrolment of students in public sector schools. Investment in education has also been increased and in 2018–19 stood at around 20% of total government expenditure. A certain proportion of these resources have been allocated to help the socially disadvantaged mainstream Chinese, Chinese immigrant students (CIS), and South and Southeast Asian students co-educated with their mainstream peers. Such issues will be examined in greater detail in the following.

Language and equity

In the SAR, language ability is the crux of the social and educational integration barrier for NCS students as for CIS, but in different ways. The policies of biliteracy (Chinese and English) and trilingualism (Cantonese, English and Putonghua) around Language in Hong Kong come with different demands on the three groups. Apart from the instrumental value of the Chinese Language for NCS students to obtain high education awards, Chinese Language skills are also crucial for them to be fully integrated with society through mainstream education pathways and professional development. Even though some of the Hong Kong-born NCS students can hold sophisticated Cantonese conversations without hindrance they usually fail in the academic (reading and writing) Chinese. The minimum requirement for students to be admitted to tertiary education is level 2 in the Chinese Language in the Hong Kong Diploma of Secondary Education (HKDSE) examination. However, parents of NCS students who are either illiterate or lack sufficient Chinese proficiency cannot offer conducive Chinese learning support to their children at home (Law & Lee, 2012; Oxfam

Hong Kong, 2014). The weak Chinese foundation of NCS students has been recognised as a significant impediment to their educational success (Leung, 2019; Loh & Hung, 2020). Annie is one typical example.

> I have been wasting a whole year since attempting the DSE examination in 2018. I had confidence in passing all DSE subjects except the Chinese Language. Unfortunately, I was so nervous about the Chinese examination that I missed it. What happened was that I had gotten very sick and had a fever on the examination day. As I was absent in the listening and speaking papers my confidence in attempting the Chinese written examination paper dissolved. In the end, I got a 'U' (unclassified grade) for that. Even the local Chinese students would have found the ancient Chinese paper challenging, not to mention NCS students like me. It was just beyond me.

Annie is a Hong Kong-born Indonesian. Despite speaking very local-accented Cantonese, she left her secondary education without recognised credentials for PSE. To pass the time and to finance her daily expenses after leaving school, she works part-time as a waitress and cashier. Her future direction is yet to be clarified. Annie's language impediment may seem very tough, but it is not uncommon among the NCS students in Hong Kong.

By contrast, despite being ethnic Chinese, the CIS encounter difficulties in language proficiency in learning. In Mainland China, the medium of instruction (MOI) is Putonghua, whereas classes in mainstream Hong Kong schools are mainly conducted in Cantonese and English. Take the case of Jiayuan as an example. Jiayuan received primary five education in Mainland China before accompanying his mother to join his father in Hong Kong. Ever since he immigrated to Hong Kong, however, his life began to break apart. Due to financial problems and expectation discrepancies, the parents broke up, and he encountered tough trajectories in learning the local dialect, Cantonese, and academic English. He recounted that:

> I had no courage even to open my mouth to buy a soft drink in Cantonese when I first arrived in Hong Kong. My classmates excluded me because of my accented Cantonese. Absolutely discouraging. I had no clue what was going on during the class, as it was conducted in Cantonese. At that time, I was really at the edge of giving everything up. My English has been failing me consistently ever since my first day of Hong Kong schooling. My English foundation is simply too weak. This, too, made me want to give it all up.

Self-efficacy is a vital factor for overcoming language barriers. As Jiayuan elaborated:

> I didn't think there was any hope for me to pass English because my standard was far below the benchmark. But currently, I have started to listen to English songs and hope this will raise my listening ability and improve my reading ability in English lessons.

Student motivation is a known mediating factor affecting academic achievements across all ability groups and cultural backgrounds. This is related to the how and what questions about helping students with different learning styles, strengths, and needs. As indicated previously, language proficiency is essential for immigrant and minority students to improve their academic achievement and promote meaningful social integration (Wong, 2014). Recent educational policy initiatives have concentrated on language enhancement for CIS and NCS students. School allocation placement is an example. Upon their arrival in the SAR, all new immigrant students, regardless of their racial, linguistic, and ethnic backgrounds, are given an option to join a full-time six-month Initiation Programme prior to the subsidised mainstream education. Alternatively, all first-time admissions to mainstream school students are entitled to a part-time government-subsidised 60-hour Induction Programme offered by a non-governmental organisation (NGO). Language is integral to learning. Both programmes place a strong emphasis on raising the new immigrant students' Chinese and/or English language proficiency. As an added benefit, this also increases their sense of belonging to the city by connecting them with society. In order to enrich the English learning environment of these newly arrived students, all public sector secondary schools are allowed to exercise greater flexibility by introducing different MOI arrangements to suit the language readiness.

Research offers conflicting findings on the issue of school allocation placement and language learning for NCS students. On the one hand, research (Yuen & Lee, 2013) suggests that placing NCS students in schools with a high percentage (50% or above) of co-ethnic peers promotes a sense of connectedness and a high level of satisfaction with life and school. On the other hand, studies (Hong Kong Unison, 2013) argue that such placements are a kind of segregated education that discourages improvement in Chinese language skills and reinforces complacency with regard to low levels of Chinese language proficiency. In mainstream schools where Chinese is the MOI and the first language of all students is Chinese, the standard of Chinese language is high. However, schools with high concentrations of NCS students usually adopt a lower standard Chinese and seldom teach for a robust understanding of Chinese among the NCS students. Furthermore, without parallel home support, learning Chinese in the absence of an immersive environment is extremely difficult, as this fails to boost students' expectations in themselves and kills motivation to integrate more into mainstream society (Burkholder, 2013).

Language may well be the critical issue in cultivating the talents of CIS and NCS students fully. Funding and educational subsidies have allowed schools to provide more learning support to boost these students' language competence. Nevertheless, public expenditure has not solved all the systematic obstacles, as many of these students fall short of the academic benchmark and fail to achieve their academic goals.

Under the impacts of neoliberalism, standardisation, and accountability, classroom pedagogy remains largely test-score oriented, and catering for educational diversity remains only a paper policy in many mainstream schools (Kennedy, 2012). As a result, meeting the educational needs of these students in Hong Kong remains an unsolved and debated issue. Before such an elusive issue can be resolved, the key factors influencing the pursuit of equal educational opportunities among CIS and NCS students need to be re-examined based upon the students' perceptions.

Family capital and language

Family background and parental support have been identified as key factors affecting the academic engagement outcomes of Chinese students in Chinese societies. As Bourdieu (1973) argues, education is understood as a means for vertical social mobility and cultural capital. The Chinese parents desire to have a high return from their educational investment in their child(ren). Moreover, under the influence of the Confucian heritage culture, excelling in public, academic examinations will mean glorifying their family and ancestors. Huang and Gove (2015) opines that these mixed interests drive the Chinese parents to pin their "only" hope on their children's educational success. Education in Hong Kong is seen as a race between the "have" and "have not" parents. The former is more than willing to pay more for their child(ren) to get extra homework and additional private tutorial lessons. Studies (Chu, 2019) show homework is positively connected with academic outcomes for senior students. However, parental expectations on academic achievement impose immense pressure upon Hong Kong students, which has been the case for decades (Chu, 2019; Tse, 1994).

As the immigrant and minority groups overlap with the low-income group, the home disadvantage is a huge obstacle to overcome (Yuen, 2018a, 2019). Entering into a digital learning era and under the threat of the unprecedented COVID-19 pandemic, the gap between home support for e-Learning has been further widened (The University of Hong Kong, 2020). As learning goes online during the prolonged suspension of in-person schooling, electronic devices have become crucial components to stay connected with school and the wider community and receive learning, conduct research, and submit homework. Students who are competent in digital learning and have full access to electronic technologies are undoubtedly in an advantageous condition. In contrast, students at the other end of the scale suffer from a digital divide, falling short in this regard with either a lack of equipment, skill deficiency, or money to afford internet charges (Garcia et al., 2020). Moreover, research (Oxfam Hong Kong, 2014) shows that low-income South Asian families are unaware of what kind of government support is available to their children. Only a small percentage of them surf the websites or visit the district offices of the Education Bureau (EDB) in person to seek information. To a large extent, these families do not have the computer and language skills necessary to access relevant resources. Again, home disadvantage matters.

Language defines success and failure

The need for competence in Chinese for both education and the workplace has been given an increasingly high priority since the HKSAR establishment in 1997, when the mother-tongue language policy was mandated in secondary schools. The mother-tongue language refers to Cantonese that is spoken by the majority of Hong Kong Chinese. However, the implementation of the mother-tongue language policy received much criticism from the general public (Hong Kong Unison, 2018). This was exacerbated by the fact that the number of secondary schools allowed to adopt English as the MOI (EMI) was downsized to 25%. By default, the rest were classified as Chinese MOI (CMI) secondary schools. This created a divisive system in that the unspoken perception was and still is that EMI schools are superior and CMI schools are inferior, whereas what was wanted was equal access to both languages. Research findings have underlined how students from EMI schools obtain greater English listening competence than their CMI counterparts due to their greater exposure to English (Coniam, 2009). Such a controversial and coercive policy magnifies structural inequalities between privileged and the underprivileged student groups in the society (Kan & Adamson, 2010). Even though the policy had been fine-tuned to allow junior secondary students to learn English in most subjects progressively, given the strong connection between the use of MOI and school performance, the discriminatory and exclusive effects of the policy on the students remain (Cheng, 2017).

A further consequence of the mother-tongue policy in Hong Kong, as Law and Lee (2012) have noted, is that this works against the government's commitment to multiculturalism by imposing exclusion and inequity within mainstream classrooms. This affects NCS students more than other groups as their languages are more distinct from the mainstream. Cunanan (2011) argues cogently that it is essential to assimilate all NCS into mainstream society and to strengthen their identity with the Mainland China. However, NCS families are bewildered in coping with Chinese, from understanding school notices to formal curriculum learning and informal communications with the school and the education system. With the growing emphasis on the Chinese language as a success factor in school and beyond, the current assessment and secondary school placement system places NCS students in a disadvantageous situation. It is already a common perception that NCS students are "inactive" as an ethnic group in Hong Kong. But researchers (Shum et al., 2016) reveal that these language hurdles are just too difficult for NCS students to overcome and so in many instances, they choose to be passive, silent, and invisible. More importantly, the policy is de facto a policy of segregation in that it pushes NCS students to cluster together in an understandable response to fears of acculturation. Out of 870 mainstream schools, 60% of NCS students are educated in just 30 schools. To cope with the language problem, NCS students tend to form ghettos in particular schools with a high concentration of co-ethnic peers and hang out together after school with their circle of friends. In this regard, Hong Kong Unison (2018) has filed an international complaint of "de facto segregation", citing the mother-tongue policy as diminishing the motivation of NCS students to mingle with mainstream peers and mainstream society.

Expansion of post-secondary education

In positioning itself to be an education hub in Asia, Hong Kong has experienced a rapid expansion of its PSE during the past decade and provides learning opportunities for more than 60% of HKDSE graduates. Such expansion was achieved mainly by offering self-financed two-year associate degree programmes (Kember, 2010). In addition, the rise of inclusive practices in post-secondary institutions (PSIs) has changed the landscape of PSE from an elite to a mass education system. Consequently, there has been a sharp increase in the intake of low-income HKMS, CIS, NCS students, and those with special educational needs (SEN), especially in self-financed and privately funded programmes and/or PSIs. As the student cohort has diversified, PSIs have more salient roles in society regarding access and participation, affordability and employability, graduate attributes, and the socio-economic impact of PSE.

The learning gap between students from low-income and high-income families in higher education is also widening. The fact is that PSE does not offer the same experience nor the same rewards for all students. Instead, each PSI seeks geopolitical significance to serve its unique mission and vision (University Grants Committee, 2019a). As university admissions hinge on HKDSE results, students in higher-band secondary schools were more likely to receive additional tutoring (free and paid) than their counterparts in lower-band schools. High parental expectations usually pressurise the former while the latter suffers from inadequate home attention and support. Elite students from privileged families are clustered in the research-intensive universities, whilst underprivileged students tend to cluster in self-financed, private, or vocational-oriented PSIs.

The segmented educational pathways of these under-represented groups lead to stratified educational and career outcomes. Unlike in the West, their educational experience and global well-being, especially in the first transitioning year, has not been given sufficient and comprehensive research attention in Hong Kong. Several local studies have highlighted that these under-represented groups in varying degrees are commonly confronted with more obstacles and fewer choices before, during, and after their PSE as compared to their affluent local Chinese counterparts (Kember, 2010). Particularly, CIS lack confidence and financial support in pursuing PSE (Yuen, 2019 & 2018a). SEN students struggle for institutional support to overcome their handicapping conditions (Siu, Tong & Lai, 2017), and EM students feel isolated in PSIs due to the language problem and the lack of social and cultural capital (Chu, 2019; Gao, 2019; Yuen, 2018a). All these empirical findings underscore the urgent need for understanding and closing the equity gaps in PSE. In this regard, only a holistic and collaborative institutional research drawing upon the synergies of each investigator can offer a big enough dataset and the depth of understanding necessary to inform a solution to the inequalities of local higher education.

Enabling access, overcoming barriers

Aiming at promoting the retention and reducing attrition rates of PSIs, Bowles et al. (2014) have examined the facilitators and obstacles in the transition to higher education. They categorise the facilitators into two groups, student-centred enablers and university-led enablers. Student-centred enablers include positive learning attitudes, eagerness to seek help, and willingness to assimilate into the institutional culture, while university-led enablers include the policy of promoting student participation and a sense of belonging. Research shows that EM students face a feeling of isolation or alienation in a higher education institution resulting from the institutional culture and/or distance between lecturers and students (Bunce et al., 2019). Others may experience discriminatory manners and treatment from lecturers, implicit or otherwise, which may hamper their learning incentive and outcomes in higher education (Urdan & Bruchmann, 2018). In Hong Kong, individual immigrant and EM students have diverse views on social discrimination and educational inclusion. The following chapters will examine these issues together with interview data.

The enhancement of educational quality, diversity, and inclusion policy will bring benefits and improvements to society. Education contributes to poverty reduction, gender equity, and the establishment of an equitable society. Inclusive and human rights imperatives drive equality education in the global policy discourse (UNESCO, 2016). As such, the government needs a more efficient public policy to equalise the conditions of public schooling and to level the playing field between the privileged and the underprivileged; instead of letting the schools compete for their market niches (Levin, 1987). This talent management strategy has been adopted by various societies aiming to equip young people with the necessary skills and knowledge for social and economic advancement and social cohesion by integrating minorities and immigrant populations in moving towards a harmonious society (Simon et al., 2007).

The following chapters will further elaborate that the Hong Kong education system has been criticised as non-responsive and discriminatory against students from non-mainstream and/or socio-culturally poor conditions (Yuen, 2018b). There is an absence of a systematic school-based policy or provision for CIS to alleviate their educational difficulties (Yuen, 2018a). They include cultural differences, insufficient Chinese or English Language proficiency and readiness leading, overage school placement, repeating class, different learning approaches in language subjects, financial difficulties, and domestic issues/tragedies (Zhang & Ting, 2011). In response to the issues above, The Chinese Language Curriculum Second Language Learning Framework was introduced in primary and secondary schools with supporting learning and teaching materials and assessment tools for NCS students (Education Bureau, 2019). To facilitate the implementation of the learning framework, the EDB increased the additional recurrent funding provided to all schools, admitting ten or more NCS students. Eligible NCS students could also apply for a subsidy to attain internationally recognised alternative Chinese Language qualifications (e.g., GCSE Chinese). Critical to note that Applied Learning Chinese is necessary for admission to University Grants Committee (UGC)-funded institutions and PSIs, including those of the Vocational Training Council (VTC) (e.g., Institute of Vocational Education/IVE) (Education Bureau, 2020a).

Recently, the government has also regulated the language standards for their admission to PSE. For example, schools can adopt a new Chinese Language framework for NCS students as second language learning provided by the EDB.

In contrast, NCS students can choose an Applied Learning (Chinese Language) subject recognised by the Qualification Framework of the HKDSE. Students are also eligible to join the subsidy scheme to take the Chinese examination under the General Certificate of Secondary Education (GCSE), International General Certificate of Secondary Education (IGCSE), and General Certificate of Education (GCE) for PSE admission. In addition, secondary schools also receive financial support for teaching Chinese History to NCS students using the Chinese language (Hong Kong Special Administrative Region Government, 2018).

Closing the unacceptable educational gaps

With regard to educational equality, all societies need to reduce the sometimes remarkable disparities present in education and life chances that result from university admission criteria that systematically exclude a large portion of the population (Gándara, 1999). The under-representation of socially disadvantaged groups such as low-income HKMS, CIS, and NCS students in PSE has raised serious concerns over education access and equity in Hong Kong. For example, the percentage of HKMS, CIS, NCS students, and low-income students who attended PSE in the 2018/2019 academic year is 42, 12, 6, and 16%, respectively (University Grants Committee, 2019b, 2020). The PSE attendance rate for HKMS is twice as high compared with other socially disadvantaged student groups. The EDB (2020b) has taken a step forward to provide additional language learning support for immigrant students in mainstream schooling. However, Hong Kong is falling short in enabling such students to compete in a rapidly evolving society, combat adversity, pursue PSE, and achieve their academic goals. As many school-aged South and Southeast Asians are out of school, their admission rate to PSE (29.2%) is significantly lower than their mainstream counterparts (50.8%) (Census and Statistics Department, 2017).

In sum, with the increasing population of various student cultural groups, Hong Kong society is becoming increasingly pluralistic and faces multiple challenges in intercultural and inter-ethnic relations. The future development of Hong Kong society is hampered by a generation of underserved youth coming from diverse socio-cultural backgrounds. The well-being and engagement of the CIS and NCS students have caused policymakers, educators, and key stakeholders to rethink how they build bridges with these young people and engage them in positive societal development. As these groups are themselves diverse in terms of ethnicity, religious faith, values, family SES, and social networks, they deserve more careful and specific attention to understand their well-being, sense of belonging, and the nature of their engagement with school and society. The right policies and support measures necessary to yield the intended outcomes are introduced with such sensitivity and knowledge.

The purpose of this first chapter has been to outline the educational policy landscape and to document the obstacles and barriers faced by the most underprivileged youth in Hong Kong. The discussion confirms a close connection between educational inequalities and socially disadvantageous conditions and casts doubt upon assertions that Hong Kong provides "equality of opportunities" that promote social mobility and inclusion for these youth. The next chapter provides a deeper understanding of the demographics of these student groups.

References

Amirkhan, J. H., & Velasco, S. E. (2019). Stress overload and the new nightmare for Dreamers. *Journal of American College Health*, 1–7. https://doi.org/10.1080/07448481.2019.1652182

Apple, M. W. (1996). Power, meaning and identity: Critical sociology of education in the United States. *British Journal of Sociology of Education*, *17*(2), 125–144. https://doi.org/10.1080/0142569960170201.

Ball, S., Macrae, S., & Maguire, M. (2000). *Choice, pathways and transitions post-16: New youth, new economies in the global city*. Routledge.

Benadusi, L. (2001). Equity and education: A critical review of sociological research and thought. In W. Hutmacher, D. Cochrane, & N. Bottani (Eds.), *In pursuit of equity in education: Using international indicators to compare equity policies* (pp. 25–64). Kluwer Academic.

Bourdieu, P. (1973). Cultural reproduction and social reproduction. In R. Brown (Ed.), *Knowledge, education, and cultural change* (pp. 71–84). Tavistock Publications.

Bowles, A., Fisher, R., McPhail, R., Rosenstreich, D., & Dobson, A. (2014). Staying the distance: Students' perceptions of enablers of transition to higher education. *Higher Education Research & Development*, *33*(2), 212–225. https://doi.org/10.1080/07294360.2013.832157.

Bunce, L., King, N., Saran, S., & Talib, N. (2019). Experiences of black and minority ethnic (BME) students in higher education: Applying self-determination theory to understand the BME attainment gap. *Studies in Higher Education*, 1–14. https://doi.org/10.1080/03075079.2019.1643305

Burkholder, C. (2013). "Just the school makes us non-Chinese": Contrasting the discourses of Hong Kong's education bureau with the lived experiences of its non-Chinese speaking secondary school population. *Journal of Educational Research for Social Change*, *2*(2), 43–58.

Cameron, S., & Daga, R. (2018). Setting out a conceptual framework for measuring equity in learning [e-book]. In UNESCO Institute for Statistics (UIS), FHI 360 EPDC, Oxford Policy Management, REAL Centre, & R. Outhred (Eds.), *Handbook on measuring equity in education* (pp. 16–45). UNESCO Institute for Statistics. http://uis.unesco.org/sites/default/files/documents/handbook-measuring-equity-education-2018-en.pdf

Census and Statistics Department. (2017). *Thematic report: Ethnic minorities*. Hong Kong Special Administrative Region. https://www.statistics.gov.hk/pub/B11201002016XXXXB0100.pdf

Cheng, Y. C. (2017). *Xianggang Jiaogai: Sanbubianzou [Hong Kong education reform: Three waves of change]*. Chung Hwa Book Co.

Christenson, S. L., Reschly, A. L., & Wylie, C. (2012). *Handbook of research on student engagement* (1st ed.). Springer.

Chu, R. (2019, October 8). Hong Kong's education gap hurts ethnic minorities as much as society at large. *Hong Kong Free Post*.

Coniam, D. (2009). The development of secondary students' English language listening competence in English medium of instruction schools in Hong Kong: A longitudinal study. *Hong Kong Journal of Applied Linguistics, 12*(1), 1–14. http://caes.hku.hk/hkjalonline/issues/download_the_file.php?f=2009_v12_1_coniam.pdf

Cunanan, M. T. (2011). Dividing classes: Segregation of ethnic minorities in Hong Kong schools (Doctoral dissertation, University of East Anglia).

Education Bureau. (2019). *Legislative Council Panel on Education 2019 Policy Address Education Bureau's Policy Initiatives.* https://www.edb.gov.hk/en/about-edb/legco/policy-address/2019_Panel_on_Education_Eng.pdf

Education Bureau. (2020a). *Acceptance of alternative qualification(s) in Chinese Language for JUPAS admission.* https://www.edb.gov.hk/en/student-parents/ncs-students/about-ncs-students/jupas-admission.html

Education Bureau. (2020b). *Education services for non-Chinese speaking (NCS) students.* https://www.edb.gov.hk/en/student-parents/ncs-students/about-ncs-students/index.html

Eglinton, K. A. (2013). *Youth identities, localities, and visual material culture: Making selves, making worlds* (1st ed.). Springer.

Gándara, P. (1999). *Priming the pump: Strategies for increasing the achievement of underrepresented minority undergraduates.* The College Board. https://citeseerx.ist.psu.edu/viewdoc/download?doi=10.1.1.190.221&rep=rep1&type=pdf

Gao, F. (2019). Ethnic minority students' progression to university in Hong Kong: Access and equity. *Multicultural Education Review, 11*(2), 135–148. https://doi.org/10.1080/2005615X.2019.1615245.

Garcia, E., Weiss, E., & Engdahl, L. (2020, April 17). *Access to online learning amid coronavirus is far from universal, and children who are poor suffer from a digital divide.* Economic Policy Institute. https://www.epi.org/blog/access-to-online-learning-amid-coronavirus-and-digital-divide/

Guittar, S. G., & Guittar, N. A. (2015). Intersectionality. *International encyclopedia of the social & behavioral sciences* (2nd ed.). Elsevier.

Harris, S. M., & Halpin, G. (2002). Development and validation of the factors influencing pursuit of higher education questionnaire. *Educational and Psychological Measurement, 62*(1), 79–96. https://doi.org/10.1177/0013164402062001006.

Hazelkorn, E., & Gibson, A. (2019). Public goods and public policy: What is public good, and who and what decides? *Higher Education, 78*(2), 257–271. https://doi.org/10.1007/s10734-018-0341-3.

Holgado, D., Maya-Jariego, I., Ramos, I., Palacio, J., Oviedo-Trespalacios, Ó, Romero-Mendoza, V., & Amar, J. (2014). Impact of child labor on academic performance: Evidence from the program "Edúcame primero Colombia." *International Journal of Educational Development, 34*, 58–66. https://doi.org/10.1016/j.ijedudev.2012.08.004

Hong Kong Special Administrative Region. (2018). *The chief executive's 2018 policy address: Strengthening support for ethnic minorities.* https://www.policyaddress.gov.hk/2018/eng/policy_ch06.html

Hong Kong Unison. (2013). *Petition to the CE for improving the Chinese language education of ethnic minorities.* http://www.unison.org.hk/index.php/en/content/petition-ce-improving-chinese-language-education-ethnic-minorities

Hong Kong Unison. (2018). *Press Statement Hong Kong Unison responds to Policy Address 2018.* https://unison.org.hk/sites/default/files/2020-11/PP20181010_Unison's_response_to_Policy_Address_ENG.pdf

Huang, G. H. C., & Gove, M. (2015). Confucianism, Chinese families, and academic achievement: Exploring how Confucianism and Asian descendant parenting practices influence children's academic achievement. In Science education in East Asia (pp. 41–66). Springer.

Hutmacher, W. (2001). Introduction. In W. Hutmacher, D. Cochrane, & N. Bottani (Eds.), *Pursuit of equity in education: Using international indicators to compare equity policies* (pp. 1–24). Kluwer Academic.

Jacob, W. J., & Holsinger, D. B. (2008). Inequality in education: A critical analysis. In B. Holsinger, & J. Jacob (Eds.), *Inequality in education: Comparative and international perspectives* (pp. 1–34). Springer.

Kahu, E. R., & Nelson, K. (2018). Student engagement in the educational interface: Understanding the mechanisms of student success. *Higher Education Research & Development, 37*(1), 58–71. https://doi.org/10.1080/07294360.2017.1344197.

Kan, V., & Adamson, B. (2010). Language policies for Hong Kong schools since 1997. *London Review of Education, 8*(2), 167–176. https://doi.org/10.1080/14748460.2010.487336.

Kember, D. (2010). Opening up the road to nowhere: Problems with the path to mass higher education in Hong Kong. *Higher Education, 59*(2), 167–179. https://doi.org/10.1007/s10734-009-9241-x.

Kennedy, K. J. (2012). The 'no loser' principle in Hong Kong's education reform: Does it apply to ethnic minority students. *Hong Kong Teachers' Central Journal, 11*, 1–23.

Knight, Z. G. (2017). A proposed model of psychodynamic psychotherapy linked to Erik Erikson's eight stages of psychosocial development. *Clinical Psychology & Psychotherapy, 24*(5), 1047–1058. https://doi.org/10.1002/cpp.2066.

Lareau, A. (2000). *Home advantage: Social class and parental intervention in elementary education* (2nd ed.). Rowman & Littlefield Publishers.

Law, K. Y., & Lee, K. M. (2012). The myth of multiculturalism in 'Asia's world city': Incomprehensive policies for ethnic minorities in Hong Kong. *Journal of Asian Public Policy, 5*(1), 117–134. https://doi.org/10.1080/17516234.2012.662353.

Leung, R. (2019, March 10). *Ethnic minority students in Hong Kong only understand 70 per cent of class syllabus because of weak Chinese...* South China Morning Post. https://www.scmp.com/news/hong-kong/education/article/2189413/ethnic-minority-students-hong-kong-only-understand-70-cent

Levin, H. M. (1987). Education as a public and private good. *Journal of Policy Analysis and Management, 6*(4), 628–641. https://doi.org/10.2307/3323518.

Levison, D., DeGraff, D. S., & Dungumaro, E. W. (2018). Implications of environmental chores for schooling: Children's time fetching water and firewood in Tanzania. *The European Journal of Development Research, 30*(2), 217–234. https://doi.org/10.1057/s41287-017-0079-2.

Loh, E., & Hung, C. (2020). *A study on the challenges faced by mainstream schools in educating ethnic minorities in Hong Kong.* https://www.eoc.org.hk/eoc/upload/ResearchReport/researchreport_20200115_e.pdf

Mortimore, P., & Whitty, G. (1999) School improvement: A remedy for social exclusion? In A. Hayton (Ed.), *Tackling disaffection and social exclusion*. Kogan Page

O'Donnell, V. L., Kean, M., & Stevens, G. (2016). *Student transition in higher education: Concepts, theories and practices.* Higher Education Academy. https://www.researchgate.net/profile/Gemma_Stevens3/publication/318947997_Student_transitions_in_higher_education_concepts_theories_and_practices/links/59877d74a6fdcc756257bb74/Student-transitions-in-higher-education-concepts-theories-and-practices.pdf

Oxfam Hong Kong. (2014). *Survey on the Chinese learning challenges South Asian ethnic minority kindergarten students from low-income families face*. https://www.oxfam.org.hk/tc/f/news_and_publication/1410/content_20711en.pdf

Shek, D. T. L. (2020). Protests in Hong Kong (2019–2020): A perspective based on quality of life and well-being. *Applied Research in Quality of Life, 15*(3), 619–635. https://doi.org/10.1007/s11482-020-09825-2.

Shum, M., Gao, F., & Ki, W. W. (2016). School desegregation in Hong Kong: Non-Chinese linguistic minority students' challenges to learning Chinese in mainstream schools. *Asia Pacific Journal of Education, 36*(4), 533–544. https://doi.org/10.1080/02188791.2015.1005048.

Simon, F., Malgorzata, K., & Beatriz, P. (2007). *Education and training policy no more failures: Ten steps to equity in education*. OECD Publishing.

Siu, A., Tong, K., & Lai, V. (2017). At college with learning disabilities: Students with special needs struggle for institutional support. *Varsity*. CUHK.

Spratt, J. (2017). *Wellbeing, equity and education: A critical analysis of policy discourses of wellbeing in schools (inclusive learning and educational equity (1))*. Springer.

Stockfelt, S. (2018). We the minority-of-minorities: A narrative inquiry of black female academics in the United Kingdom. *British Journal of Sociology of Education, 39*(7), 1012–1029. https://doi.org/10.1080/01425692.2018.1454297.

The University of Hong Kong (2020, April 21). Press Release. https://www.hku.hk/press/press-releases/detail/20915.html

Tse, J. W. (1994). Discrimination against people with mental retardation in Hong Kong. *International Social Work, 37*(4), 357–368. https://doi.org/10.1177%2F002087289403700406.

UNESCO. (2015). *Education 2030, Incheon declaration and framework for action*. United Nations Educational, Scientific and Cultural Organization (UNESCO). http://uis.unesco.org/sites/default/files/documents/education-2030-incheon-framework-for-action-implementation-of-sdg4-2016-en_2.pdf

UNESCO. (2016). *Leaving no one behind: How far on the way to universal primary and secondary education?* (Policy paper 27/Fact sheet 37). United Nations Educational, Scientific and Cultural Organization (UNESCO). https://www.west-info.eu/263-million-children-are-out-of-school/245238e/

UNESCO. (2017). *Implementation of the UNESCO operational strategy on youth (2014-2021): Summary conclusions from the first UNESCO-wide monitoring of the Strategy's implementation, 2014-2016*. United Nations Educational, Scientific and Cultural Organization (UNESCO). https://unesdoc.unesco.org/ark:/48223/pf0000247897

United Nations. (1989). *Conventions on Rights of the Child*. https://www.ohchr.org/en/professionalinterest/pages/crc.aspx

United Nations. (2015a). *Education 2030: Incheon declaration and framework for action for the implementation of sustainable development goal 4*. http://uis.unesco.org/sites/default/files/documents/education-2030-incheon-framework-for-action-implementation-of-sdg4-2016-en_2.pdf

United Nations. (2015b). *Transforming our world: The 2030 agenda for sustainable development*. https://sustainabledevelopment.un.org/content/documents/21252030%20Agenda%20for%20Sustainable%20Development%20web.pdf

University Grants Committee. (2019a). *General statistics on UGC-funded institutions/programmes*. University Grants Committee of Hong Kong. https://cdcf.ugc.edu.hk/cdcf/searchUniv.action?lang=EN

University Grants Committee. (2019b). *Non-academic information of first-year student intakes of UGC-funded full-time sub-degree and undergraduate programmes, 2017/18 to 2018/19*. University Grants Committee of Hong Kong. https://cdcf.ugc.edu.hk/cdcf/searchStatSiteReport.action#

University Grants Committee. (2020). *Key statistics on UGC-funded universities*. University Grants Committee of Hong Kong. https://cdcf.ugc.edu.hk/cdcf/searchStatSiteReport.action#

Urdan, T., & Bruchmann, K. (2018). Examining the academic motivation of a diverse student population: A consideration of methodology. *Educational Psychologist, 53*(2), 114–130. https://doi.org/10.1080/00461520.2018.1440234.

Van der Zanden, P. J., Denessen, E., Cillessen, A. H., & Meijer, P. C. (2018). Domains and predictors of first-year student success: A systematic review. *Educational Research Review, 23*, 57–77. https://doi.org/10.1016/j.edurev.2018.01.001

Voelkl, K. (2012). School identification. In L. Christenson, A. L. Reschly, & C. Wylie (Eds.), *Handbook of research on student engagement* (pp. 193–218). Springer.

Wong, R. M. H. (2014). Motivation to learn English and school grade level: The case of newly arrived Hong Kong students. *Porta Linguarum Revista Interuniversitaria de Didáctica de Las Lenguas Extranjeras, 21*, 37–50. https://doi.org/10.30827/digibug.30481

Yuen, C. Y. M. (2018a). Chinese immigrant students and cross-boundary students in Hong Kong: A call for equity through culturally relevant teaching practices. In Y. K. Cha, S. H. Ham, & M. S. Lee (Eds.), *Routledge international handbook of multicultural education research in Asia Pacific* (pp. 258–271). Routledge.

Yuen, C. Y. M. (2018b). Social equity and home-school collaboration in multicultural early years' education: A Hong Kong perspective. In Y. Guo (Ed.), *Home-school relations: International perspectives* (pp. 137–153). Springer.

Yuen, C. Y. M. (2019). *Piaoliu shaonian: Xianggang xuesheng de kuaile yu aichou [The happiness and mourning of Hong Kong students]*. Breakthrough Organization Limited.

Yuen, C. Y. M., & Lee, M. (2013). Mapping the life satisfaction of adolescents in Hong Kong secondary schools with high ethnic concentration. *Youth & Society, 48*(4), 539–556. https://doi.org/10.1177/0044118x13502060.

Zhang, K. C., & Ting, C. L. M. (2011). The education of new Chinese immigrant children in Hong Kong: Challenges and opportunities. *Support for Learning, 26*(2), 49–55. https://doi.org/10.1111/j.1467-9604.2011.01477.x.

2 The Changing Student Demographics

Hong Kong demographics

Hong Kong is predominantly an ethnic Chinese society, with around 90% being Han Chinese. For many years, this is considered a safe haven by Chinese immigrants (Chan & Chou, 2016); around one-third of the 7.3 million population of Hong Kong in 2016 was born in Mainland China. Despite the decreasing number of Chinese immigrants, down from 217,000 in 2006 to 166,000 in 2016 (Census and Statistics Department, 2018b), they still represent the most significant inflow of immigrants into the territory. As stipulated by the Basic Law, which represents the constitution of the HKSAR, Chinese immigrants can apply for permanent citizenship after living in Hong Kong for seven consecutive years. However, persons from Mainland China who have resided in Hong Kong for less than seven years are considered new immigrants. The majority of them are of low educational level and limited social capital, they tend towards low-paid employment.

The demographic profiles of Chinese immigrants are complex in terms of regional dialects, customs, beliefs, and socio-economic backgrounds. Before and after the changeover of the sovereignty from British rule to Chinese rule, these factors have made Chinese immigrants stand out as a distinct social group, and diversities within local and Mainland Chinese populations contribute to the widening divide. Hong Kong people identify themselves as Hong Kongers rather than Chinese. Hong Kong-Mainland intercultural group tensions and conflicts over employment, education, housing, and other life chances issues have become prevalent in recent times. A recent study on public attitudes towards the comprehensive social security assistance (CSSA) scheme reveals that local people have reservations about increasing the scheme's funding because the scheme benefits Chinese immigrants in Hong Kong (Yang et al., 2020).

The number of NCS ethnic minorities, by comparison, skyrocketed by 70.8% between 2006 and 2016, with a total number of 584,383 in 2016 (8% of the population), including FDHs – Foreign Domestic Helpers (Census and Statistics Department, 2018a). Among them, around four-fifths are Asians and one-tenth white. In addition, the number of Hong Kong-born ethnic minorities recorded a 120% increase within that same period. NCS South and Southeast Asians, such as Indonesians, Indians, Pakistanis, Nepalese, and Filipinos, are highly

DOI: 10.4324/9780429439315-2

heterogeneous and are characterised by distinct languages, religions, lifestyles, and customs (Table 2.1).

Table 2.1 Population of Chinese immigrants and ethnic minority in Hong Kong in 2006, 2011, and 2016

Population (percentage)	2006	2011	2016
Chinese immigrants	217,103 (3.3%)	171,311 (2.5%)	165,956 (2.4%)
Ethnic minority	342,189 (5.2%)	451,183 (6.4%)	584,383 (8%)
Overall	6,578,000 (100%)	6,852,000 (100%)	6,914,000 (100%)

Sources: Census and Statistics Department (2018a, 2018b).

Profiles of immigrant and ethnic minority students

In line with these developments, Hong Kong schools have witnessed a rapid change in student demographics due to a falling fertility rate (from 1933 in 1981 to 1051 in 2019) and a growth in the number of children born from Chinese immigrant and ethnic minority families (Census and Statistics Department, 2012, 2020).

Chinese immigrant students (CIS)

CIS are defined as students from Mainland China living in Hong Kong for less than seven years. Many had their early years and primary education in the Mainland as their mothers waited for a one-way permit to enable their children to immigrate to Hong Kong. While the number of first-time immigrant students admitted to local primary schools steadily grew from 4,403 in 2014/15 to 5,345 in 2019/20, the number of CIS admitted to secondary schools steadily increased until 2017/18 but dropped sharply in 2018/19 (Table 2.2).

Table 2.2 Number of immigrant and minority students in Hong Kong between 2013 and 2020

		2013/14	2014/15	2015/16	2016/17	2017/18	2018/19	2019/20
NCS	Kindergarten	10,670	10,368	10,481	10,708	10,773	12,968	12,956
	Primary	7,761	8,088	8,338	8,694	9,009	9,849	10,051
	Secondary	6,953	7,512	7,998	8,134	8,507	9,481	9,796
CIS	Kindergarten	–	–	–	–	–	–	–
	Primary[a]	2,656	4,403	3,824	4,039	4,202	**5,740**	5,345
	Secondary[a]	2,644	2,663	2,139	3,832	**3,804**	2,477	2,340
CBS	Kindergarten	9,287	10,364	10,406	7,846	4,610	2,031	–
	Primary	9,117	11,876	14,699	17,572	18,831	20,188	17,974
	Secondary	2,505	2,851	3,133	3,354	4,084	5,567	7,602

Source: Figures and Statistics, https://www.edb.gov.hk/en/about-edb/publications-stat/figures/index.html (Legislative Council, 2017, 2020a, 2020b).

Notes

a Figures refer to the number of students newly admitted to the respective school level.

Figures refer to One-way Permit Holders, who are newly admitted to schools 12 months prior to October of the given school year. For example, the 2019/20 school year refers to admission from October 2018 to September 2019.

Over three quarters (77%) of CIS in 2016 were enrolled in aided secondary schools. Significant variations of language proficiency exist. Around 70% of CIS, aged five or above, appeared to have greater competence than their parents in speaking the local dialect, Cantonese, and 47% of CIS can read English compared to 67.5% of the overall population (Census and Statistics Department, 2018b).

The transition of CIS from familiar Mainland schooling to their Hong Kong school is often full of frustrations, disconnectedness, and under-achievement (Yuen, 2013; Yuen & Lee, 2013). First, CIS usually take extra years to repeat one or two grades to consolidate their English foundation, improve their spoken Cantonese, connect with mainstream peers, and familiarise themselves with new examination requirements. Over-age placement is a known and detrimental factor towards low academic self-esteem among CIS. Second, using Chinese and English proficiency scores to determine class placement and eligibility for government support is controversial. Such strategy hinders rather than facilitates learning motivation and self-esteem. Third, using the English language for academic purposes is a known educational obstacle for CIS, especially in their first year of Hong Kong schooling (Chong, 2004). Fourth, most CIS have an uprooting experience, leaving their Mainland schools, teachers, and friends and, more importantly, the sense of belonging through the interim admission process. Fifth, the educational assimilationist approach to learning (Yuen, 2010) means survival of the fittest. Hence, major acculturation stressors for immigrant students are getting familiarised with the MOI – Cantonese, switching simplified Chinese characters into Complex Chinese characters, and adjusting to the Hong Kong school culture. Lastly, their accented Cantonese betrays their Mainland cultural identity, and this can lead to discriminatory attitudes. Without understanding classroom instructions, CIS can become passive and often struggle with concentration. After school, they have to work hard to find ways to overcome these difficulties. Taken together, CIS face an uphill journey in integrating into Hong Kong society (Yuen, 2018). While a few manage to stay afloat against the odds (Pong, 2009), most are overwhelmed by the Hong Kong-centric education system.

Non-Chinese speaking (NCS) students

When talking about NCS students in Hong Kong, this refers primarily to South/Southeast Asian students, most of whom are co-educated with their local counterparts in mainstream schools. It also refers to ethnic minority students from affluent families enrolled in international schools. The number of NCS students registered in local secondary schools has doubled from 7,000 (2.4% of the total student enrolment) in 2006 to 16,600 (8.4%) in 2016 (Census and Statistics Department, 2017, 2018a). The school attendance rate of NCS students aged 12–17 and 18–24 was 96.2% and 28.1%, respectively, in 2016, while the attendance rates for students overall were 97.8% and 51.8%, respectively (Census and Statistics Department, 2017). In other words, more NCS students end their schooling at the secondary level than their mainstream peers. However, the proficiency of NCS students in both Chinese and English languages for academic attainment and meeting PSE requirements is uncertain. The average post-secondary attainment rates of Indonesians (12.5%), Thais (13.3%), Nepalese (15.0%), and Pakistanis (20.5%) were far lower than that of the overall population (32.7%) in 2016 (Census and Statistics Department, 2017). The figures prompt us to rethink how to close the unacceptable attainment gap between mainstream and the underprivileged NCS students in the local schooling.

Cross-boundary students (CBS)

The third group of non-mainstream students is CBS. They are classified into two types. Type I CBS were born in Hong Kong-Mainland intercultural families, with one parent being a Hong Kong, permanent resident. Type II CBS whose parents are not Hong Kong permanent residents (mainly from Mainland China), known as "doubly non-permanent residents" (DNR) children. These Mainland mothers delivered their babies in the HKSAR with a tourist visa and returned to their Mainland homes. The public discourse about the motives of these affluent DNR parents has ensured that these children enjoy rights and entitlements that are not usually available to Mainland Chinese. All Hong Kong-born children enjoy the same entitlement as their local counterparts – a 12-year free education and visa-free travel to many overseas countries, as well as an escape from the penalty of having an additional child in the Mainland under the now shelved one-child policy. To facilitate their Hong Kong-born children's education, most families relocate to Luohu and Futian districts of Shenzhen city. It is adjacent to boundary towns in the HKSAR and offers easy access to Hong Kong schools. Despite this, geographical distance remains a challenge for early years CBS. They spend several hours each day travelling to and from school in the HKSAR. This has necessitated special arrangements for the primary school allocation process and an increase in places in North District schools to ensure local students are catered for (Legislative Council, 2015).

Commuting daily between the Mainland and the HKSAR boundary inhibits such students from developing a sense of belonging in either city, confuses their civic identity, and alienates them from both societies (Yuen, 2011). Parents of DNR CBS are alienated from the education system as they have little direct knowledge of the HKSAR society. Coping with marked educational change, family transition, and the lack of social networks, many CBS experience adjustment stress and disconnection, and some even question their place in society (Yuen, 2016). The steady increase of the CBS from DNR in Hong Kong schools in the past (Table 2.2) led to fears that public healthcare services, school places, property, welfare, and identity were all threatened by the influx, and intercultural conflicts and tensions between local parents and CBS parents intensified. Local parents consider it unfair that CBS parents have access to the same local public resources yet are not taxpayers. Such has also been compounded by the fact that Mainland Chinese now own one-fifth of the HKSAR property, leading to an over-priced property market. In order to ease such tensions and curb the numbers of DNR CBS, in 2013, the HKSAR government implemented a zero quota policy for DNR women to give birth in Hong Kong.

Consequently, it has now led to a decline in the number of CBS. Putting history aside, schools have not fully addressed the educational needs of these students. The segmentation of CBS demography cannot be overlooked. Most Type I CBS are from low-income intercultural families facing a raft of challenges ranging from transportation, education, family to personal issues. The Legislative Council (2016) has offered various service supports to CBS and their parents, such as learning support programmes, counselling services, parental services etc., to help families understand and adapt to Hong Kong's educational system, particularly those from low-income families.

With the increase of immigrant and minority student populations in mainstream schools, the dimensions of intra-ethnic and inter-ethnic student group relations and challenges are magnified. Immigrant and ethnic minority groups are over-represented in low family SES, and their children are under-represented in PSE institutions and civic participation (Yuen, 2018). The heterogeneity within and between multicultural youth is remarkable in ethnicity, religious faith, values, family SES, and social networks. Suppose the aim is to offer a more accommodating and successful learning journey to all students. In that case, schools must dedicate themselves to understand the well-being, sense of belonging, and engagement with the school and society of each student group under their care.

As discussed in the last chapter, in response to the quest for educational equity and equality of opportunity, the HKSAR has undergone a series of education reforms in the past decade. In its way, the Racial Discrimination Ordinance enactment in 2008 by the Department of Justice was groundbreaking in seeking to safeguard the rights of all races in receiving proper education, employment, and social welfare. New policies were implemented, for example, inclusive education to co-educate students with special needs in mainstream schools and the introduction of financial subsidies to enhance the Chinese learning of NCS communities. However, although the government has put in more educational resources, the promise of education for an equitable society remains an unrealised dream in the HKSAR. While investment in education has been on the rise, multiple new educational policies have left teachers overwhelmed by unrealistic expectations with little professional support for facilitating quality learning and teaching in a classroom of multiple needs, not least because of poor coordination and assessment. Despite the considerable size of student subgroups, there is no helpful indicator to monitor education quality at the individual, school, and societal levels. Learning for examinations or pedagogy directed towards test scores remains the key obstacle for realising learning equity (Yuen, 2016).

Educating the underprivileged students: Challenges and support

Discourses on the non-mainstream students, CIS, CBS, and NCS, are centred on their multiple obstacles, from underprivileged social status to negative experiences and connectedness in the new society. CIS and CBS represent two unique co-ethnic student subgroups in Hong Kong education with close Mainland ties. Each has distinctive heritage and regional culture, and each is under-resourced and under-represented in the society (Yuen, 2010, 2018). Immigrant and ethnic minority students share the characteristics of socially disadvantaged groups elsewhere (Guiraudon et al., 2005). The learning challenges of immigrant and minority students include failure in either English or Chinese learning, relatively poor academic results due to lower teacher expectations (Hong Kong Unison, 2015), early school dropouts, and limited life chances (Yuen, 2013). It also remains a significant challenge for them to gain access to PSE. The under-representation of NCS students and CIS in PSE in Hong Kong has raised serious concerns over education access and equity. Chu (2019), head of the Equal Opportunities Commission, stated that the NCS students feel pessimistic and powerless. Many low-income students lack confidence and expectation to be accepted and the financial means to realise their educational aspirations.

Table 2.3 shows that working poverty is the reality for a large proportion of South and Southeast Asians. Compared to 19.9% of the population overall, in 2017, 25.7% of South and Southeast Asians lived below the poverty line (Census and Statistics Department, 2018a; The Hong Kong Special Administrative Region Government, 2017). While half of the overall poor population lived in working households, the figure for poor ethnic minorities is 64.7%, while for poor Pakistanis and Nepalese, it was 80% (Census and Statistics Department, 2018a). The rate of ethnic minorities who joined the labour force (64.5% excluding domestic helpers) was higher than for the population overall (58.7%) (Census

Table 2.3 Household income distribution by the selected ethnic household groups in 2016

Household income	10th percentile	25th percentile	Median	75th percentile
SA	10,000	15,000	23,800	50,000
Indian	10,800	18,400	37,000	75,000
Pakistani	7,300	12,000	17,300	26,300
Nepalese	10,800	15,000	21,700	37,500
Thai	5,000	9,100	13,100	19,600
Indonesian	1,300	6,200	10,000	14,400
Filipino	6,500	12,800	20,000	35,400
Japanese and Korean	12,400	23,800	41,000	75,000
White	10,000	26,000	59,000	114,000
EM	8,300	15,800	31,300	70,000
All	5,700	12,000	24,900	45,800

Source: Census and Statistics Department(2018b, p. 12).

and Statistics Department, 2017). But these rates are misleading in that the rate for the ethnic minorities is likely to be much lower than the overall figure if Whites and better-off Asians are excluded. The highly educated Whites (88.5%), Japanese and Koreans (80.7%), and Indians (64.9%) tend to engage in higher-skill occupations (Census and Statistics Department, 2015), while the less educated ethnic minorities (primarily Indonesians, Pakistanis, and Nepalese) have limited job market choices, if at all. The distribution of professions mirrors educational attainment.

Parallel to the SES of South and Southeast Asians, the average monthly income of Chinese immigrants is lower than that of the whole population. Around 36.2% of working immigrants are service and sales workers, while a further 30.0% are workers in elementary occupations (Census and Statistics Department, 2018b). Their income level and types of professions seem to be compatible with their levels of education. In 2016, only 19.5% of them had reached the post-secondary level compared to 33.2% of the whole population (Census and Statistics Department, 2018b).

Child poverty is also an issue for immigrant families in Hong Kong. A local study reveals that more than one-third (36.2%) of Chinese immigrant children lived in poverty compared to 12.1% of local children in 2012 (Chou, 2013). Moreover, their disadvantaged background has been proven to link with at-risk behaviours (Kwan, 2007; Shek, 2002).

Studies on ethnic NCS students, on the other hand, find that they are disadvantaged by ineffective support for learning Chinese, the official language of Hong Kong (Loh & Hung, 2020), and the lack of cultural bridges between home and school (Yuen, 2014). Moreover, the uneven distribution of ethnic minority students in mainstream schools also means insufficient public care and support are being offered to address these students' educational needs.

Researching young lives – Identity and acculturation

Understanding and encouraging the sense of belonging and connectedness of these immigrants and ethnic groups in Hong Kong is part of the mission of this book. Aside from the academic discourse on their acculturation process and the construction of their cultural identity in society (Berry, 2005; Berry et al., 2013), the following chapters will provide space for them to co-construct their self-identity by listening to their opinions on life, education, friendships, and future. Schwartz et al. (2006) argue that personal identity is the spiritual anchor in the acculturation process of immigrants. Self-formation is a geo-personal construct and evolves with time and place. It is a dynamic and interactive journey (Hall, 1990), evolving with the maturity of an individual, the internal self, and interaction with social environments. As such, the identity construction of these youth in the societal context is multivariate and complex. Inner psychological change is developmental and culturally related, especially since acculturation occurs at the developmental age (Berry et al., 2013). On the other hand, youth in this critical development age are more vulnerable as well as more easily moulded in the new society than adult immigrants. Society is an agent to socialise these youth with mainstream culture (Chee, 2012). Youth, both mainstream and non-mainstream, have to acquire the essential skills and knowledge to succeed in society. Hence, school curriculum, rules and regulations, teachers' expectations, and the reinforcement approach are mediums of acculturation.

What appears vital for these immigrant and minority youth to craft their identities within and outside their ethnic groups is their integration of family heritage values, beliefs, and social ties with the mainstream societal values and cultures. This can be a challenge for some holding strong family ties. Because traditional values link with religious beliefs, they may seek to preserve their lifestyle and mediate acculturation. By contrast, immigrant youth who adopt a bicultural identity tend to develop a nuanced understanding of cultural identity and a favourable view of ethnic and mainstream cultural groups (Bennett & Bennett, 2001). Researchers (Cheung & Swank, 2019) opine that bicultural identity contributes to the well-being of immigrant youth. Making frequent shifts in their cultural frames of reference, they have greater resilience and competence in navigating both cultures. It is relatively common among second-generation immigrants to employ such a bicultural strategy.

The cultural lens of immigrant youth influences their perception of who they are in society. Positive effects of bicultural identities on psychological well-being, school adjustment, and academic achievement are documented (Cheung & Swank, 2019; Liebkind, 2001). The specific content of identity change is crucial for biculturalism. Some retain heritage values, including religion, the residing society may resist that, and the adoption of new values may be rejected by their co-ethnic group (Schwartz et al., 2006). Further, even they are armed with a basket of acculturation strategies, including assimilation, separation, and marginalisation, they are not immune to being discriminated against in the host society.

The bicultural acculturation process does not necessarily lead to local identity construction. This is particularly true in some contexts when the acculturation attitudes tend to be instrumental, such as the mastery of skills for adapting to school life (e.g., Liebkind et al., 2004). The results of research on the relationship between ethnic identity and academic achievement are divergent. In the US context, the high academic achievement of Vietnamese youth with high ethnic identity was attributed to their strong connection to the original group that attaches high value to achievement (Zhou & Bankston, 1994). In contrast, the low achievement of Mexican-American youth with high ethnic identity resulted from disengagement in school in response to discrimination (Portes & Rumbaut, 2001). Maintaining ethnic identity may be a protective factor for psychological comfort in the acculturation process. However, the construction of a strong local identity may not apply as long as local cultural involvement is fulfilled. In addition to personal volition and attitudes, the acceptance level of values in both original and new social groups significantly impacts the shaping of identities and acculturation trajectories of immigrant youth.

Hong Kong context of cultural identity

In the discourse of inclusion and equity of education, education for students' well-being applies to all, including immigrant, minority, and underprivileged students in society. Education opens many doors for personal and career advancement. Hong Kong education is just beginning to explore a bicultural approach to prepare NCS students or CIS to have a knowledge base of both heritage and receiving cultures. Take Hong Kong-born Pakistani, Indonesian and Indian students as examples. Many of them are native Cantonese speakers but cannot handle the Chinese language in their daily lives, let alone for academic purposes. The CBS and CIS fall into two categories: (1) bicultural constructivists and (2) monocultural defenders. The former is keen to cultivate their bicultural competence and serve as a cultural bridge between their parents and the local society. Unlike their parents, the bicultural immigrant youth may possess the intercultural skill set to analyse school and community interactions. They predict possible misunderstandings resulting from language barriers and expectancy discrepancy and intentionally adapt their behaviour to address the problems (Bennett & Bennett, 2001). The latter lacks a real sense of connectedness with the Hong Kong society, leads an isolated lifestyle, suffers from broken social networks, and holds a stereotyped perception of the society.

Religious identity, closely related to ethnic identity, plays a role in forming the cultural identity of South and Southeast Asian youth in Hong Kong, as with other religious, immigrant youth in other parts of the world. In the early days, South and Southeast Asians in the region exhibit a mixture of religious and ethnic communal identity. Such identity was established through their participation in activities organised by formal organisations, education in monoethnic schools, job searching through networks of watchmen and security guards, banks and other specific companies, and their extensive kinship networks (Weiss, 1991).

Compared to their place of origin, the new generation of South and Southeast Asian youth can pursue a promising life and keep their religious faith freely for their psychological well-being. Therefore, religion and language abilities are mediators for their acculturation and connectedness in society (Yuen & Leung, 2019). Learning Cantonese is often discussed as a positive factor for acculturation. However, Fleming (2015) argued that the emphasis on the importance of local language in the integration process of ethnic minorities reinforces social division because the term "non-Chinese speaking" (NCS) is a tool to distinguish local and non-local and elite and non-elite groups beyond real language competence. As NCS students are relatively stronger in English than their Chinese counterparts, they may tend to uplift the English Language value and discredit the local language (Cantonese) while negotiating their ethnic and regional identities in the acculturation process (Gu & Patkin, 2013).

School is the powerful agent for the acculturation of immigrant youth concerning teachers, peers, and the curriculum (Yuen, 2010). Unlike NCS students, CIS shares the same ethnicity with Hong Kong and uses a similar written

Chinese Language, except the former uses simplified rather than complex Chinese characters. Despite that, Chinese immigrants and ethnic minorities encounter similar cultural disparities in Hong Kong (Chee, 2012). Therefore, developing intercultural competence requires strategies in handling culture-specific and culture-general issues (Bennett & Bennett, 2001). Language proficiency and understanding the value and culture inherited from the colonial period of Hong Kong for CIS are probably the personal factors for acculturation, while historical, political, and economic backgrounds are the environmental factors. In addition to English proficiency, competence in Cantonese (Hong Kong dialect) and the complex written form are essential indicators of acculturation for CIS to master the means for effective academic learning and social communication in education (Yuen, 2010).

CIS, who are inclined to accept and follow Hong Kong cultural norms and values, appear to undergo a smooth psychological adaptation process (Chen et al., 2008). For non-religious CIS, the assimilation model seems more workable for acculturation. However, the environments for acculturation, including the school, family, and community, are influential platforms for shaping the personal beliefs and values of the youth of both immigrant groups. Parents' views and support are essential for identity development and acculturation (Yuen & Wu, 2011). These internal and external elements intertwine and contribute to the evolution of immigrant youth's cultural identity in their acculturation process. Yet, better assimilation or integration into the new society may not necessarily lead to the life satisfaction of these youth, though the status of cultural identity plays a part in it.

Self-forming and student voices

Constructing a self-identity is a critical issue for adolescents. For non-mainstream students, with their history and family roots and not yet adapted to the new society they seek to call home, they may develop a sense of marginalisation in the self-forming process. On the other hand, accepting Hong Kong culture can lead to an internal struggle between two different cultural frames of reference, especially when confronted with contrasting cultural value systems. As most NCS South/Southeast Asian students are affiliated with their family religion (Yuen & Lee, 2013), their deep-rooted religious beliefs from their ethnic tradition intervene in identity construction. In such a process, religious identity helps maintain psychological comforts when facing acculturation stress and difficulties. Simultaneously, local language development and moderate acceptance of local culture and values tend to be more instrumental than constructing a strong local identity.

Understanding student voice in schools is significant for teachers, schools, and educational sectors to improve their services. When student voice is considered in schools, students can cultivate their attachment to the learning environment. Listening to and assessing students' grievances, schools know their students' real experience, which helps achieve inclusive education. It also gives a sense of empowerment to students from various backgrounds, whether an immigrant, an ethnic minority, or one coming from a low-income family. Therefore, it is essential to consider student voice not just in schools but in the context of public involvement and discussion.

It is therefore imperative to define the term "student voice" in its more profound sense. From the perspective of children's rights, Lundy (2007) indicates that above all debates regarding student voice, it is vital to be aware that student voice represents a student's right of expression given by the identity as a child. This idea is supplemented by the United Nations Convention on the Rights of the Child, declaring that student voice is the right given to youth to freely say in all matters affecting themselves (Leitch, 2012). It is about recognising their role in contemporary society as critical stakeholders and respecting their opinions for a better future (Cook-Sather, 2006). It is not new to see students as high stakes, and increasingly they are being ascribed to participate and engage in the social and public policy arenas. Likewise, they are at the centre of education reform (Levin, 2000). How can they not be? Recollecting my private conversations with more than 200 CIS in secondary schools, the thing that struck me most is their shared feeling of inferiority in English learning in Hong Kong and their accented Cantonese. Although Hong Kong transitioned from a former British colony to a Chinese SAR over two decades ago, the education system remains highly exclusive, especially in its sociocultural complexion. English Language and Chinese Language are two significant issues for student success.

Student voice creates channels for students to engage in school and classroom activities. Participation in student voice activities promotes students' attachment to their schools and increases their connectedness with the school environment. This engagement and connectedness are caused when student voice facilitates the interactions and cooperation between students and teachers (Serriere & Mitra, 2012). The study of Baroutsis et al. (2016) indicates that conversations with students are opportunities for teachers to learn their students' experiences. Similarly, students construct their trust and understanding of their teachers while communicating with them (Sorenson, 1994). Serriere and Mitra (2012) also conclude that student voice encourages students to build positive relationships with their teachers.

Moreover, student activities enable students to voice out and get familiar with their school settings and speak about the educational environment. Actively engaging in student voice activities requires students to develop a strong understanding of education policies and curriculum reforms (Mitra, 2003). Atweh et al. (2012) further point out that this prerequisite of participating in student voice activities is an integral outcome of student participation. Engaging students are expected to gain better insight into their school reforms and policies when they have the right to speak out. Briefly, their enriched connections with their teachers, along with their increased awareness of school policies, develop a sense of belonging to their schools.

Students' attachment to school can be enhanced when they feel respected and heard. Studies on student voice and participation reveal that they consider and value respect as a vital element of their rights (Kiragu et al., 2012; Rampal, 2012). Furthermore, being capable of expressing their thoughts to schools increases students' identification (Simmons et al., 2015). By the same token, students are more willing to participate in student voice activities when they feel their words and requests are being taken by teachers and schools (Cook-Sather, 2006; Mitra & Gross, 2009). Furthermore, student voice alters the traditional power relations in classrooms and entitles students to decide matters pertaining to themselves (Rudduck & Fielding, 2006). This transformation in power relations, which is symbolised by teachers sharing part of their power with students, accentuates the value of equality between students and teachers in classrooms (Larson & Walker, 2006).

Student voice enhances the self-concept and self-esteem of engaged students. By participating in student voice activities, students feel valued (Morgan & Streb, 2001). The opportunities to express their opinions, desires, and interests to school teach them that they can make a difference in their learning (Miliband, 2006). For example, students can incorporate their learning interests into the curriculum design (Rainer & Matthews, 2002). Further, interacting with teachers is perceived as a process of mutual understanding. Students know more about adults' thoughts regarding learning content, programme design, and educational reform (Sorenson, 1994; Halliday et al., 2019). Sahin and Top (2015) articulate that the increased understanding of learning matters augments students' confidence and further inspires students to talk and communicate interpersonally. This also echoes one crucial finding of many relevant studies: Students improve their communication and negotiation skills while being involved in conversations or cooperating with adults (Atweh et al., 2012; Mitra, 2004; Mitra & Gross, 2009).

The positive causative link between student voice and student empowerment is a vivid one when perceived through the lens of curriculum equity. Mcleod (2011) asserts that, apart from reaching equality between students and teachers, student voice is crucial to empowering marginalised student groups since it offers them opportunities in school decisions. The equal chance of participation can help attain inclusive education among students from various backgrounds (Rampal, 2012; Smith & Gorard, 2006). The feeling of being heard and respected accorded by student voice to minor groups reduces their sense of alienation and develops their sense of belonging and connectedness to their classroom and to their school. This empowerment of students also applies to disengaged students who have little or no interest in participating in class activities (Mitra, 2004). These students are always labelled as lacking the skills and capacities to participate in school activities (Carrington, 2006). Nonetheless, student voice is believed to break the negative cycle by enabling disengaged students to be recognised in the class. The next chapter will take a closer look into the theoretical grounding of the well-being and connectedness of the disadvantaged immigrant and ethnic minority youth to provide a better background for subsequent case studies.

References

Atweh, B., Bland, D., Smith, K., & Woodward, A. (2012). Engaging students in research relationships for school reform. In C. Day (Ed.), *The Routledge international handbook of teacher and school development* (1st ed., pp. 233–242). Taylor & Francis.

Baroutsis, A., McGregor, G., & Mills, M. (2016). Pedagogic voice: Student voice in teaching and engagement pedagogies. *Pedagogy, Culture & Society, 24*(1), 123–140. https://doi.org/10.1080/14681366.2015.1087044.

Bennett, J., & Bennett, M. (2001). *Developing intercultural sensitivity: An integrative approach to global and domestic diversity*. Paper presented at the Diversity Symposium, June 28–29, 2001, Boston.

Berry, J. W. (2005). Acculturation: Living successfully in two cultures. *International Journal of Intercultural Relations, 29*(6), 697–712. https://doi.org/10.1016/j.ijintrel.2005.07.013.

Berry, J. W., Phinney, J. S., Kwak, K., & Sam, D. L. (2013). Introduction: Goals and research framework for studying immigrant youth. In J. W. Berry, J. S. Phinney, D. L. Sam, & P. Vedder (Eds.), *Immigrant youth in cultural transition: Acculturation, identity, and adaptation across national contexts* (6th ed., pp. 1–14). Psychology Press.

Carrington, S. (2006). Classroom relationships, pedagogy and practice in the inclusive classroom. In M. Keeffe, & S. Carrington (Eds.), *Schools and diversity* (1st ed., pp. 105–126). Pearson Education Australia.

Census and Statistics Department. (2012). *Thematic report: Ethnic minorities*. Hong Kong Special Administrative Region. https://www.statistics.gov.hk/pub/B11200622012XXXXB0100.pdf

Census and Statistics Department. (2015). *Hong Kong poverty situation report on ethnic minorities 2014*. Hong Kong Special Administrative Region. https://www.povertyrelief.gov.hk/eng/pdf/2014_EM_Report_Eng.pdf

Census and Statistics Department. (2017). *Thematic report: Ethnic minorities*. Hong Kong Special Administrative Region. https://www.statistics.gov.hk/pub/B11201002016XXXXB0100.pdf

Census and Statistics Department. (2018a). *Hong Kong poverty situation report on ethnic minorities 2016*. Hong Kong Special Administrative Region. https://www.statistics.gov.hk/pub/B9XX0004E2016XXXXE0100.pdf

Census and Statistics Department. (2018b). *Thematic report: Persons from the Mainland having resided in Hong Kong for less than 7 years*. Hong Kong Special Administrative Region. https://www.statistics.gov.hk/pub/B11201012016XXXXB0100.pdf

Census and Statistics Department. (2020). *Hong Kong monthly digest on statistics. Fertility trend in Hong Kong, 1981 to 2019*. https://www.statistics.gov.hk/pub/B72012FA2020XXXXB0100.pdf

Chan, L. S., & Chou, K. L. (2016). Immigration, living arrangement and the poverty risk of older adults in Hong Kong. *International Journal of Social Welfare, 25*(3), 247–258. https://doi.org/10.1111/ijsw.12187.

Chee, W. C. (2012). Envisioned belonging: Cultural differences and ethnicities in Hong Kong schooling. *Asian Anthropology, 11*(1), 89–105. https://doi.org/10.1080/1683478x.2012.10600858.

Chen, S. X., Benet-Martnez, V., & Harris Bond, M. (2008). Bicultural identity, bilingualism, and psychological adjustment in multicultural societies: Immigration-based and globalization-based acculturation. *Journal of Personality, 76*(4), 803–838. https://doi.org/10.1111/j.1467-6494.2008.00505.x.

Cheung, C. W., & Swank, J. M. (2019). Asian American identity development: A bicultural model for youth. *Journal of Child and Adolescent Counseling*, 5(1), 89–101.

Chong, S. (2004). Cultural minority students in Hong Kong: Critical issues and policy considerations. *Comparative Education Bulletin No. 7*, 10.

Chou, K. L. (2013). Familial effect on child poverty in Hong Kong immigrant families. *Social Indicators Research*, 113(1), 183–195.

Chu, R. (2019, October 8). *Hong Kong's education gap hurts ethnic minorities as much as society at large*. Hong Kong Free Press HKFP. https://hongkongfp.com/2019/10/08/hong-kongs-education-gap-hurts-ethnic-minorities-much-society-large/

Cook-Sather, A. (2006). Sound, presence, and power: "Student voice" in educational research and reform. *Curriculum Inquiry*, 36(4), 359–390. https://doi.org/10.1111/j.1467-873x.2006.00363.x.

Fleming, K. K. (2015). *Ideology, identity and linguistic repertoires among South Asian students in Hong Kong*. PhD dissertation. The University of Hong Kong. https://doi.org/10.5353/th_b5689270

Gu, M. M., & Patkin, J. (2013). Heritage and identity: Ethnic minority students from South Asia in Hong Kong. *Linguistics and Education*, 24(2), 131–141. https://doi.org/10.1016/j.linged.2012.12.008.

Guiraudon, V., Phalet, K., & Ter Wal, J. (2005). Monitoring ethnic minorities in the Netherlands. *International Social Science Journal*, 57(183), 75–87. https://doi.org/10.1111/j.0020-8701.2005.00532.x.

Hall, S. (1990). Cultural identity and diaspora. In J. Rutherford (Ed.), *Identity* (1st ed., pp. 222–237). Lawrence & Wishart.

Halliday, A. J., Kern, M. L., Garrett, D. K., & Turnbull, D. A. (2019). The student voice in well-being: A case study of participatory action research in positive education. *Educational Action Research*, 27(2), 173–196. https://doi.org/10.1080/09650792.2018.1436079.

Hong Kong Special Administrative Region Government. (2017). *Analysis of poverty situation in Hong Kong in 2016 announced* [Press Release]. https://www.info.gov.hk/gia/general/201711/17/P2017111700634.htm#:~:text=Compared%20with%202015%2C%20the%20pre,point%20to%2014.7%20per%20cent

Hong Kong Unison. (2015). *Submission to the panel on education of the legislative council on enhancing Chinese learning and teaching for non-Chinese speaking students* (LC Paper No. CB(4)1131/14-15(01)). Legislative Council. https://www.legco.gov.hk/yr14-15/english/panels/ed/papers/ed20150608cb4-1131-1-e.pdf

Kiragu, S., Swartz, S., Chikovore, J., Lukalo, F., Oduro, G. Y., & Day, C. (2012). Agency, access, silence and ethics: How young people's voices from Africa can contribute to social and educational change in adult-dominated societies. In *The Routledge international handbook of teacher and school development* (Vol. 1, pp. 254–264). Taylor & Francis.

Kwan, Y. K. (2007). Life satisfaction and family structure among adolescents in Hong Kong. *Social Indicators Research*, 86(1), 59–67. https://doi.org/10.1007/s11205-007-9092-8.

Larson, R. W., & Walker, K. C. (2006). Learning about the "Real world" in an urban arts youth program. *Journal of Adolescent Research*, 21(3), 244–268. https://doi.org/10.1177/0743558405285824.

Legislative Council. (2015). *Background brief on issues related to education for cross-boundary students* (LC Paper No. CB(4)925/14-15(07)). Legislative Council. https://www.legco.gov.hk/yr14-15/english/panels/ed/papers/ed20150511cb4-925-7-e.pdf

Legislative Council. (2016). *Policies and measures adopted by the administration relating to Mainland-HKSAR families* (LC Paper No. CB(2)860/15-16(02)). Legislative Council. https://www.legco.gov.hk/yr14-15/english/hc/sub_com/hs51/papers/hs5120160217cb2-860-2-e.pdf

Legislative Council. (2017). *Newly arrived pupils from the Mainland*. Legislative Council. https://www.legco.gov.hk/research-publications/english/1617issh31-newly-arrived-pupils-from-the-mainland-20170728-e.pdf

Legislative Council. (2020a). *Education support for non-Chinese speaking students*. Legislative Council. https://www.legco.gov.hk/research-publications/english/1920issh33-educational-support-for-non-chinese-speaking-students-20200708-e.pdf

Legislative Council. (2020b). *Replies to questions raised by Finance Committee Members in examining the estimates of expenditure of 2019/2020* (in Chinese). https://www.edb.gov.hk/attachment/tc/about-edb/press/legco/replies-to-fc/19-20-edb-c.pdf

Leitch, R. (2012). Student voice in a global context: Rights, benefits and limitations. In C. Day (Ed.), *The Routledge international handbook of teacher and school development* (1st ed., pp. 215–222). Taylor & Francis.

Levin, B. (2000). Putting students at the centre in education reform. *Journal of Educational Change*, *1*(2), 155–172. https://doi.org/10.1023/A:1010024225888.

Liebkind, K. (2001). Acculturation. In R. Brown, & S. L. Gaertner (Eds.), *Blackwell handbook of social psychology: Intergroup processes* (1st ed., pp. 386–406). Blackwell.

Liebkind, K., Jasinskaja-Lahti, I., & Solheim, E. (2004). Cultural identity, perceived discrimination, and parental support as determinants of immigrants' school adjustments. *Journal of Adolescent Research*, *19*(6), 635–656. https://doi.org/10.1177/0743558404269279.

Loh, K. Y. E., & Hung, O. Y. (2020). A Study on the Challenges Faced by Mainstream Schools in Educating Ethnic Minorities in Hong Kong. Research report. https://www.oxfam.org.hk/f/news_and_publication/43418/EOC_EM_Mainstream%20Schools_202001.pdf

Lundy, L. (2007). 'Voice' is not enough: Conceptualising article 12 of the United Nations convention on the rights of the child. *British Educational Research Journal*, *33*(6), 927–942. https://doi.org/10.1080/01411920701657033.

McLeod, J. (2011). Student voice and the politics of listening in higher education. *Critical Studies in Education*, *52*(2), 179–189. https://doi.org/10.1080/17508487.2011.572830.

Miliband, D. (2006). Choice and voice in personalised learning. In Centre for Educational Research and Innovation (Ed.), *Schooling for tomorrow: Personalising education* (pp. 21–30). OECD Publishing.

Mitra, D. L. (2003). Student voice in school reform: Reframing student-teacher relationships. *McGill Journal of Education*, *38*(2), 289–304. https://www.semanticscholar.org/paper/STUDENT-VOICE-IN-SCHOOL-REFORM%3A-REFRAMING-Mitra/b5b750aa72f95f02e20f2835cef25dd583ed1687

Mitra, D. L. (2004). The significance of students: Can increasing "student voice" in schools lead to gains in youth development? *Teachers College Record*, *106*(4), 651–688. https://doi.org/10.1111/j.1467-9620.2004.00354.x.

Mitra, D. L., & Gross, S. J. (2009). Increasing student voice in high school reform. *Educational Management Administration & Leadership*, *37*(4), 522–543. https://doi.org/10.1177/1741143209334577.

Morgan, W., & Streb, M. (2001). Building citizenship: How student voice in service-learning develops civic values. *Social Science Quarterly*, *82*(1), 154–169. https://doi.org/10.1111/0038-4941.00014.

Pong, S. (2009). Grade level and achievement of immigrants' children: Academic redshirting in Hong Kong. *Educational Research and Evaluation*, 15(4), 405–425. https://doi.org/10.1080/13803610903087078.

Portes, A., & Rumbaut, R. G. (2001). *Legacies: The story of the immigrant second generation* (1st ed.). University of California Press.

Rainer, J. D., & Matthews, M. W. (2002). Ownership of learning in teacher education. *Action in Teacher Education*, 24(1), 22–30. https://doi.org/10.1080/01626620.2002.10463264.

Rampal, A. (2012). Students' views on equity and justice in India's schools. In C. Day (Ed.), *The Routledge international handbook of teacher and school development* (pp. 243–253). Taylor & Francis.

Rudduck, J., & Fielding, M. (2006). Student voice and the perils of popularity. *Educational Review*, 58(2), 219–231. https://doi.org/10.1080/00131910600584207.

Sahin, A., & Top, N. (2015). STEM students on the stage (SOS): Promoting student voice and choice in STEM education through an interdisciplinary, standards-focused project based learning approach. *Journal of STEM Education*, 16(3), 24–33. https://www.learntechlib.org/p/151970/article_151970.pdf

Schwartz, S. J., Montgomery, M. J., & Briones, E. (2006). The role of identity in acculturation among immigrant people: Theoretical propositions, empirical questions, and applied recommendations. *Human Development*, 49(1), 1–30. https://doi.org/10.1159/000090300.

Serriere, S., & Mitra, D. L. (2012). Critical issues and contexts of student voice in the United States. In C. Day (Ed.), *The Routledge international handbook of teacher and school development* (pp. 223–232). Taylor & Francis.

Shek, D. T. L. (2002). Family functioning and psychological well-being, school adjustment, and problem behavior in Chinese adolescents with and without economic disadvantage. *The Journal of Genetic Psychology*, 163(4), 497–502. https://doi.org/10.1080/00221320209598698.

Simmons, C., Graham, A., & Thomas, N. (2015). Imagining an ideal school for wellbeing: Locating student voice. *Journal of Educational Change*, 16(2), 129–144. https://doi.org/10.1007/s10833-014-9239-8.

Smith, E., & Gorard, S. (2006). Pupils' views on equity in schools. *Compare: A Journal of Comparative and International Education*, 36(1), 41–56. https://doi.org/10.1080/03057920500382465.

Sorenson, D. L. (1994). Valuing the student voice: Student observer/consultant programs. *To Improve the Academy*, 13(20201217), 97–108. https://doi.org/10.3998/tia.17063888.0013.008.

Weiss, A. M. (1991). South Asian Muslims in Hong Kong: Creation of a 'Local boy' identity. *Modern Asian Studies*, 25(3), 417–453. https://doi.org/10.1017/s0026749x00013895.

Yang, S., Miao, B., & Wu, A. M. (2020). Immigration and public attitudes towards social assistance: Evidence from Hong Kong. *Journal of Economic Policy Reform*, 1–17. https://doi.org/10.1080/17487870.2020.1760102

Yuen, C. Y. M. (2010). Assimilation, integration and the construction of identity: The experience of Chinese cross-boundary and newly arrived students in Hong Kong schools. *Multicultural Education Review*, 2(2), 1–30. https://doi.org/10.1080/2005-615x.2010.11102873.

Yuen, C. Y. M. (2011). Cross-boundary students in Hong Kong schools: Education provisions and school experiences. In J. A. Phillion, M. T. Hue, & Y. Wang (Eds.), *Minority students in East Asia: Government policies, school practices, and teacher responses* (pp. 174–192). Routledge.

Yuen, C. Y. M. (2013). School engagement and civic engagement as predictors for the future political participation of ethnic Chinese and South Asian adolescents in Hong Kong. *Migracijske i Etničke Teme/Migration and Ethnic Themes*, *29*(3), 317–342. https://doi.org/10.11567/met.29.3.1.

Yuen, C. Y. M. (2014). School engagement and civic engagement as predictors for the future political participation of ethnic Chinese and South Asian adolescents in Hong Kong. *Migration and Ethnic Themes*, *29*(3), 317–342. http://doi.org/10.11567/met.29.3.1.

Yuen, C. Y. M. (2016). Utilizing pedagogical strategies of the learner-centred model in primary small class teaching settings in Hong Kong. In P. Blatchford, K. W. Chan, M. Galton, K. C. Lai, & C. K. J. Lee (Eds.), *Class size: Eastern and western perspectives* (1st ed., pp. 259–271). Routledge.

Yuen, C. Y. M. (2018). Perceptions of social justice among the South Asian and mainstream Chinese youth from diverse cultural backgrounds in Hong Kong. *Peabody Journal of Education*, *93*(3), 332–344. https://doi.org/10.1080/0161956x.2018.1449928.

Yuen, C. Y. M., & Lee, M. (2013). Mapping the life satisfaction of adolescents in Hong Kong secondary schools with high ethnic concentration. *Youth & Society*, *48*(4), 539–556. https://doi.org/10.1177/0044118x13502060.

Yuen, C. Y. M., & Leung, C. S. S. (2019). Belonging and connectedness: Identity, religiosity and aspiration of immigrant Muslim youth in Hong Kong. *Asia Pacific Journal of Education*, *39*(4), 423–435. https://doi.org/10.1080/02188791.2019.1671802.

Yuen, C. Y. M., & Wu, R. (2011). New schooling and new identities: Chinese immigrant students' perspectives. *Global Studies of Childhood*, *1*(2), 140–151. https://doi.org/10.2304/gsch.2011.1.2.140.

Zhou, M., & Bankston, C. L. (1994). Social capital and the adaptation of the second generation: The case of Vietnamese youth in New Orleans. *International Migration Review*, *28*(4), 821–845. https://doi.org/10.1177/019791839402800409.

3 Well-Being and Connectedness

Wellness, spirituality, and life satisfaction

Youth live in very different times from their parents and often find themselves transitioning due to immigration, education, career choices, wars, and other reasons. Social discontentment, relationship, identity and academic achievements are current issues facing the youth today. Therefore, there is a pressing need to re-examine the notion of the youth's well-being and connectedness for the era. Well-being can be a contested concept and has become an acronym for a favourable condition of an individual, subject to their cultural frame of reference. The issues of well-being and connectedness of the youth have been located squarely in the centre of attention across the globe. Concerning youth wellness, in an examination-oriented society, it usually refers to the desired outcomes of education, health, relationships, self-discipline, and future aspirations. Nevertheless, the notion of well-being can be rather abstract or even idealistic if we ignore the macro- and microsystemic factors affecting the youth in the contemporary world (Spratt, 2017). Their identification and connectedness with the school directly impact their subjective well-being, especially life satisfaction and self-actualisation for all school-age youth.

The impacts of spirituality and spiritual practice on young people's well-being have been widely recognised, especially on mitigating stress and anxiety. Raftopoulos and Bates (2011) warrant that spirituality fosters resilience by providing a sense of protection and security, a feeling of being meaningful, coherent, and optimistic, and consequently, the chance to increase self-awareness and self-efficacy. Increasingly researchers are interested in exploring the relationship between spirituality and health. This study of Reutter and Bigatti (2014) is an example. They interrogate the resilient role of religiosity and spirituality and conclude that they decrease stress levels and improve health status.

Fisher (1998) defines spirituality as a person's awareness of the existence and experience of inner feelings and beliefs that give purpose, meaning, and value to life. The Spiritual Health and Life Orientation Measure (SHALOM) by Gomez and Fisher (2003) focuses on the personal, communal, environmental, and transcendental domains to indicate a person's relationships with oneself, others, the environment, and the transcendental other.

DOI: 10.4324/9780429439315-3

Spirituality fits nicely within the notion of holistic and positive development. Studies confirm that spiritual health is critical for cultivating adolescents' inner strengths to tackle adverse life circumstances and inspiring hope for an uncertain future. It ignites adolescents' self-worth, gratitude, resilience, and righteousness and leads to altruistic behaviours (Yuen & Leung, 2022; Zullig et al., 2006). Milot and Ludden (2009) maintain that adolescents reporting religion as necessary in life are more motivational, while those with high religious attendance tend to have higher scores. Another study conducted by Park (2001) shows that religiousness is a significant predictor of high school students' academic achievement. In Hong Kong, studies on South and Southeast Asian students have discerned a relationship between spiritual health and life satisfaction with distinctive features across mainstream and non-mainstream student groups (Yuen, 2013; Yuen & Lee, 2016) together with their school engagement. School engagement is a vital indicator of positive youth development (Fredricks et al., 2004) because it helps combat early dropout and at-risk behaviours (Archambault et al., 2009; Finn, 1989) while improving the quality of life and promoting positive thinking among youngsters (Upadyaya & Salmela-Aro, 2013). It compels a further inquiry for a deeper understanding of this relationship.

Spirituality and religiosity are interrelated, different, and can be controversial. Some scholars considered religiosity and spirituality as two overlapping concepts, while their intersection may be examined independently. Hill et al. (2000) viewed spirituality as a central and crucial function of religion, emphasising their co-occurrence. The sense of sacredness in terms of the ultimate truth or the divine was considered the core for both. Wright et al. (2018) view spirituality as internal experiences with the sacred, and religiosity specifies individuals' relevant external practice. Some scholars perceived religion as one of the dimensions of spirituality, and spirituality is framed in a broader construct. A religious belief system may not be required in some circumstances. For instance, Briggs and colleagues (2011) illustrated the four components of spirituality as the innate capacity of searching for meaning and purpose in life: personal belief, value and ideas for success, connectedness with transcendence in terms of the divine or other supernatural power, and connectedness with a community sharing the same beliefs and values. Zullig et al. (2006) conceptualised spirituality as a way of being influenced by religion or acquired somewhere else. Fisher (2004, 2011) used a four-domain model – personal, communal, environmental, and transcendental domains – to reflect spiritual health concerning self, others, environment, and a God. In a nutshell, the broadly defined spirituality is the facilitator for searching meaning and purposes in life and determines how to view life and deal with life events (Unterrainer et al., 2014; Zullig et al., 2006).

Reaching a consensus on one unifying definition of spirituality may be a challenge. Nevertheless, spirituality contributes to life satisfaction. Both concepts relate the happiness of individuals to the internal self and external domains. Religion is a distinct domain for spirituality adding beliefs and values to the self-domain of self-actualisation. Their fundamental difference might be that life satisfaction is the cognitive dimension of comparing ideal and real situations based on personal views (Ellison, 1991). Spiritual health focuses on assessing quality relationships in relevant domains (Fisher, 2004).

Spiritual well-being and flourishing

Spiritual well-being covers the religious domain articulating life satisfaction and relates religious beliefs and participation to individuals' existential well-being (Ellison, 1983). The construct of spirituality in the contemporary discussion is multidimensional, involving several spheres of life dimensions. However, spiritual well-being may be considered independent of religiosity, but religion is a prominent domain/dimension in spirituality and is widely supported in empirical studies. Unlike the satisfaction from pleasure-seeking acts, religion brings meaning and fulfilment in life for a more endured journey of being. Voluminous research has shown that religiosity is an influential preventive factor for modifying risk behaviours such as substance use, adolescent crime, and self-harm (Carol et al., 2020; Dew et al., 2008; Milot & Ludden, 2009; Sigurvinsdottir et al., 2020; Soldera et al., 2004). Besides, religious belief is a strong motivating force for altruistic and voting behaviours (Gerber et al., 2016; Hardy & Carlo, 2005). Gibson (2008) found that the frequency of church attendance was positively associated with the likelihood of student's participation in voluntary services.

A religious cultivation environment can raise transcendental well-being (TWB) and positively affect the other domains (Fisher, 2011). Adolescent's spiritual health is connected with their religious characters and their school's religious background (Francis et al., 2012). Similarly, Malaysian undergraduate students' high spirituality and life satisfaction levels were associated with their religious backgrounds and the university's religious environment (Imam et al., 2009). In Hong Kong, the group divergence of spiritual well-being between religious NCS students and non-religious CIS suggests that the development of a community sharing the same and strong religious beliefs and values among minorities in schools benefits the overall spiritual health and life satisfaction (Yuen, 2013; Yuen & Lee, 2016).

A multidimensional measure of the religious domain is argued as more precisely predicting spiritual well-being than a general form. Kim and Esquivel (2011) viewed engagement in religion from three orientations – participation in religious activities as the intrinsic orientation, adopting a belief system as the extrinsic orientation, and the search orientation for seeking relations to the divine. The depth and importance of religious beliefs and engagement in religious activities are two common aspects of researching the interaction between the transcendental and other research studies domains. Some studies focused on faithfulness in the religious domain in discussing spirituality (Unterrainer et al., 2014) while others on rituals and participation. Kelley and Miller (2007) asserted that multiple dimensional measures of engagement in religious-related activities and religious beliefs are more predicable for life satisfaction than single-item measures. Moreover, Hall et al. (2008) also included religion such as coping, well-being, belief, affiliation, maturity, history, and experience.

Spirituality and religion have been discussed as essential systems that impact adolescent development and promote thriving, cultivating positive behaviours, and overcoming adversities at a critical age (King et al., 2013). Religious involvement is positively associated with the social capital in school, family, and community, leading to academic achievement and progress (Glanville et al., 2008; Muller & Ellison, 2001). Such findings have further confirmed spiritual health and religious faith's contributing role in individuals' global well-being. The academic measures of these studies encompass efforts to study attitudes, participation, academic outcomes, and school attachment. Some research studies suggest that religious involvement in academic outcomes is pronounced in disadvantaged and immigrant students (Bankston & Zhou, 2002; Jeynes, 2003).

So far, the discussion on the topic is mainly in the western cultural contexts. Only in recent years have there been emergent Hong Kong studies. Given the limitations of using secondary data, such as the improper measurement of the constructs and the inappropriateness of the information to address research questions (Dunn et al., 2015), our research team conducted a systematic study using primary data to unfold the relationship between religion and the civic engagement of the Hong Kong students more clearly. The two specific research questions were as follows:

1. How did gender, level of study, ethnicity, family factors, and views on religion and spirituality affect religious students' TWB in Hong Kong?
2. To what extent did prayer frequency and religious activities frequency mediate between demographic variables and TWB?

Transcendental well-being (TWB)

The 5-item transcendental domain of SHALOM (Fisher, 2008) was administrated to examine students' TWB. Students had to self-evaluate their relationship with the Divine/God using a 5-point Likert scale, ranging from very low (1) to very high (5). Internal consistency was indicated by the result of Cronbach's α (.926).

Guided by the focus of the study, the stratified purposeful sampling was employed to invite schools with a certain percentage of CIS and NCS South/Southeast Asian students. Their rights to participate or not in the study were fully respected following the ethical research procedure. Formal written consent was sought from them. The questionnaire survey was administered to all students, from secondary one to six, in each school. In total, 15,428 students aged between 12 and 19 from 28 schools were sampled. Seventy-three percent was HKCS, 16% CIS, 7% NCS, and 4% CBS. The majority (63%) indicated no religious affiliation, 24% affiliated with Christianity/Catholicism; 7% affiliated with Buddhism; 2% affiliated with Islam and others, and 1% affiliated with Hinduism and Taoism. Their views on religious activities and perception of TWB are discussed in the following.

Demographic variables

Participants were asked for their family background and religion-related activities in addition to gender, level of study, and ethnicity. Specifically, students had to report their father's and mother's highest education level coded as binary variables (secondary or below vs. post-secondary or above). Their family monthly income was also examined, and students were separated into two groups, below or above Hong Kong Dollars (HKD) 20,000. Regarding related religious activities, students were asked about their participation in prayer and religious activities. Both variables were dichotomous with never/seldom and always.

Mplus (version 7) using the weighted least squares (WLSMV) estimator was employed to conduct the statistical analyses. On the one hand, Probit Regression was performed to examine the relationship between the demographic variables, prayer frequency, and religious activities frequency, as the dependent variable is binary. On the other, significant predictors for TWB were identified by multiple linear regression, where TWB was a continuous dependent variable. Indirect effects were also investigated in which prayer frequency and religious activity frequency were treated as mediators (Figure 3.1).

There are 1,188 male and 1,104 female religious students in the dataset. Among them, 1,269 were S.1–S.3 (6th–8th graders), while 1,023 were S.4–S.6 students (9th–12th graders) at the time of the survey. Concerning their ethnicity, 1,793 were Chinese, and 559 were non-Chinese, mainly NCS South/

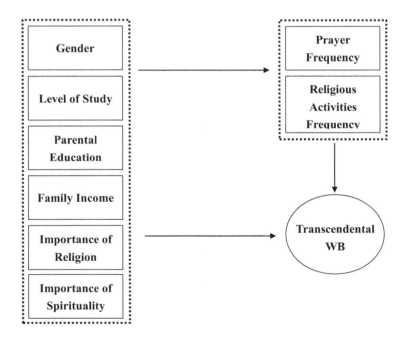

Figure 3.1 Path Analysis on Factors Affecting Transcendental Well-Being

Table 3.1 Regression coefficients on Transcendental Well-Being

	Estimate	SE	Est./SE	Two-tailed p-value
Gender (Ref: Male)	−0.117	0.034	−3.455	0.001
Level of study (Ref: Junior)	−0.107	0.031	−3.448	0.001
Ethnicity (Ref: Chinese)	0.366	0.037	9.960	0.000
Father's education	0.064	0.044	1.470	0.141
Mother's education	−0.014	0.045	−0.298	0.766
Family income	0.043	0.035	1.205	0.228
Importance of religion	0.600	0.041	14.635	0.000
Importance of spirituality	0.244	0.036	6.727	0.000
Prayer frequency	0.206	0.036	5.753	0.000
Religious activities frequency	−0.016	0.035	−0.461	0.645

Southeast Asian adolescents. Most of their parents completed secondary education (1,766 fathers and 1,831 mothers). However, only 526 fathers and 461 mothers had a post-secondary level. There were 1,638 students from low-income families, and 654 students' families earned HKD20,000 (USD 2,564) monthly.

Table 3.1 presents the findings of multiple linear regression on TWB. Remarkably, gender, level of study, ethnicity, student's view of religion and spirituality, and prayer frequency significantly predicted their TWB. Female students reported a lower level of TWB than their male counterparts. Junior students experienced a better TWB than the seniors. Consistent with previous findings, South Asian students have a higher TWB than Chinese peers. Students who viewed religions and spirituality as more critical may have experienced a higher level of TWB than those who viewed spirituality as less critical. Pray is positively related to their TWB. The more students prayed, the higher the TWB level they reported. Even though religious youth are mostly coming from religious families, the family factor has no significant impact on their TWB. Additionally, neither parental education nor family income was a significant predictor for religious students' TWB.

Table 3.2 showed the results in examining the relationship between students' information and prayer frequency. Again, a gender difference was noted.

Table 3.2 Probit regression coefficients on prayer frequency

	Estimate	SE	Est./SE	Two-tailed p-value
Gender	0.335	0.063	5.292	0.000
Level of study	−0.044	0.063	−0.701	0.483
Ethnicity	0.179	0.078	2.284	0.022
Father's education	0.094	0.092	1.029	0.304
Mother's education	0.168	0.097	1.737	0.082
Family income	0.060	0.070	0.846	0.398
Importance of religion	1.245	0.074	16.725	0.000
Importance of spirituality	0.205	0.076	2.706	0.007

Table 3.3 Probit regression coefficients on religious activities frequency

	Estimate	SE	Est./SE	Two-tailed p-value
Gender	−0.040	0.057	−0.710	0.478
Level of study	−0.003	0.057	−0.045	0.964
Ethnicity	0.173	0.069	2.497	0.013
Father's education	0.074	0.080	0.917	0.359
Mother's education	0.159	0.084	1.888	0.059
Family income	0.117	0.066	1.784	0.074
Importance of religion	0.967	0.072	13.439	0.000
Importance of spirituality	0.197	0.073	2.692	0.007

Female students prayed significantly more than male students. Additionally, ethnicity was a predictor for prayer frequency that South and Southeast Asians prayed more than the Chinese students.

Moreover, students' views on religion and spirituality's importance were positively related to their prayer frequency. Similar results could be identified for religious activities frequency (Table 3.3). Ethnicity, views on religion, and spirituality were significant predictors for their attendance at religious activities. Nevertheless, the level of study, father's and mother's education, and family income were not significant in predicting prayer and religious activity frequency.

In order to understand the mechanism underlining youth's perception of TWB, mediation analysis was conducted. Different types of mediating effects through prayer frequency were examined, as shown in Table 3.4. According to the findings, a significant indirect effect of prayer frequency on TWB was observed. Religious females prayed more frequently, and this action significantly improved their TWB, even though they still rated their TWB lower than males. South and Southeast Asian students also prayed more than their Chinese counterparts, and the practice was significantly improved their TWB. Thus, the indirect effects of the importance of religion and spirituality on TWB were also mediated by prayer frequency.

Interestingly, the family background was not significant in predicting the TWB of religious students. Previous studies suggested that religious participation was an essential factor for adolescents' spirituality (Moodley et al., 2012). The study provides insights into the differential impacts of religious participation

Table 3.4 Indirect effects to Transcendental Well-Being through prayer frequency

	Estimate	SE	Est./SE	Two-tailed p-value
Gender	0.069	0.017	3.960	0.000
Ethnicity	0.037	0.018	2.098	0.036
Importance of religion	0.256	0.047	5.478	0.000
Importance of spirituality	0.042	0.017	2.486	0.013

and its associated values on TWB development. Notably, prayer frequency, but not attending religious activities, was significant in predicting youth TWB. It might suggest that students do not equate religious activities with prayer in Hong Kong. Many people believe that going to church, fellowship meetings, and religious gatherings are part of their social lives. Sociologists argue that attending religious activities is a relational activity with people and can boost up the social capital of the immigrant and minority people. However, prayer contributes directly to personal awareness of God/the high order being. In other words, religious activities, such as worship, praise, and fellowship, can be viewed as a kind of interaction with religious institutions. In contrast, prayer has a more definite role in nurturing an individual's spirituality and awareness in seeking divine assistance from transcendental beings (Moodley et al., 2012).

Gender difference is a point of interest in religious studies. For instance, girls are spiritually healthier than boys (Brown et al., 2013; Hammermeister et al., 2005; Yuen, 2015). The Hong Kong data reveal an unexpected result that religious boys experienced a better TWB than religious girls. Nevertheless, consistent with international studies (Park et al., 2013), religious girls in our study are significantly more devoted to prayer than boys and reported a more enhanced TWB. That being said, religious girls still reported a lower level of TWB than boys. It raised a question. What are the advantages of boys becoming transcendentally well? One possible reason is that TWB is a complex concept that is affected by religious identity more than prayer. Religious identity influences boys more than girls regarding spirituality (Bryant, 2007). Religions such as Islam and Christianity have a history of male orientation. The roles of societal expectations on gender and the teaching of faith traditions on gender deserve further exploration.

Ethnicity contributes to public understanding of youth TWB. Religious South and Southeast Asian students reported a higher level of TWB than their Chinese religious counterparts significantly. As indicated previously, prayer has significantly mediated the TWB, and most of the NCS sample are self-identified as Muslims, practice five times of daily prayer. These devout Muslims treat their faith very seriously. Their perceptions of the importance of religion and spirituality significantly nurtured their subjective assessment of TWB, strengthened by their daily and regular prayers. Thus, religion is a salient predictor for TWB, with both direct and indirect effects, compared with the importance of spirituality in the sample.

The survey data unravelled how individual factors affect their awareness of the transcendental being and their subjective well-being. At the same time, there was ample evidence of religious youth's activities and their relationship with themselves, others, and the divine being. The study suggests a need for exploring the interaction between gender role, religious practice, and ethnicity. Prayer frequency mediated the effect of both gender and ethnicity on TWB (Yuen, 2015). Prior quantitative studies (Yuen & Lee, 2016; Yuen et al., 2016) have shown that religious South and Southeast Asians outscored Chinese religious youth in Hong Kong regarding satisfaction with life, school, and self even though many are of humble origin. It would be essential to identify the difference between South Asian and Chinese students' views on religion and spirituality.

Life satisfaction in a spiritual and educational context

Renewed attention has been focused on a balanced and holistic approach to examining education, spiritual health, and school engagement. Although academic achievement is universally regarded as a positive and desirable goal, it does not directly impact students' well-being. Too much emphasis on academic achievement can demoralise students and, in return, lower their life satisfaction. According to the study of 2015 PISA by the OECD, the total scores of Hong Kong students in the tests were second highest in East Asia. Achievement of such excellent international results academically, their life satisfaction score was the second lowest in East Asia. The well-being of Hong Kong students remains a pressing issue. In 2019, there were recorded 993 suicide deaths, of which 140 are in their youth, accounting for 38 more deaths than in 2018 (Dimsumdaily Hong Kong, 2019). As indicated previously, schools are charged with providing essential knowledge, skills, and attitudes for all students' adult living.

Life satisfaction is related to intrapersonal, interpersonal, and environmental variables from a broad view (Ash & Huebner, 2001). Global life satisfaction refers to individuals' subjective views of their overall life quality based on personal standards (Diener et al., 2004; Pavot & Diener, 1993). Life satisfaction is a kind of subjective assessment of personal relationships or wellness in the domains of self, family, school, and friends (Civitci & Civitci, 2009), and vice versa (Lewis et al., 2011). For adolescents, their cognitive and emotional engagement, family, social, and school contexts are facilitators and agents for their life satisfaction. The interaction of such intrapersonal and environmental variables is a valuable model for investigating youth life satisfaction (Ash & Huebner, 2001). Put differently, assessing life satisfaction not only sees how *satisfied individuals* are with their lives, but it is also a means of knowing how and why the feeling (either positive or negative affect) exists (Diener, 1984). The multidimensional nature of life satisfaction towards family, self, friends, and living environment sheds insights into different spheres of youth subjective well-being (Huebner, 1998). Indeed, life satisfaction is a full assessment of youth thinkings, and it extends from negative to positive emotions, depending on how they react to a situation.

Self

The self is an object of its reflective consciousness and a subject of its esteem. The place of self-esteem in life satisfaction has been well documented in the literature (Kwan et al., 1997; Rey et al., 2011). Self-esteem is concerned with personal perceptions of self-worth and self-importance (Rosenberg, 1965), linking intrinsic motivation and industrious learning actions. For example, global self-esteem is considered the coping resource and protective factor in aversive circumstances to help individuals stay afloat and maintain positive life satisfaction (Moksnes & Espnes, 2013). Compared with their mainstream peers, immigrant and ethnic minority students have to tackle stress and anxiety associated with acculturation issues such as language learning, cultural understanding, discrimination, and hostility in the new society. Questions such as how they handle the negative experience and how they interpret their situations require affirmative actions from society to prevent them from developing low self-esteem and the feeling of being unimportant.

Enhancement and boosting self-esteem are commonly discussed with the construction of identity among immigrant youth. Vacek et al. (2010) confirm that stress is a significant source contributing to the negative emotion of the urban minority youth's subjective well-being from low-income families. Girls reported a higher level of stress and negative affect than those experienced by boys. The findings support that the development of self-esteem and optimism is more likely to enhance immigrant students' life satisfaction and racial identity, increase their positive future expectancies, and reduce depressive symptoms (Vacek et al., 2010; Wong et al., 2012). Hope and social support are associated with higher levels of personal and relational self-esteem, which leads to decreased levels of depression (Du et al., 2016). Inspiring immigrant or disadvantaged youth to hope for the best and strive for excellence in life can give way to a sense of personal and relational self-esteem.

Chinese immigrant youth in North America with high ethnic identity enjoy positive psychological well-being, high self-esteem, and happiness. Their experience reflects that establishing stable social networks, having a sense of purpose in life, and holding a positive self-concept are all essential qualities for subjective well-being (Costigan et al., 2010; Kiang et al., 2006; Rivas-Drake et al., 2008). Hence, we should employ a positive view of the heritage and local cultures of immigrant youth. They contribute to these youth's sociocultural adaptation and psychological well-being (Berry & Sabatier, 2010). These positive notes bear implications for the curriculum policy of schools with students from different ethnic backgrounds.

Family

Parenting is a vital vehicle for positive and productive student engagement and achievement. This is especially the case for non-mainstream students. Take bilingualism as an example. Due to the lack of bilingualism policy, parental attitude towards heritage culture and language becomes prominent and affects immigrant youth choose to brush up their original language or not (Liebkind et al., 2004). The place of family in Hong Kong students' wellness and academic engagement has been reiterated. Earlier in Chapter 2, the lack of family social capital may place CIS and NCS South/Southeast Asian students in a disadvantaged school and social engagement situation. Nevertheless, their family's religious and spiritual heritage mediates their adverse life circumstances and boosts their resilience and parental support appreciation. This point will be further explored in the interview data.

In Hong Kong, our recent study (Mingpaocanada, 2021; Yuen et al., 2021) unravels that making parents happy is a motivator for positive PSE aspirations of immigrant and ethnic minority students. Hence, parental aspiration and expectation, parental support in communication and supervision, school participation, and cultural socialisation (Bingham & Okagaki, 2012) positively contribute to immigrant students' school engagement (Yuen & Cheung, 2014). The association of authoritative parenting with student learning outcomes and achievements varied across ethnic groups in western countries, while it is the weakest in the higher individualism cultural group (Pinquart & Kauser, 2018). Findings of immigrant studies have concluded that parental involvement is a robust predictive index for immigrant children's learning (Drummond & Stipek, 2004; Fan, 2001; Hong & Ho, 2005; Rumbaut, 2000). Specifically, parental aspirations/expectations for children's academic achievement substantially affect their learning outcomes (Fan & Chen, 2001). Chinese parents generally value academic achievement more than other ethnic groups, believing that education is the chief avenue for their children's upward social mobility (Eng, 1995). Confucian value emphasising education and family dynamics appears to foster students' academic achievement in the Asian contexts as parents have high expectations of education for their children and are responsive to their learning needs (Huang & Gove, 2015).

School

School provides a proximal context for immigrant students to adapt and integrate into the new culture and society. In a knowledge-based economy, satisfactory academic achievement leads to self-agency in navigating the academic turf. Naturally, it contributes to their positive academic self-esteem and enhances the sense of pride and belonging to the school (Chiu et al., 2012; Motti-Stefanidi & Masten, 2013). Positive friendship building is a significant motivator for tremendous future success leading to social integration and self-gratification of life outcomes (Chow, 2007). Fredricks et al. (2004) famously initiate the multidimensional school engagement framework looking at the behavioural, cognitive, and emotional constructs. The framework has been further fine-tuned to adopt a holistic approach to understand student engagement (Bingham & Okagaki, 2012). The behavioural domain includes elements of student participation in academic and extracurricular activities. Essential skills include learning how to be a responsible member of the community, a responsible student at school, and a trustworthy friend. Cognitively, students know how to develop a sense of purpose in life for self-actualisation. The total school learning experience should cover intrinsic motivation and metacognitive strategies for self-directed learning, aspiration towards adult living, and the ability to tackle problems. Realising all these cognitive strategies leads to global well-being and overall satisfaction of school experience (Bingham & Okagaki, 2012; Fredricks et al., 2004; Lewis et al., 2011; Motti-Stefanidi & Masten, 2013).

As spirituality and well-being affect different spheres of an individual, life satisfaction is a multidimensional construct by nature. The life satisfaction score of young people refers to the dimensions of family, friends, school, living environment, and self (Huebner, 2004). All these dimensions form a factual basis of subjective well-being. To Diener (1984), well-being is a subjective assessment of global life satisfaction involving both positive and negative affect. Given the subjective nature of well-being and life satisfaction, the personal values and beliefs issue, existential well-being issues have to be considered (Unterrainer et al., 2014).

Cultural context shapes the understanding of well-being and life satisfaction. Spiritual well-being also reflects their emotions, happiness, or sadness. CIS and South and Southeast Asian students tend to be more religious than their Chinese counterparts (Yuen, 2019). Such affiliation contributes to their sense of connectedness in their faith community (Peterson, 2017). Despite many obstacles and numerous failures, religious NCS students often stay upbeat and remain hopeful in their earthly living (Yuen & Leung, 2019).

Further, the sense of belonging in the community, school, and family will contribute positively to students' well-being and help cushion their negative emotional responses to various academic situations. For instance, religious youth can better cope with negative life factors, financial and language barriers in pursuing higher education. They tend to express higher satisfaction with life and hold high gratitude towards their parents and teachers. Some fit into the typologies, and some fall outside of them as unfolded in individual narratives in the following chapters.

References

Archambault, I., Janosz, M., Morizot, J., & Pagani, L. (2009). Adolescent behavioral, affective, and cognitive engagement in school: Relationship to dropout. *Journal of School Health*, 79(9), 408–415. https://doi.org/10.1111/j.1746-1561.2009.00428.x.

Ash, C., & Huebner, E. S. (2001). Environmental events and life satisfaction reports of adolescents. *School Psychology International*, 22(3), 320–336. https://doi.org/10.1177/0143034301223008.

Bankston, C. L., & Zhou, M. (2002). Social capital and immigrant children's achievement. In B. Fuller, & E. Hannum (Eds.), *Schooling and social capital in diverse cultures* (1st ed., pp. 13–39). Emerald Publishing Limited.

Berry, J. W., & Sabatier, C. (2010). Acculturation, discrimination, and adaptation among second generation immigrant youth in Montreal and Paris. *International Journal of Intercultural Relations*, 34(3), 191–207. https://doi.org/10.1016/j.ijintrel.2009.11.007.

Bingham, G. E., & Okagaki, L. (2012). Ethnicity and student engagement. In S. L. Christenson, A. L. Reschly, & C. Wylie (Eds.), *Handbook of research on student engagement* (1st ed., pp. 65–95). Springer.

Briggs, M. K., Akos, P., Czyszczon, G., & Eldridge, A. (2011). Assessing and promoting spiritual wellness as a protective factor in secondary schools. *Counseling and Values*, 55(2), 171–184. https://doi.org/10.1002/j.2161-007x.2011.tb00030.x.

Brown, T., Chen, T., Gehlert, N. C., & Piedomont, R. L. (2013). Age and gender effects on the assessment of spirituality and religious sentiments (ASPIRES) scale: A cross-sectional analysis. *Psychology of Religion and Spirituality*, 5(2), 90–98. https://psycnet.apa.org/doi/10.1037/a0030137.

Bryant, A. N. (2007). Gender differences in spiritual development during the college years. *Sex Roles*, 56, 835–846. https://doi.org/10.1007/s11199-007-9240-2

Carol, S., Peez, F., & Wagner, M. (2020). Delinquency among majority and minority youths in Cologne, Mannheim and Brussels: The role of religion. *Journal of Ethnic and Migration Studies, 46*(17), 3603–3629. https://doi.org/10.1080/1369183X.2019.1620415.

Chiu, M. M., Pong, S., Mori, I., & Chow, B. W.-Y. (2012). Immigrant students' emotional and cognitive engagement at school: A multilevel analysis of students in 41 countries. *Journal of Youth and Adolescence, 41*(11), 1409–1425. https://doi.org/10.1007/s10964-012-9763-x.

Chow, H. P. H. (2007). Sense of belonging and life satisfaction among Hong Kong adolescent immigrants in Canada. *Journal of Ethnic and Migration Studies, 33*(3), 511–520. https://doi.org/10.1080/13691830701234830.

Civitci, N., & Civitci, A. (2009). Self-esteem as mediator and moderator of the relationship between loneliness and life satisfaction in adolescents. *Personality and Individual Differences, 47*(8), 954–958. https://doi.org/10.1016/j.paid.2009.07.022.

Costigan, C. L., Koryzma, C. M., Hua, J. M., & Chance, L. J. (2010). Ethnic identity, achievement, and psychological adjustment: Examining risk and resilience among youth from immigrant Chinese families in Canada. *Cultural Diversity and Ethnic Minority Psychology, 16*(2), 264–273. https://doi.org/10.1037/a0017275.

Dew, R. E., Daniel, S. S., Armstrong, T. D., Goldston, D. B., Triplett, M. F., & Koenig, H. G. (2008). Religion/spirituality and adolescent psychiatric symptoms: A review. *Child Psychiatry and Human Development, 39*(4), 381–398. https://doi.org/10.1007/s10578-007-0093-2.

Diener, E. (1984). Subjective well-being. *Psychological Bulletin, 95*(3), 542–575. https://doi.org/10.1007/978-90-481-2350-6_2.

Diener, E., Scollon, C. M., & Lucas, R. E. (2004). The evolving concept of subjective wellbeing: The multifaceted nature of happiness. In P. T. Costa, & I. C. Siegler (Eds.), *The psychology of aging* (1st ed., pp. 187–220). Elsevier.

Dimsumdaily Hong Kong. (2019). *Suicide cases in HK on the rise – average of 2.72 people committed suicide everyday in 2019.* https://www.dimsumdaily.hk/suicide-cases-in-hk-on-the-rise-average-of-2-72-people-committed-suicide-everyday-in-2019/

Drummond, K. V., & Stipek, D. (2004). Low-income parents' beliefs about their role in children's academic learning. *The Elementary School Journal, 104*(3), 197–213. https://doi.org/10.1086/499749.

Du, H., King, R. B., & Chu, S. K. (2016). Hope, social support, and depression among Hong Kong youth: Personal and relational self-esteem as mediators. *Psychology, Health & Medicine, 21*(8), 926–931. https://doi.org/10.1080/13548506.2015.1127397.

Dunn, S. L., Arslanian-Engoren, C., DeKoekkoek, T., Jadack, R., & Scott, L. D. (2015). Secondary data analysis as an efficient and effective approach to nursing research. *Western Journal of Nursing Research, 37*(10), 1295–1307. https://doi.org/10.1177%2F0193945915570042.

Ellison, C. W. (1983). Spiritual wellbeing: Conceptualization and measurement. *Journal of Psychology and Theology, 11*(4), 330–338. https://doi.org/10.1177/009164718301100406.

Ellison, C. G. (1991). Religious involvement and subjective wellbeing. *Journal of Health and Social Behavior, 32*(1), 80–99. https://doi.org/10.2307/2136801.

Eng, R. (1995). *"Road to virtue": The moral world of Chinese-and Korean-American students.* Harvard University Press.

Fan, X. (2001). Parental involvement and students' academic achievement: A growth modeling analysis. *The Journal of Experimental Education, 70*(1), 27–61. https://doi.org/10.1080/00220970109599497.

Fan, X., & Chen, M. (2001). Parental involvement and students' academic achievement: A meta-analysis. *Educational Psychology Review, 13*(1), 1–22. https://doi.org/10.1023/A:1009048817385.

Finn, J. D. (1989). Withdrawing from school. *Review of Educational Research, 59*(2), 117–142. https://doi.org/10.3102/00346543059002117.

Fisher, J. (1998). *Spirituality: Women's Journeys of Discovery: A Developmental Perspective* [Doctoral dissertation]. University of Auckland.

Fisher, J. (2004). Feeling good, living life: A spiritual health measure for young children. *Journal of Beliefs & Values, 25*(3), 307–315. https://doi.org/10.1080/1361767042000306121.

Fisher, J. (2008). Impacting teachers' and students' spiritual wellbeing. *Journal of Beliefs & Values, 29*(3), 253–261. https://doi.org/10.1080/13617670802465789.

Fisher, J. (2011). The four domains model: Connecting spirituality, health and wellbeing. *Religions, 2*(1), 17–28. https://doi.org/10.3390/rel2010017.

Francis, L. J., Penny, G., & Baker, S. (2012). Defining and assessing spiritual health: A comparative study among 13- to 15-year-old pupils attending secular schools, Anglican schools, and private Christian schools in England and Wales. *Peabody Journal of Education, 87*(3), 351–367. https://doi.org/10.1080/0161956x.2012.679590.

Fredricks, J. A., Blumenfeld, P. C., & Paris, A. H. (2004). School engagement: Potential of the concept, state of the evidence. *Review of Educational Research, 74*(1), 59–109. https://doi.org/10.3102/00346543074001059.

Gerber, A. S., Gruber, J., & Hungerman, D. M. (2016). Does church attendance cause people to vote? Using blue laws' repeal to estimate the effect of religiosity on voter turnout. *British Journal of Political Science, 46*(3), 481–500. https://doi.org/10.1017/S0007123414000416.

Gibson, T. (2008). Religion and civic engagement among America's youth. *The Social Science Journal, 45*(3), 504–514. https://doi.org/10.1016/j.soscij.2008.07.007.

Glanville, J. L., Sikkink, D., & Hernández, E. I. (2008). Religious involvement and educational outcomes: The role of social capital and extracurricular participation. *The Sociological Quarterly, 49*(1), 105–137. https://doi.org/10.1111/j.1533-8525.2007.00108.x.

Gomez, R., & Fisher, J. W. (2003). Domains of spiritual well-being and development and validation of the spiritual well-being questionnaire. *Personality and Individual Differences, 35*(8), 1975–1991. https://doi.org/10.1016/S0191-8869(03)00045-X.

Hall, D. E., Meador, K. G., & Koenig, H. G. (2008). Measuring religiousness in health research: Review and critique. *Journal of Religion and Health, 47*(2), 134–163. https://doi.org/10.1007/s10943-008-9165-2.

Hammermeister, J., Flint, M., El-Alayli, A., Eidnour, H., & Peterson, M. (2005). Gender differences in spiritual wellbeing: Are females more spirituality-well than males? *American Journal of Health Studies, 20*(2), 80–84.

Hardy, S. A., & Carlo, G. (2005). Identity as a source of moral motivation. *Human Development, 48*(4), 232–256. http://dx.doi.org/10.1159%2F000086859.

Hill, P. C., Pargament, K. I. I., Hood, R. W., McCullough, J. M. E., Swyers, J. P., Hong, S., & Ho, H. Z. (2005). Direct and indirect longitudinal effects of parental involvement on student achievement: Second-order latent growth modeling across ethnic groups. *Journal of Educational Psychology, 97*(1), 32. https://psycnet.apa.org/doi/10.1037/0022-0663.97.1.32.

Huang, G. H., & Gove, M. (2015). Asian parenting styles and academic achievement: Views from Eastern and Western perspectives. *Education, 135*(3), 389–397. http://content.ebscohost.com/ContentServer.asp?T=P&P=AN&K=101708141&S=R&D=asn

&EbscoContent=dGJyMMvl7ESep684yNfsOLCmsEmeprFSs6m4TbSWxWXS&ContentCustomer=dGJyMPGqsUmyprROuePfgeyx43zx

Huebner, E. S. (1998). Cross-racial application of a children's multidimensional life satisfaction scale. *School Psychology International*, *19*(2), 179–188. https://doi.org/10.1177%2F0143034398192006.

Huebner, E. S. (2004). Research on assessment of life satisfaction of children and adolescents. *Social Indicators Research*, *66*(1), 3–33. https://doi.org/10.1023/B:SOCI.0000007497.57754.e3

Imam, S. S., Nurullah, A. S., Makol-Abdul, P. R., Rahman, S. A., & Noon, H. M. (2009). Spiritual and psychological health of Malaysian youths. *Research in the Social Scientific Study of Religion*, *20*, 85–101. https://doi.org/10.1163/ej.9789004175624.i-334.28

Jeynes, W. H. (2003). The effects of religious commitment on the academic achievement of urban and other children. *Education and Urban Society*, *36*(1), 44–62. https://doi.org/10.1177/0013124503257206.

Kelley, B. S., & Miller, L. (2007). Life satisfaction and spirituality in adolescents. *Research in the Social Scientific Study of Religion*, *18*, 233–262. https://doi.org/10.1163/ej.9789004158511.i-301.91

Kiang, L., Yip, T., Gonzales-Backen, M., Witkow, M., & Fuligni, A. J. (2006). Ethnic identity and the daily psychological wellbeing of adolescents from Mexican and Chinese backgrounds. *Child Development*, *77*(5), 1338–1350. https://doi.org/10.1111/j.1467-8624.2006.00938.x.

Kim, S., & Esquivel, G. B. (2011). Adolescent spirituality and resilience: Theory, research, and educational practices. *Psychology in the Schools*, *48*(7), 755–765. https://doi.org/10.1002/pits.20582.

King, P. E., Ramos, J. S., & Clardy, C. E. (2013). Searching for the sacred: Religion, spirituality, and adolescent development. In K. I. Pargament, J. J. Exline, & J. W. Jones (Eds.), *APA handbook of psychology, religion, and spirituality. Vol. 1, context, theory, and research* (1st ed., pp. 513–528). American Psychological Association.

Kwan, V. S. Y., Bond, M. H., & Singelis, T. M. (1997). Pancultural explanations for life satisfaction: Adding relationship harmony to self-esteem. *Journal of Personality and Social Psychology*, *73*(5), 1038–1051. https://doi.org/10.1037/0022-3514.73.5.1038.

Larson, D. B., & Zinnbauer, B. J. (2000). Conceptualizing religion and spirituality: Points of commonality, points of departure. *Journal for the Theory of Social Behaviour*, *30*(1), 51–77. https://doi.org/10.1111/1468-5914.00119.

Lewis, A. D., Huebner, E. S., Malone, P. S., & Valois, R. F. (2011). Life satisfaction and student engagement in adolescents. *Journal of Youth and Adolescence*, *40*(3), 249–262. https://doi.org/10.1007/s10964-010-9517-6.

Liebkind, K., Jasinskaja-Lahti, I., & Solheim, E. (2004). Cultural identity, perceived discrimination, and parental support as determinants of immigrants' school adjustments. *Journal of Adolescent Research*, *19*(6), 635–656. https://doi.org/10.1177/0743558404269279.

Milot, A. S., & Ludden, A. B. (2009). The effects of religion and gender on wellbeing, substance use, and academic engagement among rural adolescents. *Youth & Society*, *40*(3), 403–425. https://doi.org/10.1177/0044118x08316668.

Mingpaocanada. (2021). *News bullet: Mother's views have the greatest impacts on high schoolers' PSE decision* (in Chinese). http://www.mingpaocanada.com/TOR/htm/News/20210104/hk-gfil_er_r.htm

Moksnes, U. K., & Espnes, G. A. (2013). Self-esteem and life satisfaction in adolescents — Gender and age as potential moderators. *Quality of Life Research*, *22*(10), 2921–2928. https://doi.org/10.1007/s11136-013-0427-4.

Moodley, T., Esterhuyse, K. G., & Beukes, R. B. (2012). Factor analysis of the spiritual wellbeing questionnaire using a sample of South African adolescents. *Religion and Theology, 19*(1-2), 122–151. https://doi.org/10.1163/157430112X650339.

Motti-Stefanidi, F., & Masten, A. S. (2013). School success and school engagement of immigrant children and adolescents. *European Psychologist, 18*(2), 126–135. https://doi.org/10.1027/1016-9040/a000139.

Muller, C., & Ellison, C. G. (2001). Religious involvement, social capital, and adolescents' academic progress: Evidence from the national education longitudinal study of 1988. *Sociological Focus, 34*(2), 155–183. https://doi.org/10.1080/00380237.2001.10571189.

Park, G. C. (2001). Multiple dimensions of ethnic persons: Listening to Korean American college students. *ERIC*. Paper presented at the annual meeting of the American Educational Research Association, Seattle, WA.

Park, N. S., Lee, B. S., Sun, F., Klemmack, D. L., Roff, L. L., & Koenig, H. G. (2013). Typologies of religiousness/spirituality: Implications for health and wellbeing. *Journal of Religion and Health, 52*, 828–839. https://doi.org/10.1007/s10943-011-9520-6

Pavot, W., & Diener, E. (1993). Review of the satisfaction with life scale. *Psychological Assessment, 5*(2), 164–172. https://doi.org/10.1037/1040-3590.5.2.164.

Peterson, T. H. (2017). *Student development and social justice: Critical learning, radical healing, and community engagement*. Springer.

Pinquart, M., & Kauser, R. (2018). Do the associations of parenting styles with behavior problems and academic achievement vary by culture? Results from a meta-analysis. *Cultural Diversity and Ethnic Minority Psychology, 24*(1), 75–100. https://doi.org/10.1037/cdp0000149.

Raftopoulos, M., & Bates, G. (2011). 'It's that knowing that you are not alone': The role of spirituality in adolescent resilience. *International Journal of Children's Spirituality, 16*(2), 151–167. https://doi.org/10.1080/1364436X.2011.580729.

Reutter, K. K., & Bigatti, S. M. (2014). Religiosity and spirituality as resiliency resources: Moderation, mediation, or moderated mediation? *Journal for the Scientific Study of Religion, 53*(1), 56–72. https://doi.org/10.1111/jssr.12081.

Rey, L., Extremera, N., & Pena, M. (2011). Perceived emotional intelligence, self-esteem and life satisfaction in adolescents. *Psychosocial Intervention, 20*(2), 227–234. https://doi.org/10.5093/in2011v20n2a10.

Rivas-Drake, D., Hughes, D., & Way, N. (2008). A closer look at peer discrimination, ethnic identity, and psychological wellbeing among urban Chinese American sixth graders. *Journal of Youth and Adolescence, 37*(1), 12–21. https://doi.org/10.1007/s10964-007-9227-x.

Rosenberg, M. (1965). *Society and the adolescent self-image*. Princeton University Press.

Rumbaut, R. G. (2000). Transformations: The post-immigrant generation in an age of diversity. *In Defense of the Alien, 23*, 229–259. https://www.jstor.org/stable/23141270

Sigurvinsdottir, R., Asgeirsdottir, B. B., & Sigfusdottir, I. D. (2020). Sexual abuse, family violence/conflict, substance use, religion and spirituality among Icelandic adolescents. *Nordic Psychology, 72*(1), 51–64. https://doi.org/10.1080/19012276.2019.1638822.

Soldera, M., Dalgalarrondo, P., Corrêa Filho, H. R., & Silva, C. A. (2004). Use of psychotropics drugs among students: Prevalence and associated social factors. *Revista de saúde pública, 38*, 277–283. https://doi.org/10.1590/S0034-89102004000200018

Spratt, J. (2017). *A critical analysis of policy discourses of wellbeing in schools: Inclusive learning and educational equity*. Springer Nature. https://doi.org/10.1007/978-3-319-50066-9

Unterrainer, H. F., Lewis, A. J., & Fink, A. (2014). Religious/spiritual wellbeing, personality and mental health: A review of results and conceptual issues. *Journal of Religion and Health, 53*(2), 382–392. https://doi.org/10.1007/s10943-012-9642-5.

Upadyaya, K., & Salmela-Aro, K. (2013). Development of school engagement in association with academic success and well-being in varying social contexts. *European Psychologist, 18*(2). https://doi.org/10.1027/1016-9040/a000143

Vacek, K. R., Coyle, L. D., & Vera, E. M. (2010). Stress, self-esteem, hope, optimism, and wellbeing in urban, ethnic minority adolescents. *Journal of Multicultural Counseling and Development, 38*(2), 99–111. https://doi.org/10.1002/j.2161-1912.2010.tb00118.x.

Wong, W. K. F., Chou, K.-L., & Chow, N. W. S. (2012). Correlates of quality of life in new migrants to Hong Kong from Mainland China. *Social Indicators Research, 107*(2), 373–391. https://doi.org/10.1007/s11205-011-9853-2.

Wright, A. W., Yendork, J. S., & Kliewer, W. (2018). Patterns of spiritual connectedness during adolescence: Links to coping and adjustment in low-income urban youth. *Journal of Youth and Adolescence, 47*(12), 2608–2624. https://doi.org/10.1007/s10964-018-0886-6.

Yuen, C. Y. M. (2013). Ethnicity, level of study, gender, religious affiliation and life satisfaction of adolescents from diverse cultures in Hong Kong. *Journal of Youth Studies, 16*(6), 776–791. https://doi.org/10.1080/13676261.2012.756973.

Yuen, C. Y. M. (2015). Gender differences in life satisfaction and spiritual health among the junior immigrant and mainstream Hong Kong secondary students. *International Journal of Children's Spirituality, 20*(2), 139–154. https://doi.org/10.1080/1364436X.2015.1061485.

Yuen, C. Y. M. (2019). *The happiness and mourning of Hong Kong students*. In *Chinese*. Breakthrough Organization Limited.

Yuen, C. Y. M., & Cheung, A. C. K. (2014). School engagement and parental involvement: The case of cross-border students in Singapore. *The Australian Educational Researcher, 41*(1), 89–107. https://doi.org/10.1007/s13384-013-0124-x.

Yuen, C. Y. M., Cheung, A. C. K., Leung, C. S. S., Tang, H. H. H., & Chan, L. C. H. (2021). The success and obstacle factors in pursuing post-secondary education: The differences between Hong Kong mainstream and non-mainstream students. *Education Journal. EJ21013, 49*(2), 137–160.

Yuen, C. Y. M., & Lee, M. (2016). Mapping the life satisfaction of adolescents in Hong Kong secondary schools with high ethnic concentration. *Youth & Society, 48*(4), 539–556. https://doi.org/10.1177/0044118X13502060.

Yuen, C. Y. M., Lee, M., & Leung, C. S. S. (2016). Religious belief and its association with life satisfaction of adolescents in Hong Kong. *Journal of Beliefs & Values, 37*(1), 103–113. https://doi.org/10.1080/13617672.2016.1141533.

Yuen, C. Y. M., & Leung, C. S. S. (2019). Belonging and connectedness: Identity, religiosity and aspiration of immigrant Muslim youth in Hong Kong. *Asia Pacific Journal of Education, 39*(4), 423–435.https://doi.org/10.1080/02188791.2019.1671802

Yuen, C. Y. M., & Leung, K. H. (2022). The role of religion in civic engagement of young people from diverse cultures in Hong Kong. *British Journal of Religious Education, 44*(1), 98–111. https://doi.org/10.1080/01416200.2021.1918058.

Zullig, K. J., Ward, R. M., & Horn, T. (2006). The association between perceived spirituality, religiosity, and life satisfaction: The mediating role of self-rated health. *Social Indicators Research, 79*(2), 255–274. https://doi.org/10.1007/s11205-005-4127-5.

4 Young People's Notion of Spirituality and Life Satisfaction

The intertwine between education, spirituality, and life satisfaction: NCS students narratives

Education is the key to unlock future opportunities. As formal credentials, education is highly valued as a pathway towards a high social status, and efforts and diligence are emphasised as prerequisites for students' academic success. Schooling is the primary acculturation venue for immigrant and minority students to learn the mainstream dialect, values, and essential knowledge for upward mobility. The intersectionality among students' educational experience, life aspiration, religious, or spiritual experience has been explored in our conversations (see Appendix 4.1).

Bilingual students feel more comfortable, connected, and secure in intercultural contexts. Immigrant students who speak both heritage and local languages demonstrate a greater level of identification with their local identity and enhanced learning efficacy than those who do not (Chan et al., 2003). The Cantonese dialect facilitates CIS and NCS students to embrace the culture, accept differences in communication and social systems, and fully participate in their daily lives. Widening social circles through connecting with Hong Kong friends is conducive to immigrant and minority students' psychological well-being (Wong, 2007). Nevertheless, intra-ethnic socialisation overrides inter-ethnic socialisation in schools that have enrolled a significant number of immigrant students. Schools with CIS clusters have helped promote intra-ethnic socialisation. In such schools, bonding among Putonghua speakers and CIS from a similar cultural background is pervasive. Likewise, schools with NCS students clusters have witnessed strong inter-ethnic bonding among Pakistanis, Indians, Filipinos, and Nepalese. Intra-ethnic bubbles in schools create a safety net and a sense of intra-group belonging.

Friendship has been recognised as the most important indicator of life satisfaction for CIS and NCS students (Yuen et al., 2016). However, a high level of attachment to and satisfaction with the school cannot compensate for poor social conditions nor mediate poor academic conditions. Due to

DOI: 10.4324/9780429439315-4

the lack of knowledge and connection with mainstream society, segregated schooling creates a handicap for immigrant students (Suárez-Orozco et al., 2009). In terms of the academic attainment measure of school engagement, peer support is an effective means of academic engagement and achievement. Therefore, to improve the overall engagement of immigrant students, it is necessary to expand their social networks in schools with co-ethnic and local peers.

The study of Kwan (2008) revealed that family and school are the two least satisfying aspects for the youth. The family has an important place in the well-being of Asian youth. Asian parenting tends to be very demanding towards their children. "Tiger-mom's" parenting is known as creating enormous pressures for children to excel (Kim, 2013). In Asian societies, parental expectations of their children's educational success and future development are sources of support and stress, depending on how they are tackled. Pinky, an S5 Hong Kong-born Nepalese girl, is an example. Pinky grew up in Nepal and received all her primary education there. Aware of her ethnic-Nepalese identity, her childhood solidified her with her parental hometown, Nepal. However, when she came to Hong Kong for secondary education, she started a new journey in which parental choice played a critical role and became a springboard for her development. Pinky narrated her case.

> There is always a part of me that sees my own country as home, which is in Nepal. But Hong Kong has definitely grown on me, so Hong Kong will always have a special place in my heart. It is the place that has given me a life worth living and education that I wouldn't have been experienced if I were still in Nepal. Education in Nepal is not the most important thing, but in places more developed like Hong Kong, it is essential. Even though we are ethnic minorities, we still have a chance to make our future brighter. I was at a different secondary school when I was in junior secondary, which was a lot farther away than where I am schooling now. My parents noticed how tired and pressurized I was during those times. So my parents told me that since a few of my friends from my primary school had changed to my current school, it would be better for me to change to this school as well. At that time, I was angry at my parents for pulling me out of my former school, where I had many friends, but it turned out to be a blessing. I have made great friends here, and when I was in S1 (my previous school), I didn't prioritize education. Changing to this school, however, definitely gave me a reality check. I have since become more aware of how powerful education actually is.

Pinky is optimistic, believing that school has prepared her for a bright future. Nothing can stop her from pursuing a promising future, regardless of her ethnicity and gender. Pinky shared her vision and dream of living, in which raising the living standard of her family is the driving force for her to stay focused.

> I think S4 is actually the right stage for me to start planning for the future because time flies. When we were in S3, we didn't expect that S4 was going to be this hard. Now I understand that preparing for the future is much better than doing nothing at all. S5 may be more complex because I may be overloaded, but I think this is a good and suitable time for everyone to plan their life.

> I always have a vision that I would have a bright future – not just for myself but for my family. My mum always has a calculator in her hand. She calculates everything she spends and things like that. Instead of a calculator, in the future, I want her to hold a luxury bag. My parents always wish for me a better future so that I don't end up like them. They always tell me how hard things are for them. Watching them never minding things for themselves and always working for my education really motivates me and makes me feel very blissful in the way I'm living because some people are not as fortunate as me. Business is always portrayed as a job where you get so much income and get a wealthy life. I really want to go into business because business is something that I've always enjoyed. Although there will be many obstacles along the way, I feel this is the path for me to succeed.

Making parents happy is a source of power for Natalie as well. Natalie is a Hong Kong-born Indian girl who was taken to India for her primary education. She rejoined Hong Kong secondary education in S2. Natalie has developed a sense of purpose in life. Inspired by her cousin, she studies Biology and Chemistry and hopes to be a medical doctor someday.

> I am not interested in Business studies. My parents told me to take courses related to medicine. I have a cousin whose background is not that well-off. He didn't have enough money, and my family supported him in his education. Even though he didn't have much money, he tried his best to be a doctor. Now he is in America doing medicine. He is the only son of his family and everyone is so proud of his achievement. This motivates me to be like him. Also, my dad really wishes the best for me, and he really wants me to do my best. That's why I want to be a doctor as well.

Pinky and Natalie represent some of the resilient NCS girls in Hong Kong aspiring to reward their parents for their insightful advice for life and sacrificial love for the family. Their parents' expectations of them inspire their dreams for future success. All youth should be dream makers. Dreaming a future of hope and success carries them through all the storms in life. They need to find an anchor for navigating these extraordinary times, characterised as they are by an unprecedented pandemic, bubbled economy, and an unpredictable political situation. Anchoring themselves in aspirations helps manage expectations and increases resilience and competitiveness.

Armaan is 15, a Hong Kong-born Indian boy having mixed feelings about his relationships with his parents. The father is approachable, but his mother is rather difficult. Schoolwork is a chore to him and a source of family tension. His mother reprimands him for failing his studies. "I am not built for academics" sums up Armaan's feeling towards schooling and the sentiment he has over his argument with his mother. The English Language is his best subject, and his Chinese is fair. However, his mediocre academic achievement invites his mother's criticism. Even though he feels connected with his peers at school, the school work discourages him.

> I am generally quite happy with my school life. But last year, I was doing terrible in Chinese. I talked to my parents for extra tutorials as I felt stress at the beginning of the year. Because of the huge school workload, honestly, I am sometimes unhappy and even frustrated with life in Hong Kong. There is a vast homework difference between S3 and S4. In S3 the workload was reasonable, but since I proceeded to S4, it is just crazy. I am fed up with it. I felt the stress at the start of the year, but then I gradually caught up with the subjects ... I think my secondary school is better than my primary school as I met some really good friends whom I can stay with for these six years, and maybe even after that. My friends make me feel "very good" about school life. They understand me, and they are there to support me.

The tense relationship with his mother triggers Armaan's negative emotions towards schoolwork. He feels that things could be unpredictable.

> I usually get into arguments with my mother because of my unsatisfactory school results. Usually, my father supports me. My mother is a bit high-tempered. She gets pissed off for no reason. She is just bad-tempered and releases her stress on me. Sometimes, it makes me very unhappy, and we did not talk for two to three days. She was unhappy with my bad grades. But now it is much better.

Looking ahead to the future, Armaan does not have much knowledge of adult life. Armaan comes from a business family and is highly sensitive to money, especially since his father is in business. He believes that engaging in business could give him better life protection. He is good at Mathematics but struggles with the Chinese Language. It makes it hard for him to succeed academically.

> The local students usually can find extra support from private tutors. But I cannot. I have to handle my school work by myself. Learning Chinese is a

very discouraging experience. Even I was in a local kindergarten with all my Chinese classmates, and the teachers only gave us something for coloring, they didn't really teach the Language.

I am taking business and tourism as electives. I think I will follow in my father's footsteps to succeed him in his business. My father owns a guest house in the U.K. I really have a lot of interest in the business.

Spirituality and the source of power to navigate

Armaan does not have a firm belief in any formal religion, although he vaguely identifies himself with Sikh, his family religion.

> My entire family is affiliated with Sikhs, though not as devout as some Sikhs. I go to a Sikh temple maybe twice a month to pray. Basically, I was praying, listening to the prayers. I don't read the holy book, and even my parents don't read it either. I am uncertain about my own faith as I don't really believe in anything. To me, my religion is just a title or a religious identity. Having said that, Sikh is my family's religion, and I am still trying to be more devoted to it. Sikhs do not have a rigid prayer schedule. So whenever I have troubles, I pray… I think the school should arrange more religious classes that we can learn more about my religion. I can get more devoted to it if I know more about it.

Born in a Catholic Filipino family of four, MCR's parents have high hopes for his future. He is in S6 and reasonably optimistic about life but wishes to have more freedom in his planning for adulthood.

> On a scale of 1 to 10, my happiness score is 7. I have many like-minded friends in my photography club. They are enjoyable to be with. Also, I have mastered helpful life skills in my church. I may rate my happiness score as 9 if I don't have to think of my family. My parents have high hopes for me to get to university and be a professional in Hong Kong. They always tell me to study and study.

Aware of his parents' expectations, MCR almost anticipates the disappointment of his parents if he fails to get access to tertiary education. MCR is always puzzled about his adult life. Family pressure on further study has driven MCR away from staying focused. Compared to his elder brother's academic achievement, MCR has a sense of unease.

> My parents love my brother more than me. They always compare me with my brother as he is doing fine in higher education. I am different from him. I don't enjoy studying, and I hate Maths. I'd rather play

> computer games with friends. I know I'm a lazy student! English is the only subject I have the confidence to pass; Maths and Chinese are just beyond my ability, ok. Well, it's too late for me to catch up with the DSE exams. My level is just too low. But, somehow, my parents still expect me to follow in my brother's footsteps to enter university. That has given me tremendous pressure. I hate sibling comparison. Otherwise, I'll be much happier.

Fortunately, his church experience helps him to navigate out of his depression and to stay afloat.

> I used to be very active in my church, serving others as a volunteer in S3 and S4. In those days, I served in the church two to three times a week. However, from S5 onwards, I have been too busy to help. My voluntary service was substantially reduced and even stopped. I cannot carry on helping at church.

Finding the balance between study, church, and leisure is the most challenging task for MCR. Faith and religious attachments have sustained him during turbulences in his school life. The reality is that he needs to recognise his responsibility as a student and to prepare for HKDSE examinations.

Being a second-generation Filipino immigrant in Hong Kong, Mig has fully embraced his Hong Kong identity, calling himself a Hong Konger. Mig is 14, studying for S2, and living with his mother and sister since his parents got divorced. His mother is the sole breadwinner trying her very best to sustain the family needs. Mig has high regard for his mother.

> My mom knows my capacity, so she doesn't really expect so much from me. She trusts us in making decisions for ourselves. But I know she wants me to finish my secondary school at least. I don't need to have good grades so long as I have done my best. She learns not to give me pressure to have good grades or anything. Having said that, she supports me with what I want in the future.

English is Mig's best subject, but Chinese is intimidating to him. The university tuition fees are far too high to be affordable. Mig has several hesitations when his mother talks about accessing tertiary education in Hong Kong. Considering all, he wishes to get a degree in his parents' homeland – the Philippines.

> I'm planning to study tourism in the Philippines. It's pretty hard to get in here, and it's expensive. Even if I could afford it, there is a language barrier. I only know basic Chinese but am not fluent in Chinese at all. It would be unbearable for me to study in Hong Kong.

Settling his future education with his parent's hometown is perhaps a safety net for Mig. But he is not unhappy with his secondary school except for the teacher-student relationship.

> If the school wants the "not hardworking students" like me to work harder, the teacher has to focus more on us who are not hardworking rather than on the hardworking ones. Because teachers are supposed to bring us up to success, right? But sometimes I really feel that the school is not entirely fair, especially the teachers' attitude toward the less able students.

Everything is planned, and the only thing is to follow the pathway step by step.

> I have already planned what I would do. I would finish DSE first. Then I will work for at least one month to earn the allowance I would have in the Philippines. And after that I will enrol in the oriental school at a university in the Philippines and take the tourism course for years … I have friends there and they told me the school is a nice and cheap one. Because we have financial problems, that's why I choose the oriental school. It's already the right campus with good teaching skills, and it's not expensive. My mom also agrees to it.

Looking ahead, Mig is optimistic about his future and aspires to be a flight attendant to pay back to his hardworking mother.

> My mom told me about being a flight attendant. And I remembered I was studying tourism, so I thought about it. And I researched about it. So I think that's fine with me to be a flight attendant or anything in the tourist industry.

> Success to me is when I have a stable job for myself, when I can earn money and when I can give money to my mom, and she doesn't have to work. And success is when I can let my younger brother graduate from college because my sister gives the tuition fee to him when he is older and me. Moreover, success is when I can finally say, "I did it by myself". I just have to finish my studies, and I will be halfway to be successful.

Mig describes himself as a mediocre Catholic. Religious engagement does not attract him. However, the Catholic ethos has shaped his thinking and value development.

> I only go to church when I am with my family during Christmas Eve or New Year. I am not really a religious person … but when sometimes I really need help, I'll pray … I pray to God whenever I am sad or unhappy. I even pray after I eat sometimes, I say thank you (to God) for giving us the food that we have. Although I won't say I'm spiritual, I can really forgive people

easily, and I lower my pride for them. But for other people, they will find it hard to do so.

Like Mig, Jane is a second-generation Hong Kong-born Filipino living with her mother. She is 14 in S4. Her academic grades are mainly average. Living with her single mother, she admitted that life is quite hard for her to cope with, and she is still in trauma due to her father's death.

> There're four of us and my mom is a single mom, so we have to compromise a lot. It is hard growing up without a dad, actually … I saw him pass away in hospital. He wanted to go out of the hospital, but my aunties and uncles told me to stay with my cousin not to have to see him there. But he passed away that night. I didn't even have a chance to say goodbye … most nights I can't sleep because my dad passed away. They said I was suffering from trauma, I'm still coping with it. But it's not as bad as before. My dad passed away due to SARS. We are actually relying on the Government's subsidy. So after my father's death, my mom had to work to support us.

Jane has gone through a few turbulences during her young adolescence. Achieving the school standard stresses her out, and studying Chinese cripples her.

> It is too late for me to go for standard Chinese. So I have to go with basic Chinese. Thinking about it, my Chinese is basically OK, but if you set me out with the locals, I'm not going to win over them. Maybe I'll just go for like, I don't know, not a university, but a college. I'm going to study in Hong Kong. My sister is studying at HKUSpace. She needs to talk in Chinese and write in Chinese.

> Even though they say that you would find a place in a university if you meet the minimum requirements (3, 3, 2, 2), this is not valid. It's just there for a show. The real world, after I did some research, is that you need to get better grades than 3,3,2,2. Such a situation makes me work harder and but makes me more stressed. Hence, I get sick more frequently. My body is kind of weak.

There are streams of emotions in Jane's upbringing. She prefers to defend her own privacy in sharing. She surrenders herself to art creation.

> Sometimes, when people ask me what's wrong with me, I just tell them something else so they won't ask me about the real problem. I want my life to be private, so I don't have to be pushed … I don't share my problems with my mom because I know that she won't understand … but if the time is really getting tough, I'll talk to my friends, but I don't open up completely.

> Back home, I have to take off my mask and be myself. And then I don't really like people seeing me cry. When I really need to express myself, I will do art. It facilitates me to channel my depressive emotions.

For Jane, spirituality is a private and subjective matter. However, critical life events have led her to question God and stop attending church activities.

> Because my brother has faith in God, he always says, "God will do something; we just have to be patient". I have faith in Him (God) but not as much as my brother does. As for me, I don't have a firm religious belief, although I used to have. Spirituality is a kind of self-constructed thinking ... I think there is a destiny for all as long as you actually believe in what you believe in. Of course, it's a good thing.

Serving as a House Captain, Jane tries to set an example of fairness. She has a vision for building a fair society for all ethnic minorities.

> Being a captain, I have to be fair to everyone. So I have to work, and they have to work too. We're all equal. I won't say I have more power than them. I want to be democratic and learn to compromise ... I am a bridge for our school to reach out to society. The teachers once asked me to dance outside the school for anti-discrimination, communicate with locals in order to enhance the position of ethnic minorities.

Jane is a competent house captain at school. Her leadership has won the trust of teachers and her friends to assume greater responsibility in promoting social harmony and equity. Despite her exemplary serving heart, her inner self is unsatisfied, and this has caused her emotion to swing from one end to the other. She believes there is a destiny for those who trust in a transcendental being. Yet, she has not anchored herself in any divine being.

In Hong Kong, schoolwork dominates the majority of the time and consumes most youth at school. The NCS students' narratives unravel that they came from all walks of life and faced a myriad of critical life events. Some reported positive educational experiences, connected fellowship with peers, but some chose to bury their public emotions and cope with them within themselves. Family is a critical source of youth well-being. Coming from diverse religious family backgrounds, Catholics, Hindu, Sikh, and Christianity, they expressed a range of colours of their religious faith. Their spirituality is dependent on their family ethos and personal choice. In the following, the CIS narratives portrait a different set of the picture.

Self-saving and against the odd: CIS narratives

All CIS that were interviewed have been in Hong Kong for less than seven years. Born in the Mainland, Jia Ying is 16 and is in S3. Both of her parents were Mainland Chinese citizens prior to their immigration to Hong Kong for a family reunion. Jia Ying finished her primary schooling in the Mainland and has gone through the uprooting process by coming to Hong Kong.

> I was born in Guangdong Province, and I came to Hong Kong with my family last year. Hong Kong schooling was a big adjustment for me. No one has discussed local education with me, and my parents are both originally from Mainland China. They do not know the education system here and seldom get involved in my learning. Classes are conducted in Cantonese, and at the beginning of my schooling, I could not follow the lessons, so I just kept quiet. I didn't want to be noticed. It would be very embarrassing.

> I don't know what my parents are doing for a living and how much do they earn. I don't ask them about their job and income.

Over the years, Jia Ying has developed a sense of bonding with the school. She feels connected with her co-ethnic friends from the Mainland at school, but her friendship circle with local students is limited. Concerning her learning, she has not made substantial improvements as desired.

> I prefer to hang out with CIS in this school as we share similar cultural backgrounds and we speak Putonghua. I have a few local friends as well, but as we grew up in different societies, we have different concerns, and our conversations are superficial.

Jia Ying aspires to be a nurse. School grades will determine her future education and career prospects, but she does not have high hopes for achieving her dream.

> I wish to be a nurse, but most likely, I cannot be a nurse because of my lousy grades. So, I don't know what else I can do.

> My grades range from average to below average. My English sucks. I don't really pay attention to the English lessons as my foundation is too weak to catch up. But I quite like the teachers here. All of them are very friendly, approachable, and they joke a lot.

> Personally, I don't have a religious belief, but my parents are Buddhists. But they don't belong to any formal religious grouping, nor are they that serious about their religious rituals. So religious belief is unimportant, and it does not help me much. I would instead choose to rely on myself. At the end of the day, it is me to face reality and bear my living responsibility.

Mastering English is a giant obstacle to CIS blocking their pathway to the future. Jia Ying struggles with it. Nevertheless, even though her future does not seem to be that encouraging, she has learned to be self-reliant in handling life challenges.

Law is 16 and is in S4. She was born on the Mainland and immigrated to Hong Kong with her father four years ago. Both her parents are Mainland residents, but her grandparents are Hong Kong, permanent residents.

> My mother is still on the Mainland taking care of her saloon business. She has no plans to give up her business for a family reunion. Nevertheless, she pays us a regular monthly visit with a two-way permit. Each time she will stay for three months. My younger brother is only four years old. My parents have no idea about Hong Kong education. My father only came to the parent-teacher meeting once for my results. So he has to trust me for my own studies.

A spirit of self-efficacy and self-reliance has kept Law high up in her academic achievement.

> I repeated primary six when I first arrived to make up my poor English standard. I chose this secondary school because it is a Chinese medium school so that I have less pressure to catch up. All subjects are relatively easy except for English. I was in the top three in my grade.

> To brush up on my English, I listen to English songs, watch English movies and study the dictionary to increase my vocabulary power. You know I need to have a better English grade so that I can find a better job, such as in public relations or as a teacher. Without English, I can't really connect with people by email or other means.

Law's willingness towards acculturation in Hong Kong has been the most significant plus factor in her positive school engagement. However, Law's future is directed elsewhere.

> In my opinion, the biggest difference between the Mainland and Hong Kong regarding schooling is student discipline. In China, students will be quiet when teachers talk. But here in Hong Kong, even though teachers demand order, students carry on talking. Some local students pay no attention whatsoever to the teachers.

> I usually ignore them and concentrate on my studies. I choose to sit in the second front row to avoid the disturbances. Most of my friends are from the Mainland. We share similar values in learning. We wish to make the best of our studies. However, I have no confidence in securing a place in a university. Our school standard is far too low compared to the others. I have recently come to realize that other schools have higher standards than us. Teachers should prepare us for DSE exams earlier.

> Regarding my future career plan, I will either work in PR or as a teacher. But I will consider Taiwan for my future development as the Taiwanese economy is better than Hong Kong. There is a more significant potential for me there.

Spirituality to Law is essential but must be guarded with caution. Otherwise, it may fall into the trap of superstition.

> I have been to church a few times because I want to know what Christianity is all about. Christianity focuses on sharing. It does not seem to have much impact on me. If I have problems, I won't pray for them every day for help. Instead, I will try my own best to solve them. I don't want to be superstitious. I think spirituality is about the attitude and thinking of an individual. To me, spirituality is essential, and it can be nurtured by reading from different sorts of books … Sure, I believe there is destiny just as Buddhism tells us that there is a cause and a consequence. There are consequences for each individual's acts.

Law's academic success falls into model minority thinking. She is a successful example of a CIS who can overcome the barriers in education by devoting herself whole-heartedly to her studies. Law is unconvinced there is a God or divine being and firmly believes she should rely on herself rather than on anything else to address problems. She may have taken a longer route to enter into mainstream schooling, yet she has navigated well and with a clear focus on her future development.

Zheng Ching finished his junior secondary school in Jieyang, China, before relocating to Hong Kong. Like most CIS, he has had to repeat two years to adjust to the local curriculum. He started at S2, and now he is in S6. This is his fifth year in Hong Kong. His father left his Mainland home when he was little in order to prepare a home in Hong Kong.

> I feel bored at home as my brother is only in primary three. We have a huge age gap. So we don't have much to share. I prefer to stay at school where I can hang out with friends. My parents support me in whatever I like to do. Our family relationship is ok. If my parents want to hang out with me, I will chat with them. Otherwise, we just concentrate on our own reading. Both my mom and I love reading novels.

Zheng Ching's attitude towards schooling in Hong Kong is somewhat mixed. The science curriculum is less challenging in Hong Kong, but he has lost the motivation to press on at school.

> The Hong Kong science curriculum, such as Chemistry, is less challenging than in the Mainland by two grade levels at least. Some formulas we learn in the Mainland's junior high school were taught at the senior level in Hong Kong. However, I find the lessons not very interesting. I usually listen to the

first half, but if I feel bored, I then fall into sleep in the second half or do my homework. I prefer to finish my homework at school. I will only ask the teachers for things I have some knowledge. Otherwise, it is rather embarrassing. For the subjects in which I am weak, I'll ask my friends instead. I won't bother the teachers.

Zheng Ching aspires to be a chef.

> I dream of being a chef as I like cooking. One of my family members is also a chef. I will apply for a two-year diploma after the DSE exam.

Zheng Ching believes a divine force controls the destiny of human beings. However, he refuses to anchor his spiritual life in any formal religion.

> I don't know what spirituality is about. I don't have any religion, but I'm more inclined to believe in Buddhism. My parents like Buddhist chantings. They feel peaceful, but I feel very anxious after listening to them. I understand no Sanskrit. There is a destiny for everyone, and I firmly believe that. Things that belong to you will indeed be given to you. If not, you can never reach it, no matter what.

> I prefer to shoulder the pressures by myself. Sometimes I'll share them with friends. For more severe problems, I choose to face them myself. I like listening to music and go to eat when I am down.

CIS exhibit a certain degree of acculturation to Hong Kong society. Polarisation of academic engagement and performance is often reported. Self-reliance is a shared attitude and philosophy of life among the CIS. Their families struggle to make ends meet and have an average monthly income of USD 1,250 to 2,500. Some of them are uncertain as to their family situation and are troubled in some way by divorce, separation, living apart, arguments, and so on. CIS are anxious about their future and the prospect of gaining a place in a Hong Kong university. Academic grades tend to be average or below, especially in the English Language, and this represents the biggest impediment to them utilising their strengths and significantly lowers their chances of a university place. On the other hand, Chinese students seem less troubled by their social life in school and most have healthy relationships with fellow students.

Nevertheless, many have problems communicating and adapting to the Chinese (Cantonese) language in the first few years of their Hong Kong school life. With regard to religion, unless they are invited to a fellowship or other religious activities, CIS and CBS tend to have no firm understanding of religion. A few understand Buddhism, reincarnation, and karma because of family customs. However, in the majority of cases, they remain non-religious or unconvinced that there is a God or divine being.

Understanding NCS and CIS in schools and beyond

No conclusive findings on the psychological well-being differences between immigrant and non-immigrant students have been reached so far. Academic achievement does not seem to affect immigrant students' behavioural engagement in school (Motti-Stefanidi et al., 2015). Students who identify with the school culture and peer behaviour also exhibit a willingness towards behavioural assimilation at school. Moreover, teachers' recognition and encouragement have noticeable impacts on immigrant students' self-efficacy for academic achievement and lead to a high possibility of college enrolment. The lesson for Hong Kong teachers, especially the preservice teachers, is to recognise that what they do and do not do directly influences student behaviours. A teacher's definition of an ideal student shapes their beliefs, expectations, behaviours, and, in turn, this can affect student outcomes (Chee, 2012). Linguistic and cultural disparities between mainstream and non-mainstream students, such as CIS and NCS students, may be viewed as deficits, and this can lead to professional challenges for preservice teachers.

The positivity of NCS students towards life, in general, reflects the key role of community resources and social networks and the fact that they tend to receive significant religious resources and family, ethnic and communal acceptance and support within their community (Yuen, 2013; Yuen & Lee, 2013). A close relationship with their transcendent being is also a plus factor acknowledged among NCS students (Yuen, 2014).

Their cultural values and religious beliefs endorse work as a cushion for mediating their low points in life and enable them to work against the odds (Raftopoulos & Bates, 2011). They are more thankful for their school experiences, support from peers and teachers, living conditions, and social networks than their Chinese peers. Likewise, the quality of their relationships with others, with nature, and with the divine being tended to be rated to a higher degree. Ironically, these qualities are precisely the opposite to those that prevail within mainstream education culture, which celebrates above all else the academic success of graduates.

By contrast, the immigration process for CIS appears more of an uphill struggle (Chee, 2010). They frequently find themselves facing tensions or a disjunction between parental expectations and the reality of their schooling. They sometimes have arguments with their parents due to their low academic grades (of course, so do NCS students). Nevertheless, most of them believe that a divine being does feature in their lives and that faith is merely a means of self-comfort and stress relief. Since they want to rely on themselves more than NCS students, they have less resilience and experience more significant uncertainty about their future.

Appendix 4.1: Student interview guide

Questions regarding general well-being

1. Are you generally happy and sleeping well?
2. Who do you turn to when you are unhappy?

3. What issue always triggers your emotion?
4. What do you think about your school life?
5. How would you describe your satisfaction with your education experiences/yourself and your own identity/friendships/home environment/overall life?
6. What kinds of school activities help you the most for whole person development (e.g., learning support, home-school collaboration, pastoral care)?
7. How do you evaluate the effectiveness of support measures provided by your school/community?

Questions regarding spirituality

8. What is spirituality and how important is it to you?
9. Tell us something about your family religion.
10. Do you believe in supernatural forces/divine/God?
11. Do you have a religious group with which you identify? If yes, can you tell me how important it is to have one?
12. How often do you go to your religious group?
13. How often do you mediate/pray?
14. Are you aware of any school available support for your spiritual needs (flexible timetable for your religious practice, religious education, fellowship group, etc.)?
15. Imagine you were the principal, what kinds of school activities would you like to provide to address the spiritual needs of students?

References

Chan, S., Mantak, Y., & Lau, P. (2003). The effects of a group guidance programme on the self esteem of newly arrived children from the Chinese Mainland to Hong Kong. *Asia Pacific Journal of Education*, 23(2), 171–182. https://doi.org/10.1080/0218879030230206.

Chee, W. C. (2010). When the cultural model of success fails: Mainland Chinese teenage immigrants in Hong Kong. *Taiwan Journal of Anthropology*, 8(2), 85–110. http://dx.doi.org/10.7115%2fTJA.201006.0085.

Chee, W. C. (2012). Envisioned belonging: Cultural differences and ethnicities in Hong Kong schooling. *Asian Anthropology*, 11(1), 89–105. http://dx.doi.org/10.1080/1683478X.2012.10600858.

Kwan, Y. K. (2008). Life satisfaction and family structure among adolescents in Hong Kong. *Social Indicator's Research*, 86, 59–67. http://dx.doi.org/10.1007/s11205-007-9092-8

Motti-Stefanidi, F., Masten, A., & Asendorpf, J. B. (2015). School engagement trajectories of immigrant youth: Risks and longitudinal interplay with academic success. *International Journal of Behavioral Development*, 39(1), 32–42. https://doi.org/10.1177%2F0165025414533428.

Raftopoulos, M., & Bates, G. (2011). 'It's that knowing that you are not alone': The role of spirituality in adolescent resilience. *International Journal of Children's Spirituality*, 16(2), 151–167. https://doi.org/10.1080/1364436X.2011.580729.

Suárez-Orozco, C., Rhodes, J., & Milburn, M. (2009). Unraveling the immigrant paradox. Academic engagement and disengagement among recently arrived immigrant youth. *Youth and Society*. http://doi.org/10.1177/0044118X09333647.

Wong, S. (2007). *Exploring 'unseen' social capital in community participation: Everyday lives of poor mainland Chinese migrants in Hong Kong*. Amsterdam University Press.

Yuen, C. Y. M. (2013). Ethnicity, level of study, gender, religious affiliation and life satisfaction of adolescents from diverse cultures in Hong Kong. *Journal of Youth Studies*, *16*(6), 695–711. http://doi.org/10.1177/0044118X13502060.

Yuen, C. Y. M. (2014). School engagement and civic engagement as predictors for the future political participation of ethnic Chinese and South Asian adolescents in Hong Kong. *Migration and Ethnic Themes*, *29*(3), 317–342. http://doi.org/10.11567/met.29.3.1.

Yuen, C. Y. M., & Lee, M. S. (2013). Mapping the life satisfaction of adolescents in Hong Kong secondary schools with high ethnic concentration. *Youth and Society*, 1–18, http://doi.org/10.1177/0044118X13502060

Yuen, C. Y. M., Lee, M., & Leung, C. S. S. (2016). Religious belief and its association with life satisfaction of adolescents in Hong Kong. *Journal of Beliefs & Values*, *37*(1), 103–113. https://doi.org/10.1080/13617672.2016.1141533.

5 Teachers' Perspectives on the Civic Engagement of Chinese Immigrant and Non-Chinese Speaking (NCS) Students in Hong Kong

Citizenship and ethnic identity reconstruction

Today's students engage in multiple roles such as being self-regulated learners with digital competence, active school member, and responsible citizen. Civic participation is a part of growing up and finding one's personal identity in a society. It is expected that students get prepared for adult life as a member of the community both in and out of school contexts. Socialising with students in the school curriculum, interacting with friends and family, they develop schema to organise their thoughts, guide their actions, and formulate their attitudes towards a particular habitus. Students from diverse cultural backgrounds acquire a sense of belonging and identity from interacting with campus users through sharing views and opinions on campus, social issues and negotiating personal boundaries and space through dialogues. For more conducive campus and civic engagement, deliberate practices must be in place to foster a deeper understanding of students' life-worlds from diverse backgrounds (Young et al., 2019).

Citizens are naturally compelled to contribute to a society where they belong and aspire to shape the community's future betterment (Adler & Goggin, 2005). Civic engagement takes place in many forms depending upon the socialisation process. Volunteering oneself in community service is the most common nature of civic engagement (Diller, 2001). It is often a collective action (Van Benshoten, 2001) and sometimes involves political activities (Ronan, 2004). The indicators of civic engagement are multidimensional, consisting of cognitive (knowledge), behavioural (self-efficacy), and affective (emotional attachment) aspects. In a broader sense, civic engagement is an interactive process between individuals and society, usually driven by some form of civic values and beliefs. A robust civic identity is often associated with civic pride and national belonging or nationalism. In such a reciprocal relationship, the stronger the individuals are connected with community development, the stronger their sense of mission to contribute to society (Diller, 2001). Clearly, civic engagement is context-specific, representing a subjective approach to seeking recognition and acceptance of one's belonging in society. Cultural norms and values shape their perception of themselves and their society. Taking a broader perspective on civic engagement, the following paragraphs will discuss the relationship between CIS and NCS students

DOI: 10.4324/9780429439315-5

and local Hong Kong society and their general relationship with their school and community. In so doing, it will broaden our understanding of their engagement experience in becoming Hong Kong citizens.

Globalisation and worldwide immigration have entailed public debates and controversies on the relationships between ethnic identity and citizenship and dominant culture and ethnic culture. This debate is complicated by the fact that the terminologies of "ethnic minority", "Chinese immigrant", "Chinese", and "Hong Konger" are somewhat problematic, suggesting as they do connotations of "us versus them" polarisation (Gu et al., 2017). Ethnic Chinese are the dominant group in Hong Kong society, and CIS and NCS groups rarely challenge the marginalisation hierarchy. Both groups struggle between "Hong Konger" and ethnic identities (Chan et al., 2015). Banks (2014) argues that better ideas and practices are required to balance the rights and cultural accommodation of minority groups and the majority in multicultural societies.

Developing a sense of belonging to the community and the school is not a natural occurrence for immigrant students. Though citizens with ethnic backgrounds are guaranteed the fundamental political rights in host societies in today's world, their identities are shaped by their cultural adaptation and emotional attachment to their ethnic communities. Taking Singapore as an example, accepting Malay, Chinese, and Tamil as official languages strengthens these ethnic groups' sense of belonging and enhances their cultural roots in society (Gopinathan & Sharpe, 2004). Gutmann (2004) argues that the dominant culture should incorporate the experiences, cultures, and languages of the minority groups to help them experience civic equality and recognition. While civic engagement and citizenship of the immigrant citizens are essential issues, cultural democracy and political involvement must also be addressed (Kallen, 1924). It is accepted in many quarters that respect and tolerance should be provided for all individuals regardless of their religion, ethnic origin, colour, gender, political opinion, and philosophical beliefs. Yet, these issues nevertheless remain controversial amid the rise of nationalism across the world. Therefore, democratic societies should strive to implement the ideal for identity reconstruction.

In the opinion of Reichert and Torney-Purta (2019), schools are where civic education goals are pursued and are responsible for furthering these goals. Civic education, however, is not just confined to schools but extends to civic society outside of it. The school and civic engagement of CIS and NCS students groups imply a sense of belonging to their new society and an interest in its development. This indeed is as it should be, for they are not just a part of the society, but also a significant factor in its future.

Civic engagement of CIS and NCS students in Hong Kong

Privilege comes with responsibilities. NCS students are full members of society and see Hong Kong as home (Yuen, 2019). Many have shown concern with respect to developing their new political responsibilities and providing opportunities appropriate to their new social contexts (Yuen, 2018). Schools are entrusted with preparing the new generation for a sustainable society. Whether intentional or not, students gain a sense of belonging through schooling and community activities. School engagement and civic engagement are reciprocally reinforced (Yuen et al., 2016). This is an extension of the point already made that schools are a reflection of civic society. In Finn's model (1989, 1993), student participation and identification with the school are moderated by their engagement feedback. The cognitive dimension of student learning and the subjective assessment of the role of significant others in their learning are critical factors for their school performance (Fredricks et al., 2004; Jimerson et al., 2003). Skinner and Belmont (1993) and Elmore and Huebner (2010) have shown that the nature of student's engagement with school is affected by social and contextual factors. In a study on the ethnic identity of NCS South/South-east Asian students in Hong Kong, Yuen and Leung (2019) note that they aspired to be recognised as full members of Hong Kong society but without compromising their cultural and religious values and practice. Friendship at school is a pivotal contributor to their affective engagement, and their relationship with teachers is another critical factor influencing their behavioural engagement at school. Students with fulfilling school lives believe more readily that their efforts will lead to success, are more able to persevere in overcoming difficulties, and ascribe greater significant meaning to and satisfaction with education.

The quest for greater civic participation of youth has grown over the past decade, regardless of their cultural backgrounds (Lee, 2010). During the two major social movements and pro-democracy protests of 2014 and 2019, mainstream Hong Kong youth were visible, enthusiastic, and significant (Purbrick, 2019; Yuen, 2018). Students from the secondary and tertiary sectors were among the leaders. Yet, the role of immigrant and ethnic minority youth was relatively invisible and has received scant attention. First-generation immigrant students are usually absent in high-impact events at school due to a lack of awareness and opportunity or cultural gap (Young et al., 2019).

On the one hand, researchers (e.g., Yuen et al., 2016) acknowledge that CBS, CIS, and NCS students are confronted with a range of social exclusion from schooling to daily living. On the other hand, the cultural identities and values of immigrant students could be perceived as threats to the cultural values of mainstream society (Igarashi, 2019). Particularly for CIS, living in a conflicting social atmosphere caused by the political tension between Mainland China and Hong Kong can be a constant struggle for identification. As for NCS students, the desire for civic-based identification in the local community by taking the role as a full local Hong Kong citizen while engaging with the Chinese national identity has become increasingly incompatible with the ethnic and cultural definition of the Chinese nation (Veg, 2017). Moreover, they have to face the challenges between the conventions of their religion, the requirements of Hong Kong as a modern city, and their cultural values based on relatedness rather than competition.

Prior studies (Yuen, 2013, 2018) have noted that CBS and NCS students held the most potent convictions in defending the civic rights of ethnic and racial rights. This may be brought about by the intensities of a polarised identification between "Mainland Chinese" and "Hong Konger" labels. The geopolitical situations of the two systems certainly contribute to the Mainland-Hong Kong divide. The daily living experiences of contrary social, economic, and political systems play another role too. Hong Kong is a unique society within China, a SAR with high autonomy and civil liberties. Under the one country two systems principle, the two systems are operating under a one country framework.

Besides the identity conflict of being neither a Hong Konger nor a Mainlander, the everyday challenges of CIS include financial obstacles, communicating with people in Cantonese, and meeting school standards for a possibly unpromising future. They experience partial or whole family separation in their life transition from the Mainland to Hong Kong. This semi-detached lifestyle exacerbates their sense of disconnectedness and helplessness in society and deepens their sense of alienation, mainly if any negative emotions are prolonged. Their disadvantaged circumstances socio-economically make them very aware of their parents' hardships. More significantly, although their parents may have high expectations, at the same time, they usually cannot support their child's homework assignments.

Impact of collective family culture

NCS South Asians usually come from a culture strongly oriented towards family and community. Similarly, Chinese immigrants have a strong sense of kinship ties. The collectivism embedded in their original culture makes it natural for them to seek relatedness in the new environment. For these students, the most challenging issue in terms of civic engagement is to strike a balance between their ethnic identity and their membership or citizenship in the host society. They struggle to find a path between the host and home cultural values and form their compound identities in the new environment. Gradually, a kind of "in-between" identity emerges.

Discourse on the marginalisation of minority youth in Hong Kong focuses on their language barrier in education and society and their disadvantaged social and family conditions. However, public debates are predominantly centred on learning Chinese as a second language (e.g., Loh & Hung, 2020).

Nevertheless, what is of particular interest is how these students construct their strategies to navigate their identity both as citizens and non-mainstream students in their host society. This has not yet been covered to a sufficient degree in contemporary literature and research. How do these strategies relate to their family background, personal aspiration, community, and cultural background? To answer these questions, I interviewed frontline teachers across various disciplines such as Liberal Studies, Social Science, Mathematics, English, and Chinese to understand the rejections and involvement of CIS and NCS students at school and in society. Through this medium, it is possible to have a closer and more natural data source from a local teacher perspective to understand the obstacles faced by minority and immigrant students concerning their deeper civic engagement.

CIS and NCS students towards civic participation

School ethos shapes the interaction between staff and students and becomes the primary discursive tool for understanding their sense of connectedness and attitudes towards civic engagement. Teacher Sean expressed his observation towards CIS:

> In our school, each student must engage in Flag Day. It is good for CIS to experience this in Hong Kong as well. However, except for the mandatory school activities, they rarely participate in civic-related discussions or activities within or outside school. They do not integrate with the community and act somewhat like outsiders.

Teacher Peter reasons their detached attitudes and behaviours are due to their un-readiness in civic and political discussion.

> Some CIS don't even know the meaning and function of the Legislative Council even though they are S.4 students. They also know very little about the politics of the Mainland. At least, they can't really describe it. Influenced by the political culture in the Mainland, they have no incentives towards social engagement, whether in their hometown or in Hong Kong. Not politics, not others, but they only care about their own life.

Similarly, as Teacher William shared, NCS students show care and concern about their country of origin better than local students.

> I seldom see NCS students really care about the welfare of Hong Kong society or engage in civic activities. On Facebook, they only share news of their own country.

Teacher Sean noted that all CIS and NCS students feel segregated and isolated in the wider society. This isolation can be traced back to the educational policies of the local government. For instance, the government provided a special grant for local schools to brush up on the NCS students' Chinese from 2006 to 2013. The programme aimed to strengthen the Chinese Language study for NCS students and equip educators for teaching NCS students at school. However, the designated programme was criticised by the United Nations, calling it "de facto discrimination", which deliberately separates mainstream students and NCS students. As a result, the programme was stopped in 2014. However, the unofficial segregation seems to continue, with more than 60% of ethnic minority students attending only 10 out of 840 public schools in Hong Kong (Hong Kong Unison, 2016).

Agency and structure of CIS and NCS students civic participation

Participatory civic engagement is related to culture and social structure. Teachers attribute the conservative approach or passive attitude towards civic discussion and involvement of CIS to their limited real-life interactions both in Mainland and Hong Kong societies. Their hesitation may result from equating civic participation with radical political engagement causing disruption or threat to social stability and harmony. Under such understanding, CIS are not equipped for participatory civic engagement or accustomed to volunteer for services.

Teacher Nicholas underlined how CIS lack civic habits and are not active in doing volunteer work and offers some explanation:

> Although the school has arranged numerous voluntary service activities for the students, they are still not active in serving the community or contributing to society. I think one reason is that the activities are short-term and lack continuity. For example, when visiting a nursing home, students realise the importance of caring for the elderly, but soon after the activity they forget about it, and it does not become a habit.

Moreover, CIS have concerns about involvement in politics, and so they keep their silence. Teacher William recognised this fear:

> They do not use Facebook very often. They prefer to browse WeChat, QQ, Weibo, etc. Sharing their political opinions is not part of their culture.

Similarly, for a myriad of reasons, NCS students are also highly passive in participating in civic activities. Teacher Emma at senior management shared her observations:

> Even though they (NCS students) have been living in Hong Kong for many years, many of them prefer to identify themselves with their ethnic community, which is very firm. They also have fixed ideas about their futures. They tend to follow their parents' footsteps rather than stepping out of their safe zone to broaden their horizons. For instance, one student tells me that he will be working with his father to sell mobile phone accessories after graduation. Whether he will succeed in this business or not, he believes that copying his father's footsteps will be his life. From my point of view, they are like being trapped in their community.

Concerning NCS students inactivity in civic matters, Teacher William believes that the Chinese Language barrier is the main issue.

> I think the primary reason must be the language barrier – they don't know much Chinese. Although some South Asian students were born in Hong Kong, they are not good at Chinese. Not really. This has been common knowledge among us.

Split interest in local and "home affairs" is noted among the NCS students. Teacher Leo stated:

> I teach Liberal Studies. One of the six units is about today's Hong Kong, including political and social issues. I find NCS students are particularly disinterested in those topics because they don't have a sense of belonging in Hong Kong. When we discussed the role of the Legislative Council, public policy and etc., they were very detached and bored. We share the local news with them every day, but they lose their concentration on discussing Hong Kong issues. However, as long as the news is about their motherland, their mind is back again.

Agency and knowledge gap

Limited real-life interactions lead to a thin understanding of civic knowledge among CIS and NCS students. The crux of the problem is yet to be determined. For instance, mainstream society's acceptance of these students and their willingness to assimilate into society represent complex identity negotiation processes and interactions (Ching, 2020). For the CIS, participatory civic engagement can be contradictory to their political stance or cultural values. Teacher Nicholas observed:

> Politics are not attractive to CIS. In their mind, political parties are too complicated to comprehend. In another situation, even though some students want to understand more about politics, they still believe it's useless because they feel powerless in the current political system. They can't make any difference.

NCS students' willingness to assimilate into the Chinese society may lead to further social marginalisation of their ethnic beliefs, languages, and cultures. In addition, they have been excluded from debates about "who is the Hong Konger" (Ching, 2020) and hence are voiceless. All these lead to their limited political agency. Teacher Leo pointed out:

> This is due to their detached attitude towards social and civic affairs in society. Most of them are somewhat detached from mainstream society. They pay little attention to civic affairs. Unless they see the connection between their wellbeing and Hong Kong society, they will continue to adopt the "none of my business" attitude. We have to respect that they are who they are.

From the teachers' perspective, a primary reason for the indifference of NCS students to the community or political life is the lack of belongingness. For most of them, Hong Kong is not where they belong. Teacher Karen expressed:

> We hope to help them build up their sense of belonging to Hong Kong, just like local students. However, this is not the case. Even those living in Hong Kong since young they do not take root in the local culture.

A segregated community lifestyle shapes their sense of belonging and self-forming. NCS students prefer to keep the identity of their country of origin instead of being Hong Kongers. Teacher Leo underlines this point:

> They think they are just passers-by. Even though some of them stay in Hong Kong their whole life, they still define themselves as Pakistanis. Their involvement or attachment to Hong Kong society is minimal.

Teacher Sean argued that NCS students have their notion of "good citizen". It only differs from the label tag of "Hong Konger".

> For instance, they (Pakistanis) prefer to keep their Pakistani passports. Sometimes people identify themselves according to what passport they hold. Being a Hong Kong citizen does not mean they regard themselves as Hong Konger as we (local Chinese) think we are. They (NCS students) live in Hong Kong and obey the laws, but they may still think of themselves as guests.

Acculturation challenge of CIS

CIS face an uphill struggle in embracing themselves with a Hong Kong-centric way of living and doing. They face obstacles, including social norms, language, or learning styles. The different sociopolitical fabrics of Mainland China and Hong Kong somehow create barriers for CIS and their families from integrating with local society. Teachers acknowledge the difference and express their empathy for CIS, as Teacher Nicholas relates:

> I know it's difficult for CIS to feel at home in Hong Kong amid anti-Chinese government sentiments. The (HKSAR) government could do something to help local students know more about Mainland China. However, knowing more does not mean that you will have a greater sense of belonging. For at least half of the Hong Kong youth, they attribute the problems of Hong Kong society, such as economic and livelihood issues, to political causes, the current political system, and the governance of the central government.

Some teachers distinguish students' attachment to the motherland and acceptance of the political system. The better way to understand Mainland China is to expose students to the society themselves. To help students know more about Mainland China, schools have organised study groups to visit Mainland China every year. However, short visits may not deepen mutual understanding between locals and CIS to any significant degree. Emphasis has been focused on differentiating politics from taking up a local or an ethnic identity. For CIS, a rejection of the Mainland political system is not to denounce the achievements of their home country. Their critique of the central government is not a betrayal of their motherland or rejection of their Chinese identity. Under the sociopolitical contexts of the Mainland and Hong Kong societies, the change of CIS attitudes towards civic matters makes sense. Whilst Hong Kong society focuses on citizen's rights and entitlements of the citizens, the Mainland emphasises obligations.

Immigrant youth or minorities should achieve their membership in a polity, not by assimilation, but through the struggle to claim rights as citizens. Starting with school may be the right way to do this. Students require schools to respond to their cultural identities and incorporate their struggles, hopes, dreams, and possibilities into their curricula (Ijadi-Maghsoodi et al., 2017). Linguistically and ethnically diverse students should not be expected to be assimilated into the homogenous mainstream society. Instead, they should be granted the rights and options to become part of the polity's ethnic groups. Some teachers also agree with this approach of integration. For example, Teacher Ken declared:

> I believe the priority for integration is to respect their ethnic identities and cultural values. Based on this, we can lead them to see and to know more about the city. It's understandable for them to be kind of "exclusive" in the new host environment. Even for Hong Kong people, we would like to be together with our local peers, especially where cultures are distinctive. So maybe we can start from the community, to respect and integrate their culture is to respect their rights in the city, adopt more practical methods, and make them feel they are welcome.

The impacts of home values

Birthplace is pivotal for individual development and self-forming. Students tend to define their own identity regarding their place of origin. The cultural values embedded in the culture of birthplace also play a vital role in acculturation. Though immigrants physically have dispersed beyond the boundaries of their home country, they remain "socially, politically, culturally, and often economically part of the nation-state of their ancestors" (Basch et al., 1994; p. 48). Core values are one of the most fundamental components of cultural identity (Smolicz, 1981). Exposure to their home cultures, part of CIS and NCS students heritage values, also impacts their integration and engagement in the host society.

It could be the cultural norms of the CIS group to stay away from politics for safety reasons (Meng & Gregory, 2002). On the other hand, their values for work ethics, aspiring mobility, diligence, and their family's emphasis on academic success support their integration into Hong Kong society, while their emphasis on the value of money and individual competence may hinder their integration into Hong Kong.

For emphasis of individual competence, mathematics Teacher Sean maintained:

> CIS treasure their opportunity to study in Hong Kong, they have a stronger Math foundation than local students, and some have developed good studying habits. They could complete homework on time and think deeper when they encounter complex math problems. You can tell that they've done revision after school. Whereas the math foundation

of NCS students is thin, and if it is taught in a second language, it would be more difficult for them to get the abstracts. Moreover, they are more relaxed than CIS at home. They tend to escape from solving the learning challenges when they encounter problems. Sometimes we have to lower the school level to teach them and to motivate them.

NCS students also lack after-school supervision with their studies. Their parents tend to have long working hours and a low education level, while the students live with relatives instead of parents or do part-time jobs. Moreover, cultural values can mean that parents tend not to have the sense to follow up students' studies. Math Teacher Sean raises this concern:

> South Asian parents hold very different values from local parents. Local parents will provide homework help with their children, buy extra exercises, or send their children to tutorial classes. The learning environment after school is consistent with that at school for local students. Yet, when South Asian students return home, it is entirely another world because they have nobody to follow up with them, and students may escape all schoolwork at home.

Teacher Karen also expressed her concern about the lack of family support and part-time work taken by NCS students:

> Most of our NCS parents are busy, working ten hours a day and have no time to educate their children. I also know some students live with uncles and aunts and probably meet their parents only once a week. Some students do part-time jobs until 11 or 12 pm after school and on weekends. They not only fail to complete their homework but also lose energy to study at school.

> It is also difficult to have effective communication with NCS parents. Sometimes I could find the mother, but then she may have no position at home in a dominant male culture… so the student's problem cannot be solved at all. Sometimes I could find the father and tell him about his child's educational issues at school, but due to his limited education level, the only thing he knows, or he can do, is to punish the child at home.

The families of most CIS and NCS students are struggling with financial needs. Community engagement is far beyond their immediate concern and ability. Unlike parents of mainstream students who may often discuss the political issues of Hong Kong, civic issues are out of family domains for most CIS and NCS families. Teacher Peter articulates his concern:

> Our time with the NCS parents is minimal. And within the limited time, we have to select the essential points to discuss with the parents, such as their study, career planning, etc. Both teachers and parents will not set civic education as the priority but, maybe communities could do more on this issue.

From the perspective of teachers, CIS parents are more responsive to schools' requests than NCS parents. The former would ask leave from their employers to attend the teacher-parent meeting and always respect and be responsive to teachers' suggestions. Teacher Karen pointed out:

> On the one hand, NCS parents would like their children to be professionals rather than manual workers. They have a high expectation of their children. While on the other hand, they don't seem to care much about how their children are doing at school. They are often absent from teacher-parent meetings, even when they have promised to come. They do not show up in the end. I believe it's because of their cultural values.

The pragmatic values of success, money, and social mobility may hinder the relatedness of CIS to society and their willingness to offer voluntary community services to the needy. Teacher Faith observed that:

> Some CIS lay too much emphasis on the monetary return of their service. For example, this year, I am the class teacher of S.2, and I also teach life education. I once asked students whether they would consider being volunteers for public welfare services. But to my great surprise, four-fifths of the CIS said they would not. I further explained that they could help other people and asked them why they were unwilling to be volunteers? They unanimously answered that they could be available only if they were paid.

A headmaster Ken asserts that:

> As NCS students receive a more "relaxed" parenting style than CIS, NCS students would be happier and more involved in school cultural events, especially singing and dancing competitions. By contrast, CIS would prefer to spend their spare time on part-time jobs, playing computer games, or going home. That being said, the emphasis on the cultural aspects of life does not mean NCS students have more interest in academics.

Echoing Ken's observations, Teacher William added:

> They (NCS students) care more about whether they could have extra time to play, to hang out with friends, but not to think about their studies.

The contentment of NCS students may be associated with the family's culture. It could also be related to their preference to keep themselves to their co-ethnic community where they share a common culture, especially religion (Diller, 2001; Stepick, 2005). As such, NCS students may be good at co-ethnic socialisation and inhibited from gaining the resilience in overcoming obstacles at school and actualise their talent in society. Conversely, the instrumental cultural values of CIS may motivate them to gain competence, but nevertheless, they also show their indifference to society.

Marginalisation

Ethnic identity is a mediating factor for the degree and nature of students' civic engagement. Ethnic identity can be controversial amid the rise of nationalism. Without making a personal identification with the host society, immigrant students will not get involved in society building. It is not a natural civic act for people who do not take root in the local culture. It would be even more difficult for them to engage in politics, as this requires more profound knowledge and closer bonding to society. Feeling alienated, taking an "in-between" identity (Hong Konger and Mainlander/South/South East Asian), or feeling neither here nor there is the crux of rejection. These can be their coping strategies in facing confrontations, prejudice, and discrimination in a society where racial exclusion is still prevalent (Giuliani et al., 2018; Yeung, 2020).

Stereotyped perceptions of CIS include cutting in queues, being money-minded and being unhygienic. Their accented Cantonese often gives away their cultural background and causes discrimination. Math Teacher Sean stated:

> CIS are sometimes being discriminated against in this community. Some students have an accent, and this lets people know that they come from the Mainland. There was quite a lot of disappointing news on Mainlanders cutting in line, engaging in parallel trade. All these reports made CIS unhappy and deepened social division.

NCS students feel more attached to the society; however, they also feel marginalised and discriminated against due to cultural differences (e.g., hygiene habits, gender issues, etc.). As mentioned by the Math Teacher Sean:

> South Asian students also face the problem of discrimination. They find it challenging to integrate into society and feel isolated from the community. Many South Asian students are Muslim. In my opinion, their conception of females and traditional values are mainly learned from their usually conservative mothers. For example, some lack physical health and hygiene knowledge, such as using hygiene products and cleaning their bodies.

Teacher Peter mentioned that due to the language barriers, NCS students have minimal exposure to local Chinese media reports:

> We need to make much more effort to find appropriate teaching materials in English than those in Chinese. Obviously, in Hong Kong, more Chinese newspapers can show different positions and views, while English resources are too limited. If you ask the students to search for news by themselves, it will be an even more demanding task.

Transformative citizenship education and ethnic identities

Banks (2015) argues that teachers bring cultural perspectives to their teaching and interaction with students. They are change agents in facilitating ethnic minority students to develop democratic racial attitudes and behaviours. Teachers' perceptions of CIS and NCS students' civic attitudes, behaviours, and acculturative stressors in society are affected by their values, beliefs, and conceptions of model citizens. Therefore, teacher education is essential to raise their awareness of personal bias or in-group favouritism in their interaction with the students. For example, it may well be that CIS are more concerned about earning than offering volunteer work in their spare time since most of them come from low-income families. They have to be self-reliant financially. Again, fewer CIS are interested in politics or advocacy for democracy than their mainstream counterparts. This can be tightly linked with their cultural upbringing. Banks (2015) opines that curriculum interventions and changing school ethos can bring positive racial attitudes and perceptions among students from diverse cultural backgrounds.

NCS students generally have a culture of cleaving to their own community, and language barriers prevent them from having a rewarding integration experience in a Cantonese-speaking society. Naturally, their strong co-ethnic bonding and clanship act like firewalls to separate them from mainstream society. They acquire a sense of contentment with their ethnic identity, such as Hong Kong Pakistani, Hong Kong Indians, Fillinpios, etc. They may attach themselves more to ethnic labels as they mature and build a firmer ethnic identity (Stepick & Stepick, 2002). To raise their awareness of local issues and the interdependence between themselves and the well-being of Hong Kong society, more effective ways must be put in place to address their pass-by guest identity. Such would help them develop positive racial and ethnic attitudes and the knowledge, skills, and perspectives for deliberation among diverse groups (Parker, 2003).

As Marshall (1964) once pointed out, citizenship is developed through civil, political, and social dimensions. Citizenship is not only about the freedom of speech, the right to own property, and participating in politics. Citizenship now is about providing health, education, and other welfares needed to participate fully in cultural communities and civic culture. The political identity of NCS students has been ambivalent, even though many of them were born and raised in Hong Kong, speak perfect Cantonese, and take up a local Hong Konger identity (Yuen & Leung, 2019). The cultural values of minority groups have not been fully recognised, respected, and incorporated into the dominant culture. They have classified NCS as a category of "other". The civic education of schools has long been aimed at educating citizens who internalise their national values, honour their national heroes, and glorify their national history. However, Banks (2014) pointed out that this civic education is no longer consistent with citizenship today as people have multiple national commitments. Confronted with globalisation, civic education in multicultural societies needs to construct nation-states that reflect and incorporate the diversity of their citizens and have an overarching set of shared values, ideals, and goals to which all citizens are committed.

In a time of rapid social transition, more deliberations are needed for transformative citizenship education and helping students understand how cultural, national, regional, and global identities are constructed and interrelated. Because of incompatibility between their own cultural values and the cultural values in Hong Kong, these students are experiencing cultural conflicts. For example, the political culture of CIS is rooted in the Confucian values of respecting authority and kinship tradition, while the educational system in Hong Kong empowers students to be active citizens in social and civic affairs. In contrast, NCS students are religious, and spirituality and religion have a higher place in their daily lives than mainstream peers. Equipping them to focus more on competitive high stake examinations could be a challenge to their value system.

At the current juncture of changing a Hong Kong-centric classroom practice to a national approach to embrace the values and cultures of China, a culturally relevant pedagogical approach will make classrooms and schools more inviting for all students as they experience democracy in classrooms and schools. Teachers must examine their cultural assumptions, knowledge, attitudes, and behaviours about CIS, NCS, and mainstream students (Yuen, 2018). On the one hand, the rise of nationalism accelerates the national pride of Mainland Chinese. Taking civic and moral education as an example, teachers must recognise the differences between local and non-local student groups in cultivating their nationalism, especially when they continuously face discrimination or marginalisation from the host society. On the other hand, minority students should accept and embrace their minority identity and treasure their home country's positive cultural values. The diligence and tolerance of CIS and the optimism and relatedness of NCS students are positive cultural values inherited from their home country. At the same time, autonomy, responsibility, and freedom are also values they need to defend as Hong Kong citizens. The adoption of multiple identities would be most comfortable for them. Thus, they acquire their Hong Kong citizenship while recognising and appreciating their cultural root.

References

Adler, R. P., & Goggin, J. (2005). What do we mean by "civic engagement"? *Journal of Transformative Education*, *3*(3), 236–253. https://doi.org/10.1177%2F1541344605276792.

Banks, J. A. (2014). Diversity, group identity, and citizenship education in a global age. *Journal of Education*, *194*(3), 1–12. https://doi.org/10.1177%2F002205741419400302.

Banks, J. A. (2015). *Cultural diversity and education: Foundations, curriculum, and teaching*. Routledge.

Basch, L., Glick-Schiller, N., & Blanc-Szanton, C. (1994). *Nations unbound: Transnational projects, postcolonial predicaments and deterritorialized nation-states*. Gordon and Breach.

Chan, C. W. S., Lam, B. O. Y., Teng, Y., & Lee, M. (2015). Making sense of divergent perceptions of racial-ethnic discrimination in Hong Kong. *Multicultural Education Review*, *7*(1-2), 41–58. https://doi.org/10.1080/2005615X.2015.1048608.

Ching, L. K. (2020). *Nationalism in everyday life: Nature and membership of Hong Kong civic nationalism* [Master of Public Policy Thesis]. University of Tokyo.

Diller, E. C. (2001). *Citizens in service: The challenge of delivering civic engagement training to national service programs*. Corporation for National and Community Service.

Elmore, G. M., & Huebner, E. S. (2010). Adolescents' satisfaction with school experiences: Relationships with demographics, attachment relationships, and school engagement behavior. *Psychology in the Schools*, *47*(6), 525–537. https://doi.org/10.1002/pits.20488.

Finn, J. D. (1989). Withdrawing from school. *Review of Educational Research*, *59*(2), 117–142. https://doi.org/10.3102%2F00346543059002117.

Finn, J. D. (1993). *School engagement & students at risk*. National Center for Education Statistics.

Fredricks, J. A., Blumenfeld, P. C., & Paris, A. H. (2004). School engagement: Potential of the concept, state of the evidence. *Review of Educational Research*, *74*(1), 59–109. https://doi.org/10.3102%2F00346543074001059.

Giuliani, C., Tagliabue, S., & Regalia, C. (2018). Psychological well-being, multiple identities, and discrimination among first and second generation immigrant Muslims. *Europe's Journal of Psychology*, *14*(1), 66. https://doi.org/10.5964/ejop.v14i1.1434.

Gopinathan, S., & Sharpe, L. (2004). New bearings for citizenship education in Singapore. In W. O. Lee, D. Grossman, K. Kennedy, & G. Fairbrother (Eds.), *Citizenship education in Asia and the pacific concepts and issues* (pp. 119–136). CERC: The University of Hong Kong & Kluwer Academic Publisher.

Gu, M., Mak, B., & Qu, X. (2017). Ethnic minority students from South Asia in Hong Kong: Language ideologies and discursive identity construction. *Asia Pacific Journal of Education*, *37*(3), 360–374. https://doi.org/10.1080/02188791.2017.1296814.

Gutmann, A. (2004). Unity and diversity in democratic multicultural education: Creative and destructive tensions. In J. A. Banks (Ed.), *Diversity and citizenship education: Global perspectives* (pp. 71–96). Jossey-Bass.

Hong Kong Unison. (2016). *Hong Kong Unison Submission to the Education Panel on Education issues of Ethnic Minority* (LC Paper No. CB(4)157/16-17(02)). https://www.legco.gov.hk/yr16-17/english/panels/ed/papers/edcb4-157-2-e.pdf

Igarashi, A. (2019). Till multiculturalism do us part: Multicultural policies and the national identification of immigrants in European countries. *Social Science Research*, *77*, 88–100. https://doi.org/10.1016/j.ssresearch.2018.10.005

Ijadi-Maghsoodi, R., Marlotte, L., Garcia, E., Aralis, H., Lester, P., Escudero, P., & Kataoka, S. (2017). Adapting and implementing a school-based resilience-building curriculum among low-income racial and ethnic minority students. *Contemporary School Psychology*, *21*(3), 223–239. https://doi.org/10.1007/s40688-017-0134-1.

Jimerson, S. R., Campos, E., & Greif, J. L. (2003). Toward an understanding of definitions and measures of school engagement and related terms. *The California School Psychologist*, *8*(1), 7–27. https://doi.org/10.1007/BF03340893.

Kallen, H. M. (1924). *Culture and democracy in the United States*. Transaction Publishers.

Lee, M. R. (2010). The protective effects of civic communities against all-cause mortality. *Social Science & Medicine, 70*(11), 1840–1846. https://doi.org/10.1016/j.socscimed.2010.02.020.

Loh, E., & Hung, C. (2020). *A study on the challenges faced by mainstream schools in educating ethnic minorities in Hong Kong*. https://www.eoc.org.hk/eoc/upload/ResearchReport/researchreport_20200115_e.pdf

Marshall, T. H. (1964). *Class, citizenship, and social development: Essays*. Doubleday.

Meng, X., & Gregory, R. G. (2002). The impact of interrupted education on subsequent educational attainment: A cost of the Chinese cultural revolution. *Economic Development and Cultural Change, 50*(4), 935–959. https://doi.org/10.1086/342761.

Parker, W. C. (2003). *Teaching democracy: Unity and diversity in public life*. Teachers College Press.

Purbrick, M. (2019). A report of the 2019 Hong Kong protests. *Asian Affairs, 50*(4), 465–487. https://doi.org/10.1080/03068374.2019.1672397.

Reichert, F., & Torney-Purta, J. (2019). A cross-national comparison of teachers' beliefs about the aims of civic education in 12 countries: A person-centered analysis. *Teaching and Teacher Education, 77*, 112–125. https://doi.org/10.1016/j.tate.2018.09.005

Ronan, B. (2004). Testimony at the *White House Conference on Aging Public Forum on Civic Engagement in an Older America*, Phoenix, Arizona, 25 February 2004.

Skinner, E. A., & Belmont, M. J. (1993). Motivation in the classroom: Reciprocal effects of teacher behavior and student engagement across the school year. *Journal of Educational Psychology, 85*(4), 571. https://psycnet.apa.org/doi/10.1037/0022-0663.85.4.571.

Smolicz, J. (1981). Core values and cultural identity. *Ethnic and Racial Studies, 4*(1), 75–90. https://doi.org/10.1080/01419870.1981.9993325.

Stepick, A. (2005). God is apparently not dead: The obvious, the emergent, & the unknown in immigrant and religion. In K. Leonard, A. Stepick, M. Vasquez, K. I. Leonard, & J. Holdaway (Eds.), *Immigrant faiths: Transforming religious life in America*. Alta Mira Press.

Stepick, A., & Stepick, C. D. (2002). Becoming American, constructing ethnicity: Immigrant youth and civic engagement. *Applied Developmental Science, 6*(4), 246–257. https://doi.org/10.1207/S1532480XADS0604_12.

Van Benshoten, E. (2001). *Civic engagement for people of all ages through national service*. Unpublished manuscript.

Veg, S. (2017). The rise of "localism" and civic identity in post-handover Hong Kong: Questioning the Chinese nation-state. *The China Quarterly, 230*, 323–347. https://doi.org/10.1017/S0305741017000571

Yeung, J. (2020). Spat at, segregated, policed: Hong Kong's dark-skinned minorities say they've never felt accepted. *CNN*. https://edition.cnn.com/2020/08/21/asia/hong-kong-racism-intl-hnk-dst/index.html

Young, N., Michael, C., & Smolinksi, J. (2019). *Captivating campuses*. Vernon Press.

Yuen, C. Y. M. (2013). School engagement and civic engagement as predictors for the future political participation of ethnic Chinese and South Asian adolescents in Hong Kong. *Multicultural Education Review* (3), 317–342. http://doi.org/10.11567/met.29.3.1

Yuen, C. Y. M. (2018). Perceptions of social justice among the South Asian and mainstream Chinese youth from diverse cultural backgrounds in Hong Kong. *Peabody Journal of Education, 93*(3), 332–344. https://doi.org/10.1080/0161956X.2018.1449928.

Yuen, C. Y. M. (2019). *The happiness and mourning of Hong Kong students*. In Chinese 漂流少年：香港學生的快樂與哀愁。 Breakthrough Organization Limited.

Yuen, C. Y. M., Lee, M., & Leung, C. S. S. (2016). Religious belief and its association with life satisfaction of adolescents in Hong Kong. *Journal of Beliefs & Values*, *37*(1), 103–113. https://doi.org/10.1080/13617672.2016.1141533.

Yuen, C. Y. M., & Leung, C. S. S. (2019). Belonging and connectedness: Identity, religiosity and aspiration of immigrant Muslim youth in Hong Kong. *Asia Pacific Journal of Education*, *39*(4), 423–435. https://doi.org/10.1080/02188791.2019.1671802.

6 Inclusion and Rejection of Chinese Immigrant Students (CIS)

The colony-turned Hong Kong ethnic identity

As of 2018, there were 7,482,500 people living in Hong Kong. The Han Chinese account for over 90% of the total Hong Kong population. Most of the local Hong Kong people are descendants of Chinese nationals, residing in Hong Kong from three main time frames: post-Great Leap Forward (the late 1950s), the Cultural Revolution (1966–1967), and the other subsequent waves of migration from the Mainland (Law & Lee, 2006). With that refugee history in focus, the Hong Kong way of living has attracted Chinese immigrants to live their dreams and take up a local identity. The Hong Kong identity, or the general feeling of being a "Hong Konger", has gradually been ingrained among young people throughout the past decades (Chan & Fung, 2018). Since the changeover on 1 July 1997, there have been several waves of territory-wide social unrest and public demonstrations, starting with 1 July 2003. These demonstrations had been triggered by the proposed implementation of Basic Law Article 23 (which was then subsequently withdrawn), as well as the demand for universal suffrage regarding the election of the Chief Executive in 2014 (known as the Umbrella Movement), and the shelved proposed implementation of the Extradition Amendment Bill in 2019. Liberty, freedom of speech, social justice, and a democratic electoral system have been the core values of most local young people. All these factors distant them from the Mainland Chinese. Hence, the emergence of the ethnic Hong Konger identity has gone beyond Chinese nationalism (Chan & Fung, 2018). The Umbrella Movement in 2014 and the social incidents in June 2019 are typical examples of localism and Mainland-local inter-group conflicts.

Nonetheless, the sociocultural ties between the HKSAR and the Mainland have never been as strong as now. Cross-boundary business, cultural exchange, marriage, and relocation happen daily. In addition, every day, the HKSAR government grants a quota of 150 Mainland citizens to apply for the exit permit, known as the "One-Way Permit" (OWP). This allows them to relocate from under the Chinese government and become a Hong Kong resident (Law & Lee, 2006). In 2019, around 32,200 Chinese immigrants relocated to the HKSAR as

DOI: 10.4324/9780429439315-6

residents with the OWP (Home Affairs Department of HKSAR, 2020). Among them, around 20% are school-age children, known as CIS.

Parents of CIS share many characteristics with immigrants, namely with lower education levels, lower social and cultural capital and engagement in low-income manual work. Economically, these immigrant families are underprivileged, clustering in old built-up areas characterised by subdivided flats, public housing, and poor living environments. Socio-culturally, they are excluded from the mainstream policy discourse and marginalised as a sub-cultural group in society. Politically, they respond to the calls for Chinese nationalism more readily than their local counterparts. To them, to fulfil the civic mission is to be cooperative. All in all, they are inhibited from being fully included in local society (Law & Lee, 2006). It is against these socio-economic and political backgrounds that the self-formation of these CIS is portrayed.

The portraits of CIS

Researchers document that CIS undergo an intense and challenging journey when launching their new voyages into Hong Kong schooling and society, particularly with their first year (Chee, 2012; 2010; Yuen, 2013). Acculturation stress is associated with systemic barriers such as English proficiency, mainstream dialect (Cantonese), and adjusting to fit the host culture of learning, socialising, and climbing the social ladder to advance themselves. Discourse has been mainly on alleviating their poverty and addressing their CIS challenges in education and career prospects. Yet, little has been documented about their perspectives on education, identity, and friendship. Unlike the Mainland students who enrol in the Hong Kong education system via the international stream for credentials, these CIS are uprooted from their hometown in the Mainland to join their families in Hong Kong. Like immigrants elsewhere, the CIS are deficient in the essential social and cultural capital when re-establishing their new lives in their new society. Education is an essential platform for developing their new civic responsibilities and identity in the process of self-formation in the new society (Levine & Youniss, 2006).

Empowering CIS to speak for themselves sheds new light on their construction of civic identity and demystifies the stereotyped perceptions of CIS as socially withdrawn or disoriented in society. Their school and life trajectories are varied as they pursue their dreams in their new home. They decide their roles and identities through life course experiences and exposure. Hence, their abilities to improve their circumstances and social status directly impact their well-being and sense of belongingness. Some CIS are determined to use education to build social and cultural capital to offset their less fortunate social condition with support from parents, teachers, and friends. At the same time, some find it hard to combat the negativity. In the following, the two dimensions will shape the discussion: (1) to underscore the process of self-formation or identity construction of individual Chinese immigrant youth in the co-ethnic sociocultural context, and to (2) capture the perspectives and voices of their engagement with schools and society. By probing these two dimensions, we discover their acceptance and rejection of the cultural values of the new society and understand their intra-personal self-negotiations between their past and their new life in Hong Kong. Specifically, the interplay of handling subjective feelings and commitment to cope with life challenges will be delved deeper in the discussion.

In 2014, these individuals participated in our large-scale well-being and engagement questionnaire survey (about 15,000 student participants). Forty-seven students from four secondary schools subsequently indicated an interest in joining the interview. They gave personal and parental consent documents (if under 18) for a one-on-one interview in their school. The face-to-face and one-on-one interaction allowed them to freely express their opinions on school experience and civic/societal engagement. They could choose to have the interview conducted in Putonghua or Cantonese, whatever they felt comfortable with. The conversations usually began with introducing their demographic backgrounds, such as the length of stay in Hong Kong, parental occupations, residential area, and their original hometown. Subsequent dialogues were focused on their school experiences, perception of civic identity, life aspirations, and general perceptions of Hong Kong. It is undeniable that home always plays a major part in students' identity construction (Lareau, 2000).

Portrait 1 – Home and identity construction among CIS

One male and five female students shared their opinions on Hong Kong, especially concerning their identity and their extensive personal engagement in school and community. The participants were around 18 years old during the interviews, with varying lengths of Hong Kong residence (ranging from four months to six years). Their new school lives involved various extracurricular activities, including participation in the orchestra and athletic teams, being the Chairperson of a student welfare society, voluntary community work, and flag selling. In addition, they exhibited some forms of cultural assimilation to the local society, including embracing the local culture by mastering the Cantonese dialect, developing new social networks, and thinking of their identities as "Mainland Chinese" and "Hong Konger". To a certain extent, taking up a local Hong Konger identity is connected with a willingness to make the city their home and sharing its values. But the perceived self-efficacy and ability to handle the discrepancies between the real and ideal self is key to unravel the identity and belongingness issues (Tsang et al., 2012).

Kinyu is an 18-year-old S5 student. Embracing the new culture and values, he sees his "Hong Konger" identity evolving.

> It was such a long time since I moved here. I have forgotten my Mainland experience. As time goes by, I identify with Hong Kong people more than the Mainlanders. I could see the difference between the Mainland and Hong Kong societies. Although China's economy is getting stronger, the wealth gap is getting wider. The poor remain very poor and benefit very little from

economic development. I am learning more about the world and China in my curriculum. It provides a platform for me to be more reflective of the social circumstances across the globe. Things I was not aware of in the past but now I am. My new understanding of the world and the local society somehow shapes my identity as a Hong Konger.

Portrait 2 – Hong Kong identity

Cat, an S5 student, picks up the label of "Chinese Hong Konger". It reflects her fondness of Hong Kong society, awareness of Hong Kong's status, and her father's cultural roots. In her words, "The sovereignty of Hong Kong has been transferred back to China. Also, my father is a Hong Konger, and people say we should follow our father".

To a large extent, China's sovereignty over Hong Kong decides Cat's Chinese identity and her father's cultural origin reinforces her Chinese Hong Kong mentality. In contrast, the Hong Kong identity is not a natural outcome of other CIS residents. Instead, it is through their relationship with their teachers, peers, and schools. Kitty is one such example.

> When I first came here, my classmates were very friendly to me. The teachers were also passionate about teaching and wouldn't neglect me. They would joke with us. I feel very close to them.

Wong echoes Kitty's warm feeling regarding her new school life.

> I feel good studying here. I get along well with my classmates, and the teachers are very nice. They won't discriminate against new immigrants. I got to know really good friends here. And my teacher really cares about me.

It is the fifth year of Yu's Hong Kong schooling, she speaks highly of her teachers' helpfulness:

> I'm very satisfied with my school. Our teachers are very approachable and we talk like friends. If you (I) have anything you (I) want to ask about your (my) studies after class, they will be very willing to explain to you (me), even it costs them a lot of time to teach us.

Being actively involved in community work and mingling with local people, Yu adopts a Hong Konger identity.

> After getting more information about the differences between Hong Kong and the Mainland and knowing more about the two societies, I naturally identify myself as a Hong Konger. I'm attracted to the value of freedom. Also, Hong Kong people are polite and obedient to the law. They don't spit in the public nor jump the queue.

Portrait 3 – Unpacking Chineseness

These CIS move out of their Mainland home and relocate to Hong Kong society, and it is not easy for them to give up their Mainland mental habits and their feeling of belongingness. Loving Hong Kong and loving their cultural roots isn't mutually exclusive. For these CIS, there are some "truths" that cannot be ignored. For example, China is their birthplace. Hong Kong is part of China. All these facts constitute the core elements of the identity formation of CIS, and their Chineseness is the common thread to holding up their belonging and connectedness.

Hong Kong is part of China

Wong, an S2 student who has been in Hong Kong for about four months, is very aware of the fact that "Hong Kong is a part of China". Hence, she calls herself "a Chinese Hong Konger", meaning a Chinese person living in Hong Kong. Similarly, Tszyan, an S4 student who arrived in Hong Kong only four months ago, acknowledges that her life's trajectory began with her birthplace, Mainland China. Her civic identity is "Chinese Hong Konger". The "Chinese" identity is a dominant component, and it embodies the Hong Kong part as a whole while "Hong Konger" is more like a "subordinate identity nested within a Chinese identity" (Fu et al., 1999). They feel connected to other ethnic Chinese individuals and differentiate themselves from people of other ethnicities, like the NCS students from Southeast Asia, for example.

Rejection of anti-China sentiments

Entering the second year of her Hong Kong residence, Tung, an S5 student, describes herself as Chinese. In addition to Hong Kong being a part of China, her Mainland upbringing qualifies her to build the connections between Hong Kong and Mainland China. More importantly, Tung emphasises her objection to the anti-China sentiment.

> I know that there are many adverse reports about Mainland China, but I believe it's better to be more inclusive and tolerant. Anyway, China has done something good to promote the economic growth of Hong Kong. Don't always focus on those negative things; it also has a positive side.

Her approval of the Chinese government lies squarely within her national sentiment and patriotism. From her love of the Chinese nation and her strong emotional attachment to her birthplace, she draws her Chinese identity (thus not including Hong Kong).

Self-formation of hybrid identity

Having been in Hong Kong society for six years, Ching, an S6 student, is going to switch her new immigrant status into the status of a permanent citizen.

Ching intends to embrace both Mainland Chinese and Hong Kong cultures in her self-identity.

> I was born in Mainland China, but now I'm living in Hong Kong. So I'm both Chinese and Hong Konger. Overall, both (identities) are Chinese, but we (I) can have Mainland Chinese and Hong Konger within China despite they are two different cultures.

> However, I would put Chinese first because I was born in Mainland China and I'm more emotionally attached to it. But recently, I have formally become a Hong Konger as I have moved here. The label means that I am studying and living in Hong Kong.

Interestingly, Ching is more emotionally attached to her birthplace even though she is aware that her identity now includes a "Hong Konger" element. Such an element only makes her even more distinctive from the local Hong Konger. Her thinking further unravelled her dual-identity:

> My identity label reflects a dilemma. In the eyes of Mainland Chinese, I'm more a Hong Konger than a Mainlander. However, I'm a Chinese immigrant regardless. I'm different from the local Hong Kong people.

Ching combines the points and references of both Mainland Chinese and Hong Kong cultures when constituting her identity. She may also have consciously engaged in personal attachment to her birthplace and the current society. While her past living experience provided an alternative reference group to her identity, her more recent experiences, personal exposure, school life, and social circumstances have shaped her inner life and values. Ching's case is relatively typical compared to the self-forming experience of international students overseas (Marginson, 2014). The point being is that students can fashion their own changing identities and form their own self-trajectories between home and host societies when constructing their hybrid identities. It is key to note that the hybrid identities do not carry equal weight. The stronger is her Mainland identification and attachment, with the lesser being her Hong Kong identification. Notably, the receptivity of the host society plays a significant role in contributing to her sense of belonging and sense of detachment. For instance, in response to the Mainland-Hong Kong conflicts, Ching refrains from speaking Putonghua in public, concealing her Mainland background, and avoiding negative prejudice. Nevertheless, she affirms both her Mainland Chinese and Hong Konger identities despite her struggle. "Actually, we (Chinese immigrants) are emotionally attached to both sides enabling us to take a more neutral stance over controversial matters".

Zhen echoes Ching's experience:

> I didn't have a strong sense of belonging in Hong Kong when I first arrived. Maybe I saw myself as half Hong Konger and half Chinese at that time.

But now, I have gradually considered myself as a Hong Konger, and I think I should treat Hong Kong as my home. So my identity is gradually changing.

When CIS start to get acquainted with local society, establish social networks, and gain insight into social circumstances, they develop a stronger sense of social attachment. Almost all CIS interviewees embrace some Hong Kong values in their civic identity construction, suggesting that they recognise they are a part of the host society. On the other hand, they are also deeply anchored in their Chinese cultural roots, which is an inseparable part of their history and identity. Birthplace is a critical factor for influencing identity.

Portrait 4 – Inclusion and rejection as new citizens in Hong Kong

The patterns of civic identity construction also vary among the CIS. Ching and Zhen began to accept and embrace their new identities as Hong Kong citizens the longer they stayed. They demonstrate high interest, passion, and active participation in their schools and community organisations/activities. However, they still lack civic knowledge of the host society. Simultaneously, their attachment to the "Chinese" identity and their lower political efficacy hinders their social integration.

Deep civic interest but low civic knowledge as a future citizen

As indicated previously, schools are playing a significant role in the civic education of these students. The students see school as the platform to acquire knowledge and to exercise their civic rights by joining the student bodies, expressing their views on current and social affairs during classroom discussion, etc. Yu revealed:

> Current affairs are usually discussed in our Liberal Studies lessons. We adopt an issue-based approach to discuss social topics. In English lessons, we often discuss issues related to current affairs. The discussion motivated me to read the news and to upkeep myself with society.

Like many CIS who do not keep a distance from the local government affairs, Zhen reasons that he cannot keep track of the political parties:

> There are many political parties in Hong Kong, but I'm not that clear about what they do internally... I feel a bit confused about different parties.

Meaningful civic participation requires prior knowledge and training through education. Ching has no desire to get registered to be a voter, even though she is eligible to cast her own vote. She is not even keen to take any initiative to upkeep herself with the party development or political stance.

> Though it was mentioned in the Liberal Studies lessons, I only have a vague concept of the political parties. I don't really understand what is their main

business and have no clue how to cast a vote. I'm not familiar with the District Council members. So I haven't registered as a voter yet.

Nevertheless, she is somehow aware that politics are actually part of her daily life and deserve more attention. She added:

I'm pretty interested in politics since we live in society, and many policies are related to us. So, we need to know more about them. Then, we can get more from them and make further suggestions.

Being interested but not ready to take part in civic matters is a common phenomenon among CIS. Their knowledge does not always connect with action. Gaining first-hand experience in civic issues is critical as there is no ready-made package for young people to develop their civic-mindedness. Moreover, the lack of local civic knowledge hampers their participation. Cat is an example:

I don't know how to take part in district council matters or Hong Kong matters... I don't know what the District Council members have to do with me... I'm interested in politics, but when asked whether I'd like to be a District Council voter, I said I'm not sure as I don't know what they do.

Textbook knowledge of civics and citizenship education fails to engage the mind and hearts of CIS. Although schools provide opportunities for these students to discuss or learn more about current affairs or public issues in Hong Kong, CIS have been adopting a wait-and-see approach and are not keen on applying their civic knowledge to civic behaviours.

Regardless, Wong is an exception. He develops a habit of reading the newspaper every day and is familiar with government structure. Of course, even he can provide the names of many chief officials within the Hong Kong government does not mean he has developed a personal perspective on civic engagement.

Portrait 5 – Inclusion inside/outside school and high expected civic engagement

One indicator measuring the level of civic engagement is community engagement, inside and outside school. Due to their positive learning attitude and behaviours, these CIS have been assigned to take up leadership roles at school.

School can surely play a role in raising students' awareness of civic obligations and rights by orchestrating their learning experiences. In comparison to others, Cat is the most committed example to service at school. She was the former Chairperson of the Student Welfare Society and is currently the Chairperson of the Drama and Astronomy Clubs. She is also the Vice-chairperson of the Senior Students Group. Outside school, she participates in the AYP (The Hong Kong Award for Young People) and flag selling. When asked about her civic engagement in the future, she is also the most proactive and determined. She has already registered as a voter and plans to vote in the upcoming elections. Her words show her interest and foreseeable action in civic activities. She elaborated that:

> If there is meaningful policy advocacy that I support, I will join. Or, if I find something unfair to fight against, I will gather more information and take part for the benefit of Hong Kong.

Through serving, Ching has ignited her sense of commitment to the school community. At school, she is a Prefect, the Chairperson of the Chinese Society, and the Vice House Captain. Her leadership gifts are being acknowledged, and hence she actively takes part in voluntary work inside and outside school.

Wong belongs to the school's athletics team. But so far, he has yet applied his interest in public service to community engagement. However, he did indicate that he might run for the local district council should there be a chance for him in the future.

Self-efficacy is vital to cultivate civic-mindedness. Yu and Wong are less active in comparison to Cat and Ching. However, in regard to future civic engagement, they believe that they will get involved. Yu is a Prefect and a member of the Chinese Society. She said: "If there are issues I find important, I may take part in them in the future".

Often there is a gap between aspiring to serve and taking it into action. Tung is a member of the House Committee and Calligraphy Club at school. Her involvement in voluntary community work is restricted to charitable service: selling flags. She mentioned:

> It is better to give than to take. When you help others, others will help you too. One day we may need help from others. This is what my mom told us we should do. Our school also encourages us to take part in these activities...helping others makes me happy. My family will support me too as it is about charity.

Zhen is quite active at school, serving as a prefect and being a member of the Chinese Orchestra and the English Society. She has also participated in the Speech Festival and flag selling outside school. However, she does not indicate her aspiration for future civic engagement in society.

There is no consistent correlation between the nature of engagement at school and the degree of students' expected civic engagement in the future (Torney-Purta, 2002). Nevertheless, most of these students have assumed one or more leadership roles in the student organisations at school. They unanimously offer their good wishes to serve in society. Wallin (2003) has pointed out that students' leadership training could raise their political awareness and enhance their democratic skills in tackling controversial issues and having empathy for others, etc.

The significance of student leadership training concerning their future civic engagement has been articulated by Cat as follows:

> The role as the Chair of the Student Welfare Society is the most helpful for my personal development. Through serving in society, I have learned many things, like communication skills and how to deal with different problems. My teachers also taught me how to talk to others and the necessary attitude... Besides, as the Chair, I needed to promote activities, have meetings with fellow students and teachers, and speak on stage. All these made me a lot braver. Before that, I used to be very timid and quiet, dare not to talk to students from other classes and forms.

The leadership opportunity not only builds up Cat's self-confidence but also sharpens her communication and public speaking skills. Sharing Cat's views, Tung believes school activities are a good training ground for holistic development.

> Participation in school activities certainly influences participation in social activities to some extent. It lets me gain experience and cultivate more interest in engaging in social activities. It definitely improves my ability and self-confidence.

Besides skills, Tung added that participation in school activities actually enhanced her interest in social activities. School is a miniature society. As students get involved in school matters and activities, they are recognised as members of the student organisations, developing a stronger sense of school belonging and pride in their activities. They may then be prompted to care more about the school community, and such interest may be further shifted to the broader society.

Rejection of active political participation

Despite the fact that CIS are keen to immerse into school and community, none of them are passionate about civic or political participation. There is a vast divide between social integration and personal civic engagement. Zhen and Tung are keen to offer public services to the needy, but distance themselves from political participation. Zhen has her own reasoning as follows:

> I will pay attention to current affairs but personally, I disapprove behaviours like demonstrations. It causes discomfort to others with so many people gathered together... I like serving and helping others so I will participate in community services, but for controversial issues involving many people, I may withdraw.

Drawing reference to her family education, Tung expressed her reservations over public demonstration.

> My family members will discuss current affairs but we won't take actions like going on demonstrations... In general, people participating in

demonstrations are more emotional and some use more violent language and behaviour. That scared me. Also, my family thinks demonstrations are not good. They would say it is stupid to go on demonstrations and it is better to spend time studying instead...maybe that's related to my family's education. It's okay to discuss current affairs, but we don't like people using too much foul language to express opinions.

The way in which significant others respond to the political climate contribute to CIS attitudes towards civic engagement. Tung's impression of civic engagement was rather negative. She attributes this to her family education. Another reason for their low passion for political demonstration may be their lower self-efficacy in politics, just as most Mainland Chinese choose to distance themselves from politics whilst burying their heads into studying (Zhai, 2018).

Portrait 6 – Future aspirations

Torney-Purta (2002) accentuates that student expectations about their future educations are a powerful predictor of civic knowledge and participation and demonstrate their attachment to the city. Senior secondary students have half a foot into adulthood, so future aspirations become a key concern. Four CIS expressed their aspiration to study or develop their career in Hong Kong, with different reasons behind them. Wong aspires to further his studies in Hong Kong: "I think it is better to further my studies in Hong Kong as the qualifications I get here will be better recognized than those I get in Mainland China in the future".

Zhen aspires to be a teacher, and she believes that pressure drives her further. "I prefer to develop my career in Hong Kong because the keen competition here can motivate me to study harder".

It shows that these students see the advantage of the education and atmosphere in Hong Kong. Ching would like to study at a university in Hong Kong. If she fails, she plans on enrolling in an associate degree or higher diploma course first and hopes to get into university afterward. Accounting is Ching's dream job, as it offers a better career prospect for her. Aspiring to serve Hong Kong is another source of her motivation to lead a life of flourishing and productivity.

> I'm determined to work hard and contribute to Hong Kong society to prove that not all Mainland immigrants just wish to take advantage of this society. No matter whether what I have learned, my experience, or the money I earn, I will contribute them to Hong Kong.

Resilience is a personal quality that stands out in conversations with these CIS. Despite the huge stress associated with the high-stakes HKDSE, they look beyond the challenge and fix their eyes upon the returns of the hard work. Even though not all students set their goals in the academic field, many of them have clear plans about their future, like fashion design, hydropower engineering, driving, teaching at preschools, and maintaining aircraft. They also have plans to explore different societies should they fail to secure a place in a local university. Taiwan is an alternative learning destination. Japan and Mainland China are also options. Alternatively, better yet, they can apply for technical and vocational education in Hong Kong if foreign educational opportunities do not knock. Neither shame nor guilt is involved. Taking Yu's thinking as an example. "It doesn't mean that you have no future if you can't go to the universities".

All CIS need to find a path that was themselves. Even many of them felt that they were not well prepared for secondary education exit nor were informed of the social change, they dared to dream to be a change agent.

Portrait 7 – Chinese ethnic identities: Inclusion and rejection

With the fact that Hong Kong is a SAR of China, the CIS are inclined to include "Chinese" in their civic identity. Nevertheless, most of them identify as "Chinese Hong Konger" or "Hong Konger", showing their definite and simultaneous attachment to Hong Kong society. There may be different connotations, but it is evident that these students are gaining a sense of belonging to their schools through positive relationships with classmates and teachers. As they spend long hours at school, it becomes a significant part of their life, and being accepted at school is an essential arena for measuring acceptance as a community member.

However, though they are pleased to accept their new identities as Hong Kong citizens, the connotations with the identity of "Chinese" seem to be more ambivalent. Although, as students explained, Mainland China is their birthplace, they have deep connections with friends, teachers, and family members there and thus have attachments for both sides.

CIS contest that they are not a "quiet" withdrawn group, as one may think. Should they be given more chances to exercise their muscle, they too can be excellent student leaders at school, contributing to the welfare of all students. Indeed, students with leadership roles have a higher sense of connection with schoolmates, teachers, and the school. This probably cultivates a stronger sense of belonging to the school, which can be transferred to the broader society. Of course, school attachment breeds civic belonging and pride.

It can also be seen that the leadership roles equip them with confidence and skills, which are vital for civic engagement. These skills include developing the confidence to speak to others, voice out opinions, hold discussions, and negotiate. Besides this, they probably also have a greater sense of being able to bring influence to situations and events, through actions like organising various activities and negotiating preferences with teachers or the school. It is, therefore, sensible that these students have expressed their willingness or certainty to take part in future civic activities.

CIS participants gave a somewhat positive note on community service provided by schools. Their sharings reveal that engaging in voluntary activities has enabled them to gain real-world experiences, connect with the local community, serve the needy, and eventually cultivate their vision and mission to contribute to society as a full member.

Because of the connotations regarding their Chinese identity, some still carry lower political efficacy of the characteristics of Mainland Chinese political culture. They still lack local civic knowledge as newcomers, although they are interested in politics and express willingness or certainty with civic engagement in the future. As CIS revealed, schools are essential contexts for them to acquire knowledge and discuss current affairs. On the one hand, civic development is context-specific. Through sharing their beliefs, values, and lived experiences, students develop their connectedness with the school and the community.

On the other hand, schools often overlook the need for these CIS to understand the foundational and common civic knowledge they do not have from their Mainland Chinese background. Researchers (Crocetti et al., 2014; Denney, 2019) opine that civic knowledge is the foundation for active and meaningful engagement. Not surprisingly, there is a unanimous view on the government and schools to include immigrant youth in the local society and to familiarise them with the local political structure (Stepick et al., 2008). For example, on how different political parties run for the District and Legislative Councils, Tung said:

> I think more resources are needed to let newly-arrived immigrants know more about Hong Kong, as we are really not familiar with things here.

Yu emphasised that the government has a critical role to play in enhancing effective civic engagement of CIS:

> The government should do more to encourage students to care about society because students are members of Hong Kong. We really should participate in society and it is absolutely appropriate (for us to be so). It doesn't make sense that a student does nothing except waiting passively for reading the news and doing nothing afterward.

On the other hand, Ching emphasised the role of the school:

> It is most effective to promote civic engagement through school, like holding talks or through Liberal Studies lessons.

Apart from student voices and suggestions, it may be more profound for schools to understand their identity dilemma and their attachments for both sides. Most CIS explored the social issues in Liberal Studies, which seems to be the general practice across schools. However, their belongingness to Hong Kong society cannot be boosted without professional guided discussion and intentional teaching strategies.

Furthermore, Hong Kong has to address a balance between high autonomy and the genes of Chinese culture and to distinguish people-to-people connections from political conflicts, especially when the economic and social interactions between the two societies become more frequent and interdependent.

For instance, the nested Greater Bay Area development offers excellent opportunities for CIS to serve as a cultural bridge and resources for the tomorrow of Hong Kong development.

It may be a heavy burden for CIS to figure out the best negotiating and adaptive strategies for their dilemma, however, understanding may be the first step for further integration, and more guidance may be needed to help them distinguish home town from the government and political issues. Besides, these immigrant students are likely to further their studies and work in Hong Kong and are an important asset to our society. Their voices about their identity, future civic engagement and life aspirations reflect a great desire to be included as functional and capable citizens of Hong Kong.

Currently, Hong Kong schools have been entrusted with promoting the latest version of nationalism aligned with the National Security Law. These young people come from different cultural backgrounds and have attempted to forge new lives in Hong Kong. They have created and will be creating new identities and roles in society. It will be interesting to see how their civic and political responsibilities are nurtured with opportunities appropriate to the new sociopolitical construction of the HKSAR.

References

Chan, C. K., & Fung, A. Y. (2018). Disarticulation between civic values and nationalism: Mapping Chinese state nationalism in post-handover Hong Kong. *China Perspectives*, 41–50. https://doi.org/10.4000/chinaperspectives.8106

Chee, W. C. (2012). Envisioned belonging: Cultural differences and ethnicities in Hong Kong schooling. *Asian Anthropology*, *11*(1), 89–105. https://doi.org/10.1080/1683478X.2012.10600858.

Crocetti, E., Erentaitė, R., & Žukauskienė, R. (2014). Identity styles, positive youth development, and civic engagement in adolescence. *Journal of Youth and Adolescence*, *43*(11), 1818–1828. http://doi.org/10.1007/s10964-014-0100-4.

Denney, S. M. (2019). *Adolescent Identity Exploration and Civic Identity Development in a US Government Classroom* [PhD Dissertation]. University of South Florida.

Fu, H. Y., Lee, S. L., Chiu, C. Y., & Hong, Y. Y. (1999). Setting the frame of mind for social identity. *International Journal of Intercultural Relations*, *23*(2), 199–214. https://doi.org/10.1016/S0147-1767(98)00035-2.

Home Affairs Department of the Government of the Hong Kong Special Administrative Region. (2020). *Support Services for New Arrivals from the Mainland and Ethnic Minorities*. https://www.had.gov.hk/en/public_services/services_for_new_arrivals_from_the_mainland/surveys.htm

Kim, S. (2013, July). What is "tiger" parenting? How does it affect children? Retrieved from https://www.apadivisions.org/division-7/publications/newsletters/developmental/2013/07/tiger-parenting

Lareau, A. (2000). *Home advantage: Social class and parental intervention in elementary education*. Rowman & Littlefield Publishers.

Law, K. Y., & Lee, K. M. (2006). Citizenship, economy and social exclusion of mainland Chinese immigrants in Hong Kong. *Journal of Contemporary Asia*, *36*(2), 217–242. http://doi.org/10.1080/00472330680000131.

Levine, P., & Youniss, J. (2006). Youth civic engagement: An institutional turn. Circle working paper 45. *Center for Information and Research on Civic Learning and Engagement (CIRCLE), University of Maryland*.

Marginson, S. (2014). Student self-formation in international education. *Journal of Studies in International Education*, *18*(1), 6–22. https://doi.org/10.1177%2F1028315313513036.

Stepick, A., Stepick, C., & Labissiere, Y. (2008). South Florida's immigrant youth and civic engagement: Major engagement: Minor differences. *Applied Development Science*, *12*(2), 57–65. https://doi.org/10.1080/10888690801997036.

Torney-Purta, J. (2002). The school's role in developing civic engagement: A study of adolescents in twenty-eight countries. *Applied Developmental Science*, *6*(4), 203–212. https://doi.org/10.1207/S1532480XADS0604_7.

Tsang, S. K., Hui, E. K., & Law, B. (2012). Positive identity as a positive youth development construct: A conceptual review. *The Scientific World Journal*, 1–8. http://doi.org/10.1100/2012/529691.

Wallin, D. (2003). Student leadership and democratic schools: A case study. *NASSP Bulletin*, *87*(636), 55–78. https://doi.org/10.1177%2F019263650308763606.

Yuen, C. Y. M. (2010). Assimilation, integration and the construction of identity: The experience of Chinese cross-boundary and newly arrived students in Hong Kong schools. *Multicultural Education Review*, *2*(2), 1–30. http://doi.org/10.1080/2005-615X.2010.11102873.

Yuen, C. Y. M. (2013). School engagement and civic engagement as predictors for the future political participation of ethnic Chinese and South Asian adolescents in Hong Kong. *Multicultural Education Review*, (3), 317–342. http://doi.org/10.11567/met.29.3.1

Zhai, Y. (2018). The gap in viewing China's rise between Chinese youth and their Asian counterparts. *Journal of Contemporary China*, *27*(114), 848–866. https://doi.org/10.1080/10670564.2018.1488102.

7 Belonging and (Dis)Connectedness of Chinese Cross-Boundary Students (CBS) in Hong Kong

Schools on the Hong Kong boundary towns

Following the merger between the HKSAR and the Mainland governments in1997, education for cross-boundary students (CBS) has generated a great deal of public policy debate. CBS represent a particular student group in Hong Kong mainstream schools. The number of CBS increased greatly up to 2013, when the government implemented a zero quota policy for Mainland residents to give birth in Hong Kong. In the 2021/22 school year, there were 26,971 CBS enrolled in 825 schools across the kindergarten to secondary sectors. These schools are clustered in the western (228) and northern (147) districts of the New Territories of Hong Kong (HKSAR Government, 2021). The majority of CB secondary schools are located in Yuen Long, Tuen Mun, Sheung Shui, and Tai Po in which towns are located the nearest East and West Mass Transit Railway (MTR) stations in Hong Kong to the Chinese Mainland boundary districts of Futian, Nanshan, Luohu, and Yintian in Shenzhen.

On the one hand, geographical proximity allows Mainland-based students to make daily journeys to attend schools in Hong Kong. On the other hand, the physical Mainland-Hong Kong boundary is heavily guarded with immigrant checkpoints and is restricted to citizens with valid visas or permits to travel (Chan & Ngan, 2018). Consequently, each CB school journey may take one to two hours, depending on their Mainland residential location. CB schooling can be very costly for families in terms of time, effort, and expense. CBS have to be disciplined and independent to observe the restrictions on passing through immigration checkpoints in both the Mainland and Hong Kong four times a day without getting themselves into trouble. Aside from the physical journey, CBS also have to secure a place in a desirable secondary school in competition with their mainstream peers through the central pre-secondary one allocation system. Their academic grades, conduct, extracurricular activities, and teachers' comments from primary school are all considered under a standard procedure, regardless of the many parents who come "knocking on the school doors" seeking to secure a placement for their child(ren).

Bourdieu (2010) argues that education is part of cultural capital and school credential is essential for vertical mobilities. The mode of inheriting or acquiring

DOI: 10.4324/9780429439315-7

cultural capital matters. CB parents equate Hong Kong education with a good investment for promoting their children's better future life chances and economic returns. Hence, access to Hong Kong schooling is understood as the habitus (Bourdieu, 2010) to achieve the necessary conditions for desirable life outcomes and is highly valued. It is expected that the merits of Hong Kong schooling will bring symbolic and legitimate capital for a better life (p. 168). Under the one-country two systems rule, acquiring Hong Kong educational capital can increase legitimate membership in the society and pave the way for an opportunistic future, especially and specifically within the English domain. English as a lingua franca is an essential medium for global learning and communication. As English teaching in schools in the Mainland is at a relatively low level, the Hong Kong English curriculum has consequently become all the more desirable.

Residing in Shenzhen and studying in Hong Kong is an optimal plan for many families, geopolitically and economically (Yuen, 2010), especially for those families with one or both parents who are Mainland residents or without the right of abode in Hong Kong. For the sake of maximising the habitus, CB families pay the price for facilitating their child(ren) to commit to a long-term CB educational placement (Yuen, 2018). For strategic reasons, therefore, making the daily boundary-crossing for education has generated momentum among Mainland parents, usually at the expense of the comfort of their young children. Studies (Chan & Ngan, 2018; Yuen, 2010, 2018) have shown that CB schooling is associated with various levels of acculturation stress across the age levels. Such stress includes meeting academic standards, mastering Cantonese and English language proficiency, and integrating into mainstream society.

It is worth noting that most CBS were born in Hong Kong and did not have a registered residence (hukou) in the Mainland. Without hukou, they could not enrol in the public non-fee paying schools in Shenzhen until 2017, when this regulation was lifted. However, Hong Kong-born CBS are entitled to all educational and social welfare benefits as a Hong Kong resident. They have the right to be placed in government-funded schools in Hong Kong (Chan & Kabir, 2014) for quality education without extra cost. Waters and Leung (2020) highlight that CB schooling involves arduous and burdensome daily journeys in order to acquire educational and cultural capital. After having committed to the hefty daily itinerant expenses, CB parents would naturally want the best for their children in terms of academic returns.

Indeed, Xu (2017a, 2017b) argue that the boundary is a public space for CBS to share their cultural habitus, exchange ideas, and build bonding. Through the process, they develop a sense of resilience in mitigating their disadvantaged learning conditions, such as heightened self-discipline, time management, and problem-solving skills. Nevertheless, the intersection between poor socio-economic conditions and academic linguistic barriers has not been fully explored. CBS in kindergarten and primary schools are known for struggling with security, self-efficacy, and subsequently adverse learning outcomes, especially in English (Yuen, 2011a, 2011b). But when CBS proceed to secondary schools, they become independent and have a stronger sense of purpose in life. However, their family conditions and academic capabilities are factors in their CB schooling. The effect of varied living conditions and livelihoods among CBS deserves further deliberated attention. Recognising their life course and educational trajectories helps to unravel the meaning, challenge, and construction of CB schooling as a phenomenon. In this regard, the in-depth dialogues and personal conversations we held with CBS have allowed us to understand and recognise their individuality and notions of education, relationship, and aspirations for life.

Portraits of CBS

Due to daily mobility between the Mainland and Hong Kong, CB youth are very aware of the sociopolitical and cultural differences between the two societies. Seeing the pros and cons of both societies and with various levels of personal attachment, some find it hard to form a strong ethnic or civic identity. For example, some may feel that they are neither a "Hong Konger" nor a "Mainlander" (Yuen, 2010, 2019). To probe their identity and belongingness further, seven CBS student participants of my previous project were chosen for in-depth interviews. All student names and school names are pseudonyms to conceal their identities. The interviewees were aged 16–19 and came from two secondary schools and were chosen to examine their education experience in general and their engagement with school and society. Among the seven, two were born in Hong Kong and then stayed in the Mainland during their childhood but re-engaged in Hong Kong schooling (Table 7.1).

CBS families

It is often the case that CBS from intercultural (Mainland-Hong Kong) families come from humble origins. Some are living with a single parent and some are co-living with siblings from different parents (Chee, 2017; Yuen, 2011a). However, in a typical CBS family, the father (a Hong Kong resident) is usually the sole breadwinner, working long hours in a low-skill-low-income job, such as construction, catering, or logistics. The mother (who is a Mainland resident) is usually a full-time homemaker coping single-handedly with the parenting. Father absenteeism is relatively common, while homework help is unavailable. For the kindergarten and primary CBS, well-being and integrity are often at risk due to limited social capital, dysfunctional intercultural marriages, and mother-child conflicts (Yuen, 2011a). For secondary CBS, their rich though strenuous boundary-crossing experience may well be instrumental in cultivating a resilient mindset to combat adversity.

The seven CBS interviewed were from non-traditional families that reflect the unique nature of Mainland-Hong Kong intercultural marriages. Commonly, the father or mother had multiple marriages before their current situation. As the data reveal, family issues are a source of worry for CBS that significantly influences their well-being. For example, Finly was in S4 during the interview.

Table 7.1 Profile of the cross-boundary students (CBS)

Name / gender	Age	School	Grade level	Place of birth	Current residence	Year of CB schooling	Parents civic origin	Self identification	Family structure
Jong (F)	19	Di-San Secondary School	S6	HK	Shenzhen	6	Father: HK Mother: Mainland	Chinese	She lived with both parents and two younger siblings
Muhan (F)	16	Di-San Secondary School	S4	Futian Shenzhen	Lung Gong, Shenzhen	2	Father: HK Mother: Guangxi	Hong Konger	Cohabited family, with one half-sister, father has another family in HK
Xiyi (M)	17	Di-San Secondary School	S4	Sichuan Province	Shenzhen	1	Father: HK Mother: Mainland	Mainlander	Reconstructed family with a stepfather
Finly (F)	16	Di-Si Secondary School	S4	Shenzhen	Sha Tau Kok	4	Father: HK Mother: Mainland	Chinese	She lived with her father alone
Wang (M)	16	Di-San Secondary School	S4	Hunan	Shenzhen	2	Father: HK Mother: Hunan	Hong Konger	He lived with his mother, stepfather, and a stepbrother
Nihai (M)	17	Di-Si Secondary School	S5	Sichuan	Luohu, Shenzhen	2	Father: HK Mother: Sichuan	Chinese	Reconstructed family, the father stays with his HK family
Wendy (F)	16	Di-Si Secondary School	S4	HK	Man Kam To, Shenzhen	4	Father: HK Mother: Hubei	Chinese	She lived with her mother alone

Coming from a single-parent family, she chose to stay with her Hong Kong father in Shenzhen to continue her schooling in Hong Kong. After the divorce, her Mainland mother relocated back to her home town in Hubei province in the northern part of China. Despite missing her presence very much, Finly was only able to see her mother once a year. Living alone with her father, who unfortunately has a gambling addiction, she often finds herself in tense situations with him about money:

> My father gives me HK$3000 each month. I'm trying to save it, but it's impossible because he always asks me for money whenever he loses in gambling. He is always hanging out with friends, leaving me alone at home. I have no mood to study, and I'm always worried about my future. Even if I've tried very hard to do something, my father still says I'm useless compared to others. I used to be heartbroken, but now I just don't really care about what he says because I can't change who he is.

Finly's narrative reveals that CBS are prone to complicated family issues and parental relations concerning financial circumstances they have to deal with. But her case is not an exception, Nihai is another example. He was in S5 living with his mother in Shenzhen while his father was residing in the HKSAR. Although his parents only got married a few years ago, Nihai realised that his father was running another family in Hong Kong. He is envious of his half-brother from his father's first marriage and feels sorry for his mother as she is denied the opportunity to live in Hong Kong with his father. He believes his mother is perceived as a threat to his father and his first family.

> (Nihai) I've never met my half-brother, and I doubt he is even aware of my existence, but I know my father loves him more than me. For example, my half-brother is allowed to study in Australia but I don't have the opportunity to study abroad. They live in Hong Kong, but my mother and I are left in the Mainland to stand on our own feet. This is totally unfair.

Wang comes from a reconstructed family and his interactions with his stepfather and stepbrother are somewhat superficial.

> (Wang) When I was in primary four, my mother asked my stepfather to divorce his former wife and to marry her. My stepfather is from Hong Kong and they wished me to study in Hong Kong. I seldom talked to my younger brother. We are from different mothers and I don't know much about him. I only shared my feelings with my mother.

The complication of CB marriages and the challenges imposed on their children is beyond description. Familial conflicts and tensions are often compounded by incompatible cultural values, upbringing, lifestyles, and challenges caused by distance and discrepancies in expectations between couples regarding financial and caregiving duties and so on (Ho, 2012; Yuen, 2019). Domestic instability is a detrimental factor for school engagement, adding challenges and burdens for CBS. Conversely, a functional family acts as a stabilising factor in the affective development of CBS and promotes cognitive and behavioural engagement. Jimmy from S5 is an example. He lives with both parents and prides himself as a hardworking student. He reported a high level of school identification and attachment, demonstrated a high level of academic performance, and was athletic and caring for his friends. During a family financial crisis, Jimmy remained positive and focused. Moreover, he often goes to school early to help junior students with Math tutorials and be the class monitor and president of the sports union.

Atypical cases of CBS

The diversity within the CBS population is noticeable and needs to be recognised. Two categories have been identified among the many atypical cases of CBS, namely the outperformers and the minority within a minority. "Outperformers" are CBS achieving fantastic grades and performing well in school. These outperformers are understood as "model minorities" for their achievements. By contrast, a minority of CBS have the same mindset as the outperformers, but they cannot perform as well for various reasons. English remains a significant obstacle for them to aspire for a better HKDSE grade and tertiary education, even though they have proficiency in speaking Cantonese. There is no clear-cut criterion for categorising a particular student into one category or the other. Some may not fit in the stereotypical understanding of an outperformer, yet neither are they typical of what the general public or teachers expect CBS to be – they fall just in between. The message here is that CBS must be recognised individually as to how they see themselves and, most importantly, how they motivate themselves forward in their different circumstances.

As mentioned above, CBS are considered a distinct minority in Hong Kong due to their Mainland-Hong Kong intercultural family background, linguistic diversity, and physical mobility between the two boundary locations. However, any negative label aside, their occupation of social space in commuting between the boundary checkpoints and on the school journeys has given them a unique social tag or identity and, most importantly, an opportunity to construct their cultural capital. For example, atypical CBS maximise their travelling time by engaging in academic revisions, doing assignments, gaming, or sleeping. The role of self-agency in driving success will be further elaborated below.

School lovers

As Appadurai argues (2004), aspiration comes with wants, preferences, choices, and calculations (p. 67). It is a collective decision or action usually affected by significant others, such as parental expectations. For most CBS, going to a secondary school in Hong Kong is more of an opportunity for future advancement than a burden for them. These motivated and aspiring students appreciate teachers' efforts, friendships, and support from family even though homework support is not always available. For those who received basic education in the Mainland they compared the former "examination-oriented" and restricting teaching styles with the Hong Kong's open school culture, cherishing mutual respect and the right to speak. They express their sheer joy of learning in Hong Kong schools with autonomy and unconditional respect in the new environment. The beginning of CB schooling is notably challenging due to the legal procedures in boundary checkpoints, adjusting to a Cantonese-speaking school environment, new school routines and curriculum, and missing friends. However, as time goes by, the above obstacles are overcome, they begin to enjoy the school ethos and develop a sense of fondness towards learning and teachers. In this regard, Xiyi shared his observations:

> People here are very friendly to me; they have no segregation or discrimination against us Mainland students. I feel comfortable turning to classmates for help, regardless of whether they are local or non-local students. They all would like to offer me help.

Similarly, Jimmy compared his school experience with his former Mainland experience and praised his Hong Kong education. He has a remarkable academic performance, ranking top in his class.

> My previous teachers are very strict and authoritative. I think because Mainland education is all about getting good grades in exams. It does not allow us to have open dialogues with teachers. By contrast, Hong Kong education offers me lots of freedom and autonomy to raise questions and express my own thinking in learning. I find the local students are also very friendly to me. I can easily make friends with local and CBS here.

Jong echoed Jimmy's observations on the differences between the Mainland and Hong Kong school ethos. She elaborated her educational experience as follows:

> First of all, the teachers here are amiable even though my grades are not good. My previous Mainland teachers only loved elite students and ignored me. But here, this is just the opposite. It seems that teachers love the weak students more than the strong students. They know our class is full of Mainland students and our English standard is poor, so they don't push us too hard.

The above narratives of CBS reveal that they appreciate a warm and caring school ethos. The sense of acceptance promotes their sense of belonging and fires up their learning motivation. An open system and a student-centred structure characterise Hong Kong education to facilitate independent and critical thinking about knowledge.

When there is a will, there is a way. Nihai did not let the three-hour travelling time become an obstacle for his extracurricular activities. He is a devoted player for the school basketball team, a scout-in-training in the Scout Association of Hong Kong, and a committee member in his school. These diverse activities and community engagement make his school life colourful and fruitful. Participating in three fields, Nihai does not "spend much time at home until 8 pm, and sometimes there is not sufficient time for me to study at all". Even so, he decides not to relinquish his hobbies and interests.

> Being a committee member has trained me up for taking a leadership role. However, since leaders must take the initiative and for other students to listen to you (me) humbly, the only way to improve myself is to continue and engage in the experiences.

Muhai is another example. She is a prefect, librarian, monitress, and a student counsellor. Yet, to manage all her leadership responsibilities, she has to sacrifice her comfort.

> Sometimes I have several meetings after school and do not get back until 10 – 11 in the evening. But all these are worthwhile because my educational experience becomes enriching.

Stories of CBS highlight how vital Hong Kong schooling is to them by offering them alternative education opportunities with an empowering learning approach. The happy and informal inquiring classroom ethos has driven them to a strong emotional attachment to their schools, teachers, and fellow classmates. Most CBS reported having friends at school, including other CBS and local Hong Kong students. Although Nihai's and Wendy's friendships are limited to other CBS, nevertheless, they have developed good relationships with their friends and have not felt disconnected and isolated at school. A caring and inclusive school environment contributes to the life satisfaction and positive engagement of CBS and enhances their sense of belonging to the school as well as to the HKSAR. According to Jong, Muhan, and Wang, smaller class sizes, well-equipped facilities, student-oriented teaching values, flexible teaching methods, enjoyable curricular and extracurricular activities, and individualised care for diverse needs give merit to their CB education.

The immigrant paradox and resilience in CBS

Sadowski (2013) points out that many teachers underestimate students' capabilities from immigrant families, mainly due to evident issues with language and false assumptions regarding their family and perhaps educational backgrounds. It is a common trait for most teachers to base their judgements on what they see and hear. As apparent as any case might be, most teachers do not give enough credit towards the disadvantaged and do not have the expectation of resilience and life aspiration sown from the unseen, unknown motivation passed onto them through their backgrounds. Yuen and Cheung (2014) have observed that Malaysian students crossing the border to receive education in Singapore daily are highly motivated and engaged in academic learning. Social scientists term this phenomenon as the *immigrant paradox*, which indicates that first-generation immigrants take on resilience and strive for success. At the same time, the motivations decline from the first to the next generations (Zehr, 2009).

Within the context of Hong Kong, this paradox exists among immigrant families as well. Corroborating with the findings of Hu-DeHart and Garcia Coll(2010), some secondary CBS are among the top 10% of students in the school. English still proves to be the biggest hurdle, and they have an abysmal start in the race. Nevertheless, many report a jump start in their schooling thereafter with heightened intrinsic motivation to perform better. This is another unexpected immigrant paradox. The seven CBS are clear about and can identify the obstacles they face in the new environment. They appreciate that their level of English is a crucial advantage for them in the future. As a minority among mainstream Hong Kong students, they also know that they are at a disadvantage to start with and that their grades will significantly affect their chances to study in a university in Hong Kong. Interestingly, most CBS do not consider crossing boundaries every morning and after school to be an issue and have become used to it. When having a casual chat with CBS, it seems that a significant level of resilience is displayed and it appears that resilience is an expected quality among CBS.

For example, Wendy has excellent grades in Chinese and Liberal Studies but performs poorly in English and Mathematics. Due to the family's poor financial situation and with a disabled father and self-employed mother, she needs to work at a fast-food shop, part-time and in her spare time – 5 hours on weekdays and 10 hours on weekends – to make ends meet. In Nihai's case, he takes the most indirect route home to minimise the transportation cost. He goes a cheaper route home by taking the train, then changing to a bus afterward, and finally walks 10 minutes home. As a result, he returns home late at around 8 p.m., sometimes 9 p.m. School ends at around 3 p.m., and if he has afterschool activities, he will stay until 5 p.m. or 6 p.m. and arrive home 2–3 hours later.

Echoing the observations of Xu (2017a, b), CB schooling is recognised mainly as habitus by CBS and educational mobilities are somehow well embedded in CBS thinking. Nihai reflected:

> My parents believe that there are more opportunities for work in Hong Kong in the future than in the Mainland, and the education is better here too, and I think they are right.

Nihai copes with his ordeal travelling to school each day because he shares his family's aspiration for a better future.

> You can learn things outside of textbooks. For example, right now I'm learning the art of face-changing. We can't imagine learning this in Mainland

schools. Because it is not an academic subject, you simply don't have many opportunities to reach into subjects like this one.

There seems to be an unspoken contract between parents and their children in which parents invest their resources in schooling, hoping to promote their child's vertical mobility. Such expectation has generated motivation for CBS to work hard and pursue good grades. The atypical CBS are more likely to engage and willingly improve their skills and capabilities to aspire for a better future, become more disciplined and resilient against the odds, have self-efficacy beliefs, and perhaps be interested in mastering a skill and not just achieving good grades.

Aspiring vs. disillusion

Family expectations and self-agency motivate CBS to pursue upward social mobility dreams in Hong Kong. Nevertheless, they have to face the reality that their geographical location and social networks have restricted them as newcomers from getting access to the top educational recourses in the city. Schools admitting a significant segment of CBS are usually of the lowest banding (band 3) and with the lowest university enrolment rate (under 15%). This fact has negative impacts on future aspirations. Finly stated:

> One of my teachers said that the best scenario would be that one student in my grade would be able to enroll in a university in Hong Kong, and of course, I'm not the top student, so I know there's no hope for me to go to university. So even if I spend more time studying much harder, it wouldn't change the situation, and sometimes I feel desperate.

Based on her six years' CB schooling, Jong was better positioned to see student-centre education philosophy and practice benefits. This, however, does not take away the reality that being educated in a Band three school, she has not been fully equipped for a competitive higher education entry portal. Jong unfolded her feelings:

> Although I enjoy the friendly teaching atmosphere here, my chance to get into university is meager. The English passing rate of our graduates is far below the required and our teachers told us that maybe one of two students could make it to university. This makes me sad and feel very uncertain about the future.

With their attachment to Hong Kong, most CBS expressed their intention to live in the city for further career development. However, as mentioned above, the relatively scarce educational resources and school atmosphere make it difficult for them to fulfil their Hong Kong dreams. For most local students, the university is not the only way to have a good life in the future.

However, CBS parents seem to be more rigid in fastening their children's future to a university education. Therefore, the future of CBS is more uncertain as their academic scores may not allow them to study in Hong Kong universities. Moreover, it would be more difficult for them to stay in the city by themselves since their families are in Mainland China. As Xiyi said:

> My mother doesn't accept alternative PSE programmes like IVE (Institute of Vocational Education). She believes such are not a real qualification and only appreciates university degrees, which becomes a big burden for me.

Disconnectedness – lost in the two cultures

On the one hand, CBS appreciate the relatively relaxed and equal education opportunities in Hong Kong and enjoy the respect and trust from the new school. On the other hand, they are confronted with dilemmas both in their learning and daily life involvement. As stated at the beginning of this chapter, space and distance are significant obstacles to CBS acculturation. Since CBS have a long way to travel back and forth from their home and schools, it is not easy for them to be wholly engaged in school activities. Some students may get the momentum to engage with society, but choose to give the time for study or related school activities. As a result, a fair amount of CBS return home directly after school and give up on any sort of involvement in other extracurricular activities. It is not because they have no interests – many students said they quite enjoy activities like playing chess, being scouts, or visiting the elders.

Living between Hong Kong and Mainland societies, their understanding of Hong Kong is superficial and often restricted to school and textbook experiences (Yuen, 2011b). As they go back to Shenzhen every day, this offers them more opportunities to communicate and interact with previous friends, familiar neighbours. These interactions are embedded with cultural values that strengthen their attachment to Mainland China. As Wang related, most of his friends are still in Shenzhen:

> My friends are generally from my primary school, and we are now living in the same block; we grow up together, we hang out together, my friends are all living there.

Muhan, who is good at English, compares the school atmosphere she feels on two sides:

> I feel it's more joyful in Shenzhen because the school was spacious, and more students love sports. Of course, some students are not in the same class, even not in the same grade, but it's quick for us to be familiar with each other by playing basketball or football together. In Hong Kong, I have only five friends, there's no cross-grade communication, and even within one class, we don't often do sports together.

Wang pointed out the reasons for his restricted social engagement in his current school:

> Well, I live in Shenzhen. So almost all of my outside school activities are confined to Shenzhen. We (CBS) only go to Hong Kong to study. In my case, I had studied in Shenzhen from primary school to secondary 3, I have many friends in the Mainland; we often do sports and hang out on weekends in Shenzhen.

Without having much exposure to the local social landscape, CBS feel like tourists in the city. They visited the tourist sites as tourists. Typically, they are only familiar with the New Territories (near the boundary) even after studying in the city for about three years. For example, Finly confounded her after school activity in her school neighbourhood vicinity. She visited Mongkok (a local shopping hub) when she was seven or eight years old.

Self-identity, belonging and defending the Chinese identity

Identity can be a self-ascribed label and an indicator of one's belongingness to a group, a community, and a culture. However, compared to local students and CIS, the reflections of being CBS were more complicated. They were asked about their self-identification in the interview, and three options were provided: Hong Konger, Mainlander, or Chinese. Students have varied answers to this question according to their own perceptions on their place of birth, their attachment, and their judgement on the different values of the two societies.

In choosing identity, some CBS are confident to make a quick response. For instance, Nihai thought of himself as a "Hong Konger" and a "Chinese" because he held a Hong Kong Identity Card and believed Hong Kong is part of China. Jimmy also. He asserted that:

> Freedom is the core value of Hong Kong, and I have no negative experiences of being discriminated against by other Hong Kongers.

Nevertheless, the CBS participants did not identify themselves between the "Mainlander" and "Hong Konger" categories. They would instead select a more inclusive identity as a "Chinese". Muhan identified herself as "Chinese" but definitely not as a "Mainlander", because she was confident that she could adapt to the Hong Kong lifestyle and immerse in the local culture. Conversely, Wendy and Xiyi were perplexed and hesitant when asked about self-identity. They identified themselves as "Chinese" but for different reasons. Wendy was perplexed by the question because her self-identification with Hong Kong and the Mainland were both strong. Born in Hong Kong and having lived in here for the entire seven primary school years, Wendy has not forgotten her immigrant past, "I am from the Mainland", and it was natural for her to say so. Xiyi expressed being caught in between, neither a Mainlander nor a Hong Konger. He has no place to settle his sense of belonging. To him, location only represents a temporary stop in his life journey, whether residing in the Mainland or in Hong Kong.

Wang was puzzled with his identity too:

> I have the right of abode in Hong Kong. So I think I am a Hong Kong resident. But actually, I don't really know. If you ask me to choose between Chinese and Hong Konger, I think I am a Chinese Hong Konger.

CIS are more prone to identify themselves with "Hong Kong-Chinese (Or a Chinese in Hong Kong)", CBS incline to identify themselves as Chinese. Although, they have more bonds with their families and friends in Mainland China, integration into local society seems to be a more relaxed, even passive process. For example, Nihai identifies himself as a "Chinese" because the economic outperformance of China makes him proud of his country, but he would identify himself as a "Hong Konger" in Mainland China as the identity brings him a sense of superiority.

> Maybe it's because of the CCP (Chinese Communist Party) education, I feel proud of my country's accomplishments in many fields, so I'm more prone to identify myself as Chinese. However, as Hong Kong's identity is in high favour in the Mainland, I would say I'm a Hong Konger when I'm there. It could help me get rid of many troubles, for example, the Huhou (residence registration) issue.

In addition, some voices indicated that the sense of belonging to Hong Kong might decline outside of school. Wendy believes it is common for Hong Kongers to discriminate against Mainlanders, though she does not have any personal experiences of being discriminated against directly herself. She reasons that she is surrounded by good friends who do not discriminate against her. We are not qualified to talk about politics.

As most CBS identify themselves as Chinese, and they do not have enough extra time to integrate into the local society, and grades are a more proximal pressure for them to fulfil their parents' expectations, civic engagement is even more scarce among such students compared with CIS. For most CBS, the only interactions with local communities are looking after elders in nursing homes or visiting tourist sites on invitation from local friends. None of the interviewed CBS stated that they have ever participated in the demonstrations in the city. Jimmy expressed that he would vote in the future but would not join any demonstrations or protests. Although he was a member of the Civic Education Team, Jimmy avoided discussing political issues so as not to worry his parents. He explained as follows:

> The Mainland immigration officers will confiscate any Hong Kong newspapers we take into the Mainland. It may be OK to discuss the political issues

in Hong Kong, but I don't know the exact dangers of talking about politics in the Mainland. Anyway, my parents don't allow me to talk about politics. They believe it's very dangerous.

As far as Hong Kong politics is concerned, CBS see themselves as outsiders. Wendy pointed out that "we are not qualified and capable of participating in Hong Kong politics". She added:

> I'm interested in helping the weak and the elderly. These are more important and there are more meaningful things to do than to talk about politics. As I live in Shenzhen I don't know much about the politics in Hong Kong. I don't think I'm qualified to participate in politics and I think studying is my priority.

Nevertheless, CBS showed awareness concerning the social conflicts relating to Mainlanders in Hong Kong, for example, the shortage of milk powder, the parallel trader issue near the boundary towns, and the double-non-permanent stay families and children. It has been brought to Muhan's attention:

> I believe that some CBS were parallel traders, although I don't know them in person. It was very tempting for them as they could earn up to RMB 60 per i-pad transaction. Also, it does not involve much effort. They just go to the shop to get one (i-pad) after school…But I personally have never done that.

Xiyi noted that these conflicts had brought some controversies into the classroom though these conflicts were not obstacles for their friendship:

> We often had fierce discussions on issues such as parallel traders in class. I know some Mainlanders are wrong to engage in parallel trading, but I can't accept the local students' unfound criticisms of the Mainland culture. I don't think everything about China is negative, I think this kind of mentality is problematic … sure, we have different, even opposite opinions, but these differences don't hurt our friendship. After the quarrels, we are still friends.

Belongings and disconnectedness of CBS

We have elaborated in this chapter that CBS have embraced their respective schools/schooling in the HKSAR and gradually developed their attachment towards new teachers and peers. They enjoy the equality, respect, and abundance of activities in schools. This being said, they also face struggles and challenges between parental expectations and personal capacities in meeting their aspirations. Their parental goals, values, and aspirations are reflexively sown like seeds, ingraining the conceptual frameworks. Therefore, they are more inclined to demonstrate stronger motivational traits than HKMS.

However, the intrinsic motivation of CBS may not be paralleled by their expected outcomes. They are based both on the boundary of Hong Kong and the border of educational resources, which may not be sufficient for them to fulfil their educational dream in Hong Kong. Therefore, their school lives in Hong Kong are filled with enjoyment but mixed with anxieties. Jong elaborates below:

> I really wish to make it to university in Hong Kong. Since I was born in Hong Kong and it has cost my mom a good fortune, I must repay her. However, sadly, it looks pretty unlikely that I will be able to get to university. I am lazy. My academic results are not good enough, plus I never pass the English tests. Even my parents make it explicit that it is up to me to go to university or not so long as I can take care of myself financially. I think they say this is just to comfort me. My dad is very concerned with filial piety, and he treated his mom very generously. I wish to be like him and go to university and earn more to support them in the future. So I am under huge stress.

Wang presented his thought on honouring his parents' aspiration for his future.

> I aspire to be a medical doctor because my parents want me to be. Although I don't really like studying, I need to fulfill my parents' dream. I like Maths, and I do well in it. However, English is hard and my Cantonese is insufficient. I'm not used to the teaching approaches here. But all I have to do is to study harder.

Concluding remarks

Generally speaking, CB schooling has been well received by the CBS and their families as a habitus for personal capital, even though it comes with a price for the whole family. Physical mobility shapes their belonging and attachment to the schools and fellow CBS rather than to society. CBS appreciate the educational opportunities for vertical mobility but not as much as being a Hong Kong resident, since they reside outside of Hong Kong. Thus, their educational aspiration intertwines with future Hong Kong dreams. Academically, they are prepared to embrace as much as possible in school learning, especially knowing that English proficiency is their biggest obstacle and also the key to tertiary education and career advancement.

Socio-politically, due to the lack of sufficient real-life exposure to Hong Kong society and participation in public affairs, CBS see themselves as outsiders and, consequently, feel alienated from society. Moreover, the boundary-crossing experience has shaped their identity, which combines Chinese and Hong Kong elements. As such, CBS embrace a more sophisticated cultural identity than their Chinese immigrant peers. This being said, CBS have settled their future goals. They have made choices from the different cultural values in two societies. However, as they construct their aspiration for a better future, they need to know more about the city, enhance their criteria to judge, and engage in self-negotiation when confronted with unexpected cultural conflicts.

References

Appadurai, A. (2004). The capacity to aspire: Culture and the terms of recognition. In R. Vijayaendra, & W. Michael (Eds.), *Culture and public action*. Stanford University Press.

Bourdieu, P. (2010). *Distinction: A social critique of the judgement of taste*. Routledge.

Chan, A. K., & Ngan, L. L. (2018). Investigating the differential mobility experiences of Chinese cross-border students. *Mobilities*, *13*(1), 142–156. https://doi.org/10.1080/17450101.2017.1300452.

Chan, P. W. K., & Kabir, A. H. (2014). Education across borders in Hong Kong: Impacts and solutions. In H. Zhang, K. P. Chan, & C. Boyle (Eds.), *Equality in education* (pp. 155–166). Brill Sense.

Chee, W. C. (2017). Trapped in the current of mobilities: China-Hong Kong cross-border families. *Mobilities*, *12*(2), 199–212. https://doi.org/10.1080/17450101.2017.1292777.

Ho, S. Y. P. (2012). Hong Kong men's stories of intra-national cross border romances. *Asia Pacific Journal of Social Work and Development*, *22*(3), 176–186. https://doi.org/10.1080/02185385.2012.691717.

Hong Kong Special Administrative Region Government. (2021). Press release, LCQ18: Cross-boundary students. https://gia.info.gov.hk/general/202106/23/P2021062300304_370335_1_1624420284415.pdf

Hu-DeHart, E., & Garcia Coll, C. (2010). The immigrant paradox in children's education and behavior: Evidence from new research. Brown University.

Sadowski, M. (2013). *Portraits of promise: Voices of successful immigrant students*. Harvard Education Press.

Waters, J., & Leung, M. W. H. (2020). Rhythms, flows, and structures of cross-boundary schooling: State power and educational mobilities between Shenzhen and Hong Kong. *Population, Space and Place*, *26*(3), 1–16. https://doi.org/10.1002/psp.2298.

Xu, C. L. (2017a). Mainland Chinese students at an elite Hong Kong university: habitus-field disjuncture in a transborder context. *British Journal of Sociology of Education*, *38*(5), 610–624. https://doi.org/10.1080/01425692.2016.1158642.

Xu, C. L. (2017b). Transborder habitus in a within-country mobility context: A Bourdieusian analysis of mainland Chinese students in Hong Kong. *The Sociological Review*, *66*(6), 1128–1144. https://doi.org/10.1177%2F0038026117732669.

Yuen, C. Y. M. (2010). Assimilation, integration and the construction of identity: The experience of Chinese cross-boundary and newly arrived students in Hong Kong schools. *Multicultural Education Review*, *2*(2), 1–30. https://doi.org/10.1080/2005-615X.2010.11102873.

Yuen, C. Y. M. (2011a). Cross-boundary students in Hong Kong schools: Education provisions and school experiences. In J. Phillion, M. T. Hue, & Y. Wang (Eds.), *Minority students in East Asia: Government policies, school practices, and teacher responses* (pp. 174–192). Routledge.

Yuen, C. Y. M. (2011b). Towards inclusion of cross-boundary students from Mainland China in educational policies and practices in Hong Kong. *Education, Citizenship and Social Justice*, *6*(3), 251–264. https://doi.org/10.1177%2F1746197911417416.

Yuen, C. Y. M. (2018). Chinese immigrant students and cross-boundary students in Hong Kong: A call for equity through culturally relevant teaching practices. In Y. K. Cha, S. H. Ham, & M. S. Lee (Eds.), *Routledge international handbook of multicultural education research in Asia Pacific* (pp. 258–271). Routledge.

Yuen, C. Y. M. (2019). *The happiness and mourning of Hong Kong students* (in Chinese). Breakthrough.

Yuen, C. Y. M., & Cheung, A. C. (2014). School engagement and parental involvement: The case of cross-border students in Singapore. *The Australian Educational Researcher*, *41*(1), 89–107. http://doi.org/10.1007/s13384-013-0124-x.

Zehr, M. A. (2009). Scholars mull the 'Paradox' of immigrants. *Education Week*, *28*(25), 1–12.

8 Educational Assimilation and Inclusion of South/Southeast Asian Students

Educational exclusion and inclusion

Chapter 1 has shown how a Hong Kong-centric education fails to include students from diverse backgrounds and with multiple intelligences (Arat et al., 2016; Hong Kong Unison, 2010; Loh & Hung, 2020; Shum et al., 2011; Yuen, 2019). First and foremost, the prevailing assimilationist educational ethos is not altogether the best for society, and neither does it promote success for all spirits. Mainstream schooling adopts a melting-pot approach to socialising the ethnic minorities into the mainstream culture and values. This leads to teacher intercultural insensitivity and ineffectiveness in classroom praxis (Yuen & Grossman, 2009). The meritocratic social system represents a hegemony over ethnic minorities and is reinforced by the high stake examination-oriented culture. The curriculum structure is primarily geared towards the college application examination, the HKDSE, and the subjects offered by government-subsidised secondary schools aim to prepare students for university applications rather than any other applied track.

The whole education system is governed by the golden market rules of the struggle for survival and the survival of the fittest. Academically, streaming is adopted to allow elite students to study alongside their peers of similar capability or aspiration for PSE and vice versa. The study of Yuen et al. (2021) on 4,800 plus secondary students underlines how ethnic culture is a significant hurdle for NCS students in their PSE pursuit. The intersectionality of their multiple challenges needs to be better acknowledged. Generally, such students tend to be educated in low-banding schools with under-resourced learning environments, and this is not conducive for cultivating dreams (Loh & Hung, 2020). Challenges include limited subject options, additional risk factors, lack of homework support from parents, lack of resources, lack of role models, and a lack of confidence in achieving one's full potential. Poor financial conditions further compound these educational hurdles. As shown in Chapter 2, working poverty is the reality for the majority of the Southeast and South Asian population in the city.

DOI: 10.4324/9780429439315-8

Acculturation strategies

Acculturation is a natural process for immigrants to embrace the new cultures, values, and modifications in the host society. In this, the length of stay makes a significant difference in the sociocultural and psychological acculturation process, as does their demographic profiles such as age, gender, religion, and family socio-economic status (SES; Berry & Sam, 1997). Moreover, the adoption of an acculturative strategy also depends on the quality of intercultural relations in the cultural context of the host society (Berry et al., 2006). In societies sympathetic towards multiculturalism, immigrants would prefer/opt for integration or inclusion, while in monocultural societies, many immigrants would remain separated or marginalised (Phalet et al., 2018). Berry et al. (2006) highlight four acculturation strategies of immigrants in coping with adaptation stress in host societies. These strategies are associated with their intercultural knowledge, skills, and attitudes towards the host society. They are, in descending order, integration (which combines both host and home cultures), assimilation (prioritising the adoption for mainstream culture), separation (the preference for maintaining heritage culture) to marginalisation (neither maintaining heritage culture nor interacting with host cultures).

Challenges in schooling

It has already been highlighted how Chinese learning for NCS ethnic minority students in Hong Kong is a long-standing factor hindering their educational, social, and economic inclusion. Chinese language proficiency and the exclusion of NCS students are complex and interrelated issues and have been highly contested. Those who favour the lowering of the Chinese requirement of NCS students in PSE admissions insist that Hong Kong is a metropolitan city in that both Chinese and English are the official languages. South Asian students speak a language or dialect other than Cantonese or English at home. Some researchers (Patkin, 2020) argue that emphasising Chinese proficiency in Hong Kong schooling comes at the cost of losing their mother tongue. Therefore, it can be seen as discriminatory to require NCS students to be as good in Chinese as their local peers (Patkin, 2020).

Viewed from a different perspective, Cheuk (2020) argues that lowering the Chinese Language proficiency of non-ethnic Hong Kong students could lead to another kind of social and educational discrimination. Chinese language skills are fundamental for NCS students to integrate into mainstream schooling and the job market. Without giving them an option to learn the Chinese Language alongside their mainstream Chinese peers, this may also be a discriminatory act in that without this option, their future social and economic mobility in the Chinese society can be compromised (Hong Kong Unison, 2010, 2020). South Asians tend to be clustered in the low-skilled and low-income employment sectors in the labour market, working as security guards, construction workers, and waiters and waitresses. To compromise their Chinese standard, therefore, has the effect of obstructing them from pursuing dreams in society and shielding them from the reality of their situation (Loh & Hung, 2020).

For most NCS students, the Chinese language still presents itself as an obstacle, even for those who attended local primary schools. Some may be good at speaking while still having difficulties in comprehension and writing. For NCS students who attended designated ethnic minority schools, language would undoubtedly be an even more significant barrier. It has always been a controversy about whether these students should be allocated to mainstream or ethnic minority schools, a decision related to their Chinese capabilities and their identities. Research (Yuen & Lee, 2016; Yuen et al., 2016) shows that NCS students from high co-ethnic schools rated their life satisfaction higher than those from low co-ethnic schools. When their life experiences unfold, NCS students have formulated close and meaningful relationships with local peers at mainstream schools. Given this, widening their social circle by connecting them with local peers is conducive to their connectedness and belongingness. Cultural identification affects language learning (Lai et al., 2015), and schools should consider linguistic and psychosocial adjustment factors when teaching Chinese to NCS students.

Social controversies always provoke policy responses. For example, the EDB proposed in 2007 that minority students would be able to take overseas Chinese Language examinations, such as the General Certificate of Education (GCE) and International General Certificate of Secondary Education (IGCSE), as a replacement to HKDSE Chinese (Education Bureau, 2007). Subsequently, the University Grant Commission (UGC) introduced flexible language admission policies for UGC-funded institutions, including GCE and IGCSE, as alternative qualifications for admission. The EDB also encouraged local tertiary institutions to consider the language requirement on the admission of minority students on a case-by-case basis (Education Bureau, 2007). However, as each local tertiary institution has its own admissions criteria and mechanism, there is a lack of uniform Chinese Language benchmarking. In addition, the recognition of IGCSEs across universities is also a concern (Hong Kong Unison, 2020), as the HKDSE results are preferred by most higher education institutions (Gao, 2019). This is one major reason for the admissions disparity between mainstream (52.6%) and ethnic minority (43.3%) students in tertiary institutions (Department of Census and Statistics, 2017).

Aspirations for higher education

It is a fact that disadvantaged students have fewer capabilities to aspire for higher education (Appadurai, 2013). One of the main reasons is a lack of faith in themselves, thinking that they are inferior, second-class citizens than their more affluent peers. Hence, higher education is skewed towards the more privileged (Hutchings & Archer, 2001; Reay et al., 2001). In other cases, such students may even perceive higher education as "unattractive" and "not for them", and this breeds a reluctance to pursue higher education. Corredor et al. (2020) reveal the disadvantage of fitting in and how the inequalities experienced by disadvantaged students in higher education bear a close relationship with their constraints on its cultural norms and guidance to support their transition to higher education. The findings of Reay et al. (2010) align with this and note that disadvantaged students often position themselves in second-tier institutions.

Differentiated student profiles are a universal phenomenon. In Hong Kong, over 48% of research-intensive university students came from upper-middle classes or resource-rich band one schools (Yip & Peng, 2018). Around 30% of self-financed, private, or vocational PSE students were from families below the poverty line. It is noteworthy that these self-financed programmes are important PSE choices for most NCS students. Yuen et al. (2021) further reveal that NCS students rate ethnic culture as a significant obstacle for their PSE pursuit. Such social barriers are strongly related to social stereotypes and linked to perceived challenges in pursuing PSE. Such findings corroborate international studies (Marsh & Scalas, 2010). My previous interview data show that NCS students lack the essential knowledge of HKDSE requirements and associated academic planning for the Joint University Programmes Admissions System (JUPAS). The participants listed in Table 8.1 all struggled with Chinese Language proficiency, especially for academic purposes.

All about learning Chinese

It can be argued that language should be learned at a younger age. NCS students who studied Chinese from an early age (kindergartens and primary schools) find Chinese learning easier, although not to the point where they would keep up with their local peers. Many Hong Kong-born NCS students are failing in their Chinese.

How hard is it for NCS students to learn Chinese? A second-generation Nepalese, Maurice, gives his verdict. Being a Hong Kong-born Nepalese, he was educated in the city all his life. Yet, Chinese is just like a distant friend he can never understand.

> My parents were also born and raised in Hong Kong. My parents never taught me Nepalese at home. They talk to each other in Nepalese but talk with me in English because they want me to learn better English… I went to a local primary school where all my classmates were Chinese, I can speak Cantonese without problem. But I'm not good at Chinese reading and writing and I still fail in Chinese.

SAH's perspective on learning Chinese is a mixture of bitter and sweet. When asking to rate the difficulty in learning Chinese, he expressed the following:

> It is tough for me to learn Chinese - I'd say from 1 to 10 it is 7 or 8 out of 10 (most difficult). But my Chinese foundation is good as I graduated from a local primary school, which emphasizes learning Chinese.

122 *Educational Assimilation and Inclusion*

Table 8.1 Profile of the non-Chinese speaking (NCS) students

Name	Arjun	Pingping	Arian	Maurice	Sung	SAH
Basic information	Male, 15, S4	Female, 18, S6	Female, 16, S5	Male, 16, S5	Male, 15, S4	Male, 16, S4
Birthplace	HK	HK	HK	HK	HK	Pakistani, came to HK since a baby
Ethnic identity Civic identity	Indian HK resident	Pakistani HK citizen	Filipino Filipino living in HK	Nepalese Third generation HK Nepalese	Indian HK citizen	Pakistani HK citizen
Self-identity	HK citizen	Pakistani Hongkonger	Filipino-Hongkonger	HK Nepalese	HK citizen	HK Pakistani
Civic interest	x	Not really interested	Watch local news, but not interested	HK Nepalese	Watches Indian TV in English	Read Chinese books and papers, but not interested in local issues
Father's ethnicity and occupation	Indian, Driver	x	Filipino, operator	Nepal born in HK, unsure	Indian, businessman	Pakistani, security guard
Mother's ethnicity and occupation	Indian, Housewife		Filipino, customer servicer	Nepal born in HK, chief	Indian, housewife	Pakistani, housewife
Religion	Sikh	Islam	Catholicism	Hindu	Sikh	Islam
Family monthly income (HKD)	19,000	No data	20,000	25,000	20,000	10,000
Primary school (local Chinese ethnic concentration)	x	Local Chinese school	Ethnic concentration school	Local Chinese school	Local Chinese school (but taking GCSE)	Ethnic concentrated school

Educational Assimilation and Inclusion 123

Table 8.1 Profile of the non-Chinese speaking (NCS) students (Continued)

Name	Arjun	Pingping	Arian	Maurice	Sung	SAH
Speaking language	x	English and Cantonese	English	English and Cantonese	English and Cantonese	English, Cantonese, and Urdu
Feeling excluded or included by the society	x	Included	Included in school	Included, but sometimes is ignored	Included	Excluded in the community
Future plan	x	Study in a local university	x	Study science or engineering in a local university	Help in family business	Study in a local university

Name	Bana	Arthur	Rhea	Anaya	Karen	Vera
Basic information	Female, 15, S4	Male, 15, S4	Female, 16, S5	Female, 18, S6	Female, 17, S6	Female, 18, S6
Born in	HK	HK	HK	HK	HK	HK
Ethnic identity	Pakistani	Filipino	Filipino	Pakistani	Indian	Filipino
Civic identity	HK Pakistani	HK citizen	HK citizen	Not a full HK citizen	Not a full HK citizen	Not a full HK citizen
Self-identity	HK citizen	HK citizen	Filipino in HK	Pakistan Hongkonger	Indian Hongkonger	Filipino Hongkonger
Civic interest	Not interested	Not interested, parents watch Filipino news	Not interested in politics	Not interested	Interested in fighting for family and social betterment	Interested in social events but never got involved
Father's ethnicity and occupation	Pakistani, Businessman	x	Passed away	Pakistani, clerk	Indian, fashion designer	x
Mother's ethnicity and occupation	x	x	x	Pakistani, Housewife	Indian, Housewife	Digital manager in Central

(Continued)

Table 8.1 Profile of the non-Chinese speaking (NCS) students (Continued)

Name	Bana	Arthur	Rhea	Anaya	Karen	Vera
Religion	Islam	Sikh	Sikh	Islam	Sikh	Catholicism
Family monthly income (HKD)	x	x	Unsure, but on government subsidy scheme	x	x	x
Primary school (local Chinese ethnic concentration)	x	x	Ethnic concentrated school	x	Ethnic concentrated school	Ethnic concentrated school
Language	English and Cantonese	English	English and Tagalog	English	English and some Cantonese	English
Feeling excluded or included by society	Included	Included	Excluded, we are not equal with the system	x	x	x
Future plan	Be a flight attendant in HK	x	University/college in HK, to be an art therapist	Get a bachelor degree Marketing or Psychology)	Want to be a flight attendant, study tourism in Canada	Be a ground staff or flight attendant, study tourism in the Philippines

In spite of being educated in a local primary school and learning mainstream Chinese, Pingping has less confidence in attempting the HKDSE Chinese.

> I study in a local Chinese primary school with other local Chinese students. I can improve my English, but my Chinese remains poor. I know I should put more effort into Chinese as it is very important here, and I will be taking the Chinese version of the DSE for Chinese, so I'm very nervous about it.

Passing the HKDSE Chinese benchmark is regarded as beyond reach, in that the Chinese Language is a compulsory core subject requiring a deep understanding of the selected classic and contemporary Chinese writings, history, and cultures. Without fulfilling the required HKDSE Chinese proficiency, students have little chance to be admitted to UGC-funded universities. As pointed out by researchers (Gao, 2019; Loh & Hung, 2020; Shum et al., 2011), minority students are significantly disadvantaged as the education system assumes that all the students have a native-level command of Chinese and a high level of Chinese Language and culture.

PSE pathways

Clearly, insufficiency in the Chinese language and passing the DSE Chinese or alternative GCSE Chinese are major obstacles in pursuing the academic dream in Hong Kong. Given this, can this common language barrier be eradicated by self-efficacy? Unfortunately, there is no simple answer to that question. The narratives of ethnic minority students give a hint that they would instead seek alternative academic opportunities elsewhere. For example, educated in a high co-ethnic school from primary to secondary, Filipino Vera's Chinese foundation is very weak.

> It's not possible for me to get a place at college in Hong Kong. I am seriously thinking about going back to the Philippines. I would like to be a flight attendant so I plan to study tourism at college where (Chinese) language would not be a barrier for me any more. I like Hong Kong, but it's not possible for me to face Chinese here.

Karen has also identified an alternative for her PSE. She believes Canada would be a good option for studying tourism.

> I shall explore other options outside Hong Kong for college. Canada is an option. They have many colleges opportunities, and there I will not have to face the Chinese language and it will no longer be an obstacle to me anymore.

Sung planned to study computer engineering in his home town in India.

> My Chinese is not good. And India is at the top of Computer Science, and Indian universities welcome Indians around the world. And I also want to make my country a better place. So I plan to go back to study.

By contrast, Maurice aspires to build his dream in his birthplace. Maurice explains:

> I plan to invest my future in Hong Kong because both my parents and I were born in this city. I would like to do Medical Science or something related to Physics in the future. I hope that I can learn something that can contribute to the world or Hong Kong.

Significant others' support – parents

Generally speaking, NCS have good relationships with their parents who positively impact them and motivate them. Parents are the primary sources of NCS students support and inspiration. They tend to be self-motivated and aspire in life, showing a strong sense of self-discipline when confronted with different obstacles. However, NCS parents may well be intimidated by the local Chinese school culture and the environment if they have little Chinese understanding or have little knowledge about the local education system. Usually, they are absent from school activities due to family engagement or other reasons. Under such circumstances, this may reinforce the impression of teachers and local parents that NCS parents seem uninterested in their children's schooling or their future education choices. This study has shown the opposite to be true. Parents of NCS students are supportive of their children, even if not pushing them too hard. As Arian explained:

> I have a good relationship with my parents, and we talk about school and discuss it a lot. They want me to get good grades as they could bring a higher chance to go to university and, eventually, a better career.

For some NCS students, their careers are not only for their own sake but are also used to set an example for their siblings or to honour the family. SAH shared:

> My parents have high expectations of me and tell me to study hard. I am the eldest child in my family, and I should be a good role model for my younger sister. My father wants me to be a university student and I want to become a teacher to give back to society in the future. If I cannot find work in that area, I want to become a translator.

Most parents of NCS students have high expectations for them but are also understanding if they find that they are too demanding. Vera articulated these views.

> Because my mom knows my capacity, she does not really expect so much from me, but wants me to finish my studies. She does not pressure me to have good grades and supports me with what I want in the future. I want to study tourism in the Philippines and become a flight attendant or ground staff in the airport.

This sense of understanding from parents helps Karen to stop self-questioning and provides her with more space for what she really wants. Karen shared:

> My parents want me to have good grades and want me to enter university. My mom used to want me to become a medical doctor when I was young, but slowly, I've realized and come to know myself better. I told her that I want to become a flight attendant and she supports me. I really appreciate that. My parents pay for my education but they do not force me to do anything I don't want. I want to achieve my dreams and have a good life as well as a happy family.

As international studies (Sadowski, 2013) show, immigrant parents somehow impress their children that pursuing a better life for the future is desirable. Education is the lever for a better life. Hence immigrant students often aspire for a good life through education. Family capital is often equated with educational capital. Some NCS students feel academic pressure from their Chinese peers, and sometimes they would like their parents to play a more active role in their studies. It seems that they struggle to reconcile their parents' traditional values and their emerging values as Hong Kong youth. For example, Vera desires more parental support on homework.

> Sometimes I see my friends' parents pressuring their children to study more. I've never really felt that from my mom since she's the type of person who would just go with the flow. She wouldn't ask you to do much if you can't do it.

Significant others' support – teachers

Teacher support is a known plus factor. Below is how Arthur appreciates the care and assistance that the teachers offered to him.

> I feel happy at school. Our teachers are always kind, and they care about us. If my grades are dropping, teachers would ask me what's happening. People in my school are all nice, and we get along very well.

> The teachers here are really…like open-minded. They share their feelings, too, so we become more comfortable with each other.

Anaya, who works a part-time job to support her family, is anxious about her future career. Her perspective on teacher support focuses on experience sharing as this can broaden her horizons.

> Our school provides preparation programmes to help students consider their future after secondary education. Our teachers guide us in discovering

what we want to become in the future. That gives me more ideas to think about it. Also, my school invites graduates to share their tips in working out graduation plans. All these help me become more knowledgeable about future educational options. Their sharings really help.

Educational transition is a part of life course. It always comes with stress and uncertainties. Homework is the source of Sung's stress.

> I feel generally happy in both primary and secondary schools, but occasionally I feel stressed. I sleep less when I have extra schoolwork to do. Getting to senior secondary is a real challenge to me. I began to sleep less as there is more and difficult homework to complete.

In a meritocratic society, academically strong students get more teacher support than their counterparts. Anaya is very sensitive to differential teacher treatment. She complains that schools and teachers are biased against academically weak students, and they are neglected.

> Sometimes I feel like there's inequality in this school because teachers usually pay more attention to smart students and ignore us (the less able). Teachers even offer after-school activities exclusively to 6D (the elite class). Maybe they think that the other students are not as hardworking as them. But this is unfair to us.

Involvement in the school activities

Davis III and Kiang (2016) establish a close link between demographics, race, family SES, and school engagement. For example, ethnic group identification, religious affiliation, and family income are all key variables for adolescents' school engagement (Davis III & Kiang, 2016). Within a local context, though most families of NCS students are of low SES, they are generally more appreciative towards their families, teachers, and social networks than their Chinese peers. Their strong religious affiliation and ethnic identity reinforce students' involvement in school life as well as their life satisfaction in their host society (Yuen, 2016).

For most NCS students enjoy the school activities and appreciate their teachers' assistance in their studies. Moreover, they express a heightened sense of belonging as they can speak their mother tongue in their Hong Kong school. Sung Dasu, a S6 student, said:

> I love school because there are lots of people who understand me and know how I feel living here. It is really fun as I can communicate with my language - Panjabi. I also have tutorials where I get support for my Chinese writing.

School activities also make students feel involved. Karen, a S6 Indian girl, said that she participated in the student union and organised activities such as the singing competition and a fashion competition, which helped her become responsible. Karen revealed that:

> I am a House Committee member and the prefect in the student union, which builds up some leadership capacity for me in the sense that it makes me feel confident and responsible. I can learn many different things and learn how to handle and organize them, which are important skills for my future life. I have joined many events, like the multicultural festival. I have been doing our traditional dance for many years organized by the community centre.

Rhea found herself passionate about getting involved in extracurricular activities, despite working a part-time job to make ends meet after losing her father. She was also voted as a House Captain:

> I enjoy the democratic atmosphere created by me for the House. As a Captain, I want to be fair. I organise the House's work equally among members. Being a Captain doesn't mean that I'm the most powerful one. It only means that I'm there to guide others. And I try to be more democratic - for example, if I want something that others may not want and vice versa, we learn how to make a compromise.

Self-identification and civic engagement

Waterman (1985) has pointed out that the development of identity is the primary task for adolescents. The process of identity construction is viewed as a delineated self-definition comprised of various domains, including career choice, political ideology, worldview, and other social and sex roles. Race and ethnicity have a profound effect on people's personalities and psychological growth. Ethnic minorities are constantly faced with multiple demands and possible conflicts regarding alternative cultural frames and discrimination in the host society. Hence, race and ethnicity are pivotal factors for the identity construction of ethnic minority adolescents (Robinson, 2009).

All the youth featured so far in this chapter were Hong Kong-born, except for SAH who was born in Pakistan but was brought to Hong Kong as a baby. These students are *de facto* fully fledged Hong Kong citizens. However, only three out of the 12 students assume such an identity. The most straightforward reason for their self-identification is their birthplace and citizenship. For example, Sung, the S4 student, said:

> I identify myself as a Hong Kong citizen. Because I live here, I learn more about Hong Kong than India. I know a lot more about Hong Kong than India. If I see myself as an Indian, I then realise that I know nothing about India.

To Sung, he names himself as a "Hong Kong citizen" because he has the same rights as other local people:

> I am a Hong Kong citizen, because I also have a Hong Kong passport. I believe I am a Hong Kong citizen and I have the same rights that other people.

Family history has a direct bearing on the NCS students identity and belongingness. Arthur's family has a longer history in Hong Kong, and his acculturation strategy in the host society is integration. Arthur is happy to take up a local boy identity as unfolded below:

> I'm a Hong Kong citizen and I see myself as a Hong Kong person because my parents were born here. I'm used to the environment, I'm not that type of Filipino who just wishes to hang out with their own Filipino peers. Instead, I mingle well with locals.

But aside from the above students, the others identify with a two-dimensional identity, adding a Hong Kong identity with an identity from their home country. They have various reasons for their self-identification. Sociopolitical factors such as discrimination, exclusion, and job opportunities/unemployment affect young people's perceptions and attitudes towards adapting to their host societies (Modood, 2005). Some NCS students have reservations about their Hong Kong roots because of discrimination. Rhea argued that society is not equal:

> I still don't get it. Why we ethnic minorities have our schools and locals have their schools, it's like we are separated? They can't expect us to be friends if we have separate schools. I was supposed to go to a Chinese secondary school, but my class teacher said, "you'd be bullied there, you'd be an alien because you're an ethnic minority student". My mother had approved for me to go to a local Chinese school, but after talking to my teacher, she made me to come here. That is kind of hassle for me.

Vera recalled her unpleasant childhood experience of being singled out. She believes that there is also discrimination in the job market. She made her point by sharing one news article discussing the discrimination ethnic minorities face in the job market. In the quote, "an Indian man was initially offered a job after the interview. However, due to his ethnicity, they finally rejected him even though his Cantonese proficiency is like a native". Vera continues:

> The root problem is that they don't accept ethnic minorities, so they don't employ them. I have a feeling that I'll have that same problem too after my public (DSE) exams. Also my Chinese is poor. I'll try my best but I will go back to the Philippines to study.

Intercultural competence is one outstanding element that can be celebrated in local schools where it occurs. Pingping went to a local primary school, is fairly proficient at Cantonese, and has close friends from both local Chinese and ethnic minority backgrounds. She feels attached to both cultural groups:

> I'm a Pakistani Hong Kong citizen. Because my parents belong there (Pakistan) but my relatives are also here and I speak the language (Cantonese), I somehow feel that I belong there too...I identify with Hong Kong - first and foremost because I have permanent residence, and I was born here so I can speak Cantonese. I have Chinese friends and I think I'm the same as most Chinese people and they're just like us too. We sit together, eat together and we share stuff together.

Students with dual involvement and identification with the host and their ethnic cultures report a more positive acculturative process and demonstrate better psychological adjustment than those who are marginalised or separated in society (Berry, 2003). Most NCS students who identify themselves as both a Hong Konger and with their ethnic identity understand that they have the same rights as local citizens. For example, Arthur, having gone to a local primary school and engaged in school activities, identifies himself as someone in between:

> I am a Filipino living in Hong Kong. I wouldn't really go to the Philippines, I watch local news with my mother rather than the Philippine news. I'm personally not interested in the Hong Kong issues discussed in Liberal Studies, but we live here, so we should help local people.

NCS students are concerned with their rights in society and people's respect for their ethnic cultures. For example, Karen had participated in protests with her family for their welfare issues. In addition, some of them see their rights in seeking a better society. Below are some examples:

ANAYA – You should voice out for what you want. Being a good citizen is to be yourself. If you don't want to see something happen, you should voice out against it.

KAREN – I think a good citizen is to respect his/her own country and other countries as well, they should respect diversity.

ARTHUR – If I was Chief Executive, I would make ethnic minorities feel that they are being considered. Make them feel like "we care about them".

Religious identity and adaptation in the host society

Religious identity is the sense of belonging and affection towards one's religious group. Commonly, religious people define their identity by their religious beliefs (Chan et al., 2014). As for adolescents' identity formation, they rely on a system of beliefs that constitutes their worldview. In such a way, religious beliefs shape the identity formation of religious youth (Davis & Kiang, 2016).

Prior studies on religious identity and acculturation have shown positive associations between religious involvement and positive peer networks, well-being, a sense of purpose, especially among last generation immigrant adolescents (e.g., Phalet et al., 2018). The cultural values associated with religious identity are interdependence, tradition, conformity, and benevolence. These values are affirmed through the context of acculturation and also inherited across generations of immigrant families and communities (Phalet et al., 2018). Moreover, for religious adolescents, their religious identity may become a more significant marker for their identity than their nationality, even for immigrant students born in their host societies or who have spent a long time there (Feliciano & Rumbaut, 2018).

For religious NCS youth, attending church activities was an important part of their social and spiritual lives in Hong Kong. By being involved in church, students were able to find a greater sense of belonging to their respective ethnic groups and strengthen their religious identity by playing active roles in church services. For example, Arthur is heavily involved in his church.

> I'm one of the leaders in the youth group in my church. Even when I'm busy with school I still go to church. I need to be connected with my cultural community. Our church activities are primarily for the Filipino communities. Very few are designed for the local community.

Religion is also a strong sustaining motivator for some NCS students who are faced with difficulties in life. For example, Rhea and her three other siblings often struggle with financial needs. However, her faith can harbour her life storms.

> Patience, patience, I just need to be patient in time of trouble. My brother often says, "God will do something; just be patient". I also have faith in God, though not as much as him.

Viewed from her Muslim perspective, Bana disapproves of the secular cultural values in Hong Kong.

> You must believe in something. Nowadays, teenagers always do stupid things. They cannot predict the future. I think they should have religion and know that they still have hope regardless. Without faith, it is impossible to face disappointments in life. Hong Kong culture is too materialistic and draws teenagers away from seeking the meaning of life.

Studies conducted in Europe and the US found polarising discrepancies within religious practices amongst Muslim minority youth, with great increases in religious practice in some groups and significantly decreased levels of practice in others (Simsek et al., 2019). As revealed in the interview data, contradictions between some religious traditions and the cultural values in Hong Kong society have challenged the aspirations of NCS girls for the future. For example, Bana lives in a traditional Muslim household. Aware of her life aspirations, she learns how to negotiate between the different cultural realms.

> I'm different from my family. Although I'm a girl, I want to have a career, to work and create my future. They (My parents) want to marry me off and get settled with a family... I'm not that sort of religious person, even though I go to the mosque every week, I wear a scarf every day, and I pray five times a day when I have problems. I think my destiny isn't to marry someone but to change my family's will, to do something different from my family's decision. My father wasn't going to let me study in my senior years, but he pays a lot for my brother to study, and that's not fair.

Despite Bana's aspiration for further studies immediately after her secondary education, her family wishes her to settle for marriage with her relative instead. Hoping to pursue her dream and be an English teacher, she eventually compromised with her parents to get married. Her strong belief in goal-seeking motivated her to stay optimistic about her desired future. She is an example of how self-agency may mediate personal intersectionality in their uphill social mobility journeys.

Conclusion

On a positive note, the interviews have unfolded that NCS students feel connected with their schools, peers, and teachers, albeit this is not a simple or straightforward process for most of them. They appreciate the opportunities for knowledge, social, and holistic development, but at the same time, they face a myriad of challenges in education. Among them, the Chinese language is the most ubiquitous obstacle to be overcome. They are regularly frustrated by challenges and/or lack of interest in learning Chinese at school. Family relationships and parental expectations represent significant levers for boosting their confidence and aspiration for PSE development. However, their academic focus and aspirations are encapsulated by the assimilationist education system and underprivileged socio-economic family background. Seeking diversified PSE pathways, they tend to enrol in focused vocational programmes in self-financed institutions or return to their parent's home town. In order to better address disparities in their educational attainment and PSE enrolment, their access to academic-focused higher education institutions must be improved, for this would be a significant lever for reducing the socio-economic gaps between the non-Chinese population and their mainstream peers. Data reveal that ethnic minorities faced with cultural conflicts particularly conflicts caused by their religion and the social upward cultural values find the processes of self-identity difficult. However, each society has an obligation to empower students of different races, nationalities, and abilities to become valuable members of society. An inclusive society should create an inclusive educational system as intentional. In this, a suitable set of quality assurance mechanisms will help promote equitable school campuses.

References

Appadurai, A. (2013). *The future as cultural fact*. Verso.

Arat, G., Hoang, A. P., Jordan, L. P., & Wong, P. W. (2016). A systematic review of studies on ethnic minority youth development in Hong Kong: An application of the ecological framework. *China Journal of Social Work, 9*(3), 218–237. https://doi.org/10.1080/17525098.2017.1254716.

Berry, J. W. (2003). *Conceptual approaches to acculturation*. American Psychological Association.

Berry, J. W., Phinney, J. S., Sam, D. L., & Vedder, P. (2006). Immigrant youth: Acculturation, identity, and adaptation. *Applied Psychology: An International Review, 55*, 303–332. https://doi.org/10.1111/j.1464-0597.2006.00256.x

Berry, J. W., & Sam, D. (1997). Acculturation and adaptation. In W. Berry, M. H. Segall, & C. Kagitcibasi (Eds.), *Handbook of cross-cultural psychology, vol. 3, social behavior and applications* (pp. 291–326). Allyn and Bacon.

Census and Statistics Department. (2017). *Thematic report: Ethnic minorities*. Hong Kong Special Administrative Region. https://www.statistics.gov.hk/pub/B11201002016XXXXB0100.pdf

Chan, M., Tsai, K. M., & Fuligni, A. J. (2014). Changes in religiosity across the transition to young adulthood. *Journal of Youth and Adolescence, 44*(8), 1555–1566. https://doi.org/10.1007/s10964-014-0157-0.

Cheuk, M. (2020). Cantonese is the key to success for Hong Kong's ethnic minorities. *Hong Kong Unison*. https://hongkongfp.com/2020/08/21/cantonese-is-the-key-to-success-for-hong-kongs-ethnic-minorities/

Corredor, J., Álvarez-Rivadulla, M. J., & Maldonado-Carreño, C. (2020). Good will hunting: Social integration of students receiving forgivable loans for college education in contexts of high inequality. *Studies in Higher Education, 45*(8), 1664–1678. https://doi.org/10.1080/03075079.2019.1629410.

Davis, R. F. III, & Kiang, L. (2016). Religious identity, religious participation, and psychological wellbeing in Asian American adolescents. *Journal of Youth and Adolescence, 45*(3), 532–546. https://doi.org/10.1007/s10964-015-0350-9.

Education Bureau (EDB). (2007). *Flexibility in the application of Chinese language requirement for the admission of non-Chinese speaking students into UGC-funded institutions*. http://www.legco.gov.hk/yr06-07/english/bc/bc52/papers/bc52cb2-2573-1-e.pdf

Feliciano, C., & Rumbaut, R. G. (2018). Varieties of ethnic self-identities: Children of immigrants in middle adulthood. *RSF: The Russell Sage Foundation Journal of the Social Sciences, 4*(5), 26–46. https://doi.org/10.7758/RSF.2018.4.5.02.

Gao, F. (2019). Ethnic minority students' progression to university in Hong Kong: Access and equity. *Multicultural Education Review, 11*(2), 135–148. https://doi.org/10.1080/2005615X.2019.1615245.

Hong Kong Unison. (2010). *Hong Kong Unison's submission to education bureau – Use of language fund to enhance Chinese language proficiency of EM people in HK*. Retrieved from https://unison.org.hk/sites/default/files/2020-11/PP201007_2010July_Submission3.pdf

Hong Kong Unison. (2020). *Hong Kong Unison's response to the paper submitted by the Education Bureau to the penal on the education of the Legislative Council*. https://unison.org.hk/sites/default/files/2020-11/PP20111212_HK_Unison_Submission_Response_to_Paper_submitted_by_EDB_to_Panel_on_Education_of_LegCo_English.pdf

Hutchings, M., & Archer, L. (2001). 'Higher than Einstein': Constructions of going to university among working-class non-participants. *Research Papers in Education, 16*(1), 69–91. https://doi.org/10.1080/02671520010011879.

Lai, C., Gao, F., & Wang, Q. (2015). Bicultural orientation and Chinese language learning among South Asian ethnic minority students in Hong Kong. *International Journal of Bilingual Education and Bilingualism, 18*(2), 203–224. https://doi.org/10.1080/13670050.2014.887054.

Loh, K. Y. E., & Hung, O. Y. (2020). A Study on the Challenges Faced by Mainstream Schools in Educating Ethnic Minorities in Hong Kong. *Research report*. https://www.oxfam.org.hk/f/news_and_publication/43418/EOC_EM_Mainstream%20Schools_202001.pdf

Marsh, H., & Scalas, L. F. (2010). Self-concept in learning: Reciprocal effects model between academic self-concept and academic achievement. In P. L. Peterson, E. L. Baker, & B. McGaw (Eds.), *International encyclopedia of education*. Elsevier.

Modood, T. (2005). *Multicultural politics*. Edinburgh University Press.

Patkin, J. (2020). *Should we expect non-Chinese Hongkongers to learn Cantonese? Hong Kong Free Press HKFP*. https://hongkongfp.com/2020/07/13/should-we-expect-non-chinese-hongkongers-to-learn-cantonese/

Phalet, K., Fleischmann, F., & Hillekens, J. (2018). Religious identity and acculturation of immigrant minority youth. *European Psychologist, 23*(1), 1–32. https://doi.org/10.1027/1016-9040/a000309.

Reay, D., Crozier, G., & Clayton, J. (2010). 'Fitting in' or 'standing out': Working-class students in UK higher education. *British Educational Research Journal, 36*(1), 107–124. https://doi.org/10.1080/01411920902878925.

Reay, D., Davies, J., David, M., & Ball, S. J. (2001). Choices of degree or degrees of choice? Class, 'Race' and the higher education choice process. *Sociology, 35*(4), 855–874. https://doi.org/10.1017/S0038038501008550.

Robinson, L. (2009). Cultural identity and acculturation preferences among South. Asian adolescents in Britain: An exploratory study. *Children & Society, 23*(6), 442–454. https://doi.org/10.1111/j.1099-0860.2008.00179.x.

Sadowski, M. (2013). *Portraits of promise: Voices of successful immigrant students*. Harvard Education Press.

Shum, M. S., Gao, F., Tsung, L., & Ki, W. W. (2011). South Asian students' Chinese language learning in Hong Kong: Motivations and strategies. *Journal of Multilingual and Multicultural Development, 32*(3), 285–297. https://doi.org/10.1080/01434632.2010.539693.

Simsek, M., Fleischmann, F., & van Tubergen, F. (2019). Similar or divergent paths? Religious development of Christian and Muslim adolescents in Western Europe. *Social Science Research, 79*, 160–180. https://doi.org/10.1016/j.ssresearch.2018.09.004

Waterman, A. S. (1985). Identity in the context of adolescent psychology. *New Directions for Child and Adolescent Development, 1985*(30), 5–24. https://doi.org/10.1002/cd.23219853003.

Yip, P., & Peng, C. H. (2018). How higher education in Hong Kong reinforces social inequalities. *The South Morning Post*. https://www.scmp.com/print/comment/insight-opinion/article/2129659/how-higher-education-hong-kong-reinforces-social

Yuen, C. Y. M. (2016). Linking life satisfaction with school engagement of secondary students from diverse cultural backgrounds in Hong Kong. *International Journal of Educational Research, 77*, 74–82. https://doi.org/10.1016/j.ijer.2016.03.003

Yuen, C. Y. M. (2018). Perceptions of social justice among the South Asian and mainstream Chinese youth from diverse cultural backgrounds in Hong Kong. *Peabody Journal of Education*, 93(3), 332–344. https://doi.org/10.1080/0161956x.2018.1449928

Yuen, C. Y. M. (2019). *The happiness and mourning of Hong Kong students* (in Chinese). Breakthrough Limited.

Yuen, Y. M. C., Cheung, A. C. K., Leung, C. S. S., Tang, H. H. H., & Chan, L. C. H. (2021). The Success and obstacle factors in pursuing post-secondary education: The differences between Hong Kong mainstream and non-mainstream students (In Chinese). *Education Journal*, 49(2), 137–160.

Yuen, C. Y. M., & Grossman, D. L. (2009). The intercultural sensitivity of student teachers in three cities. *Compare*, 39(3), 349–365. https://doi.org/10.1080/03057920 802281571.

Yuen, Y. M. C., & Lee, M. (2016). Mapping the life satisfaction of adolescents in Hong Kong secondary schools with high ethnic concentration. *Youth & Society*, 48(4), 539–556. https://doi.org/10.1177%2F0044118X13502060.

Yuen, C. Y. M., Lee, M., & Leung, C. S. S. (2016). Religious belief and its association with life satisfaction of adolescents in Hong Kong. *Journal of Beliefs & Values*, 37(1), 103–113. https://doi.org/10.1080/13617672.2016.1141533.

9 Aspirations of Mainstream Youth from Underprivileged Backgrounds in Post-Secondary Education

The challenges of the youth

Poverty is undoubtedly a significant issue concerning young people in Hong Kong. Nowadays, youth may be caught in a cycle of poverty, which ultimately reflects the status quo in which the different social classes in Hong Kong are entrenched. Often, underprivileged youth are prone to early drop out of schooling and lack educational resources to upkeep themselves with the necessary knowledge, skills, and networks for the changing society. Moreover, their circumstances hinder them from seeking quality employment in the job market, which arguably has become more demanding in terms of academic qualifications over the years.

The problems faced by these youth are complicated and their experiences differ significantly (Wong, 2016). Spires (2016) gives a detailed account of Hong Kong's disadvantaged youth. In his words, these youth "face a variety of issues: lack of care, limited world view, lack of confidence, lack of opportunity, lack of choice, weak social networks, communication issues, family background issues, unhappiness, lack of hope, negative image, social problems, and issues associated with the low-ranked Band 3 Schools" (p. 5). It is a fact that students from low-income families are less likely to pursue PSE than their middle-class counterparts. Indeed, the chance for students from low-income families to pursue PSE is far less than those from middle-class families (Ho et al., 2017).

Similarly, middle-class students have more chances to pursue higher education overseas than lower-class students. Hong Kong students need to undergo the challenging HKDSE examinations and pay a heavy price to find alternative education if they fail to achieve the necessary grades (Yuen et al., 2017). Moreover, students from low-income families are often pressured to shoulder the family's economic burden as soon as possible and forgo further education. At the same time, their more affluent peers generally aspire towards tertiary education as a matter of course for better earning and a good life. Additionally, the structures of society and soaring house prices further impede upward social mobility and make it difficult to realise the Hong Kong dream. In this way, the differences of economic background leading to inequalities in the distribution of educational resources are highlighted.

DOI: 10.4324/9780429439315-9

The estimated earnings premiums associated with PSE are significantly more positive for low-income youth than for their more affluent counterparts across the distribution of income (Frenette, 2019). Hence, it is even more desirable for low-income students to acquire PSE skills, knowledge, and attitudes. Under the performative system of secondary education, teachers and students alike believe that the HKDSE is an inescapable "life and death" hurdle that exacerbates stress and frustrations in learning (Ho, 2015). The HKDSE scores are the portal for tertiary education in Hong Kong and have become symbols of advantage. Students place great emphasis on achieving high marks in the HKDSE in the hope of "breaking out of the disadvantaged loop". The disproportionate emphasis placed on the test-taking strategy leads to an examination-oriented drilling practice, especially in senior secondary education. This survival of the fittest mechanism fuels the growth of the commercialisation of education. Such an educational ethos is not only a direct violation of the original meaning and intention behind education for self-actualisation, but are also highly detrimental to students' physical and mental health. Aspirations for higher education vary from individual to individual, subject to the capacity to aspire for the future in terms of hopes, goals, and targets (Appadurai, 2004; p. 60).

Self-reflective narratives and life experiences of freshers in tertiary education

The discussion below was drawn from multiple interviews with first-year students in different higher education institutions in Hong Kong, as part of the qualitative study of the government-funded project titled *Transition from Secondary to Post-Secondary Education: Access, Obstacles, and Success Factors of Immigrant, Minority and Low Income Youth in Hong Kong*. The interviews began with the students introducing themselves and their family backgrounds, college specialism, followed by answering the following questions: Were there any possible obstacles in your pursuit of PSE? If yes, how did you overcome them? In what way did your secondary education programme prepare you for your pursuit? What are the main reasons for you to choose your current major? What is your future career plan, and do you think your current PSE programme is helpful to equip you for that? Does it bring you closer to your goal? Why?

These dialogues gave fresher students a voice to express their thoughts and strengthen their capacity to reflect on the changing values of the times and their personal experiences. Through their retellings and expression of feelings towards their schooling, academic results, aspirations for the future in education, and career development, their wants, hopes, expectations, aspirations, and calculations are revealed.

The case of Cornia (aged 18) is one example. Both her parents had primary education only. The father was a taxi driver and the mother was a homemaker. Both parents never discussed the PSE plan with her nor the associated challenges. However, they put much emphasis on her education and always encouraged her to aim at university. She relied on full subsidies from the government when she was in secondary school. Before her father's bankruptcy was caused by unwise investment, they were financially adequate and comfortable. Even back then, Cornia's parents encouraged her to set her life goal as going into one of the top three universities.

> I doubted that they (my parents) would ever imagine a scenario where I wouldn't be able to go to a university as they always kept telling me about going to university ever since I was in primary school... as a result, I only have two life goals: going to university and being a teacher...So when DSE results were released, I shared with my parents that I had got enough scores to apply for a place in this university. For them, my current university education was somewhat expected.

Her university dream drove Corina, and she gave her undivided attention to get prepared for the university. Her strong motivation for achievement is exemplary. However, her HKDSE results were the biggest hurdle for her and lower than expected.

> I worked hard at school, and I attended many talks and university open days. No matter how well I did at school, I would be done if I failed in DSE. Anyway, my DSE scores were lower than I predicted. That's why I had to compromise with second-best – doing education as my major. I don't really like this campus, and it is so inconvenient to travel.

When the HKDSE results were released, Corina felt most grateful for her supportive secondary school environment. She invited many teachers and senior schoolmates to help other recent graduates to apply for universities and select majors. After being admitted to the university, Corina has to face the reality of finding the means to settle her fees.

> My parents told me that I don't have to worry about the tuition fees. All I need to do is to borrow a loan from the government.

Being a fresher at the university was a novel experience for Cornia, but the boarding life helped her to adjust to university quickly.

> My current education programme is helpful. I like Child Psychology, it is really useful. I can apply the knowledge to teaching. For this first semester I would actually like to enrol for more courses. But I listened to the professors that I should lessen my load so I could adjust to university life more easily. I enjoy living in hall. It saves lots of traveling time and money.

She wanted to join a university exchange programme, but it was beyond her budget.

> I wanted to go for exchange and I discussed this idea with my mother. But because this involved one extra year fees, she immediately told me not to go.

> I also told myself to forget about it. It is quite depressing. Even before I get a job, I will owe the government a huge sum of money upon my graduation.

Corina worked part-time as a private tutor and piano teacher to help pay her living expenses. She tried applying for a student assistantship and only to find that the threshold was too high, as it requires students to have a scholarship or outstanding academic achievement. So she applied for a government loan to cover the tuition fee, but found the lack of information regarding the application process caused great inconvenience.

Looking ahead, she hoped to be a teacher in her alma mater and planned to pursue a master's degree after one or two years of teaching.

> I want to go back to my secondary school and be a teacher. Teaching is a stable job, and the monthly salary is quite attractive for a fresh graduate. I can save some money, and I may do a masters after teaching for a few years. I wish to be a panel head and I need to upgrade myself… Anyway, every teacher starts as a contract staff. If there is too much competition, then I will change job.

Harrison (aged 18) shared many similarities with Corina. Parents had received education up to the primary level, were a working-class family, and received full subsidies from the government during secondary education. In addition, Harrison has a younger sibling under his mother's care.

Harrison did not have a clear vision of his future. He recognised himself as not academic material nor a lover of learning. His parents, who have a significant influence on him, constantly reminded him that studying hard can increase his opportunity to enter university, get better employment, and have a better life.

Why did he choose education as a major?

> My DSE scores decided my current major. My initial thoughts were only for getting a degree, I didn't care in which discipline. In my JUPAS, my first choice was Business Studies. But I missed it by two DSE points. I'm not interested in other subjects. Cultural Management was my second choice. I wanted to study the Chinese Language as I like it very much. Unfortunately, I only got a "4" in Chinese. So I put education as the third choice. I have some interest in education and I like a close student-teacher relationship very much. Anyway, my parents were very proud of my DSE results and I could study at this university.

Despite the fact that Harrison articulated his university pathway in a rather causal way, he worked hard for it, especially during his final secondary education stage (S4–S6).

> My school's senior secondary education is more or less the same as for other schools. In S4 and S5 they teach basic knowledge. But in S6 they simply

focus on DSE drilling. There were lots of after-school tutorial classes, from 3:30 pm up till 5 pm or 6 pm, Monday to Friday, plus doing tests on Saturdays. Running September through February, we were on study leave. We had to do self-study.

Regarding my ability in attempting exams, I think my biggest strength is my answering skill. I knew how to apply my understanding to answer the exam questions. Perhaps, the Chinese Language is my strength in that I could do well. I also took some private tutorials – that helped raised my grade, except in my English. They did not help my English at all, so I stopped.

The HKDSE stress is public knowledge, and to know how to handle the stress is crucial for all students. Below is Harrison's recollection of his coping strategies:

I went back to school for self-study during the study leave period. The DSE stress was overwhelming. I like basketball so I used to play basketball to release my stress. Occasionally, I talked with my mum about my worries. She supported me and just told me to focus on the exams. Although we are not rich, my family certainly helped me, even to borrow some money from my uncle. My job was only to get into university.

At university, Harrison had a reality check. The University campus is a middle-class construct and that created some problems.

I realized that friends who played sports with me were from affluent families and went to Band 1 schools. I initially felt a bit uncomfortable hanging out with them. I grew up in public housing, and my family is not wealthy. You know the university is characterized by middle-class culture. I am also not used to the shared accommodation … But so far, I am adjusting fairly well. I enjoy learning Chinese and interacting with my professors and classmates.

To be competitive in the future job market, Harrison puts extra effort into catching up.

People think university life is all about having fun. It's not true. Instead, it is all about studying. I feel that I'm not prepared for the future. I've decided to work harder. I usually run through the readings before attending the lectures. That helps. Other students are doing the same, though. It's just like doing exercise to keep fit so that I can compete with the others.

The future is yet to be decided. Although studying education, Harrison has yet to determine his career pathway.

I don't have any career plans for my future at this stage. I am still searching. I believe many HR (human resources) organizations will hire major education graduates. I don't think I will be a teacher. It may be more likely that I'll work as a HR person. Perhaps, I'll be clearer after the internship...I understand teachers are well-paid in Hong Kong. Even though I won't be a teacher, my teaching licensure will give me advantages in job hunting. My dream is not about earning much money as such. I only look for a stable lifestyle so I can play basketball at my leisure. If I am too busy, I will have to sacrifice my hobbies.

Commenting on senior secondary education, Harrison opined that knowing the options is critical for informed PSE choices. Unfortunately, this aspect has been neglected by teachers.

I suggest not only focusing on the admission mark but also putting greater emphasis on knowing more about the subjects and knowledge when selecting a major. I am still exploring the future, though without much planning, in the hope I can have a secure and pleasant life in the future.

Winnie (aged 20) addressed herself as an over-age fresher. "I studied two years for a higher dip (diploma) before being admitted to this university". Living with her mother and two siblings, her biggest challenge is finance. Her father passed away, and her mother has to shoulder the whole family's expenses.

I come from a family with poor economic conditions. Since I graduated from secondary school, I have never asked for pocket money from my parents. I got a grant from the government to do my study. Sometimes, I worked part-time as an event helper or waitress to keep me going. But now I'm getting busy and I've no time to do part-time. I did apply for a grant and loan, but I don't know the results yet. I've thought of doing part-time, but I'm afraid that it will take my focus away from my academic studies. So I want to wait till the end of this semester before deciding whether I need to find a part-time or not. So far, my family and friends have given me lots of support and encouragement.

Claiming herself as a HKDSE looser, Winnie lamented that she did not receive sufficient support from her teachers as she would have liked. However, reflecting on her experiences with HKDSE, she maintained that:

it was a nightmare for me to prepare for the exams and more, I have endured much pressure after receiving unsatisfying results. You know, my secondary school offered minimal support to mediocre students like me! They have not been fair. They showed favoritism in helping the outstanding students obtain better results in DSE to boost the school's university enrollment rate. My teacher used to challenge me by saying, "are you really thinking about going to university? Your grades won't make it!" The grade is everything. Personal interest doesn't count.

University choice is entirely determined by DSE scores, not by a student's potential or passion. A progression of exit examination hurdles at the kindergarten, primary and secondary levels offer students multiple crunch points of success or failure. From her personal experience, Winnie disagreed with her teachers' judgement on students and advised her junior fellow students to follow their dreams.

> They should not take all their teachers' saying into account. My experience tells me that teachers' help is somewhat limited. Most of the time, they just wish to boost the university admissions rate and advise students to try different programmes. A friend of mine obtained enough scores to study at university. But his teacher advised him to try a HD (higher diploma) instead, and he did. I think he just missed the chance to be a university student.

The teacher expectancy effect really exists. Winnie stressed that teachers could encourage students more and that secondary schools could provide more information and additional options concerning alternative paths for those who had taken the HKDSE.

> When I received my DSE results, I was so anxious that I didn't know what to do. My brother was overseas, and my mother had no idea. Hence, I just picked a programme to give myself a choice. Luckily, I have no regrets about my decision.

> I think the teachers should not hail the DSE as the be-all-and-end-all. I hope they can provide extra information about the pros and cons of different options, such as if students cannot enter university, they may think about pursuing an Associate Degree. Although it may take another two years, I've walked this road and it was the happiest time in my education journey. Even though I was aimless at the start of the programme, I felt relieved after talking to the lecturers. They told me many concrete examples of how to bridge my study with a degree. I've had to learn about many different subjects, not all of them I liked. I could then select the subjects I liked for my associate degree. The degree had many mid-term exams, and I felt overworked, yet I had still enjoyed my experience.

Winnie added that she completed her associate degree with an outstanding grade point average (GPA) of 3.7. She also engaged in other activities such as the Rotary Club and being a Health Ambassador. Her classmates were also supportive and brought her more confidence.

> Most of my secondary school teachers want to help us improve our grades, but some teachers may tell me directly that I could only get a "2" for that subject, which destroyed my confidence. I was so stressed and anxious to the point that I just wanted to give it up altogether. You know, I really hate school, for my teachers seldom encouraged us (the non-elite students) nor let us practise more for the exams. However, the lecturers in my Associate Degree were quite different - they gave us more encouragement and support.

Emmigration is Winnie's future plan. Her dream is to study nursing, she wants to emigrate to Canada because she thinks life in Hong Kong is too stressful and the pace of living is too fast.

> For the sake of myself and my family, I wish to earn more money when I am young so that I can enjoy my retirement life. My family's economic situation is not stable. My sister has tried all sorts of jobs that you can think of, sales, tourist guide, secretary, but never for long. Nursing is in high demand overseas, and Canada is a slow-paced place. Pollution is low too.

Joy (aged 18) did not have a chance to develop her hobbies because her family could not afford her when she was a child. As a result, she was jealous of others who seemed to have had an exciting experience in school.

> Many students have a chance to develop their hobbies, such as dance, piano etc. I also wanted to join them but my father told me not to waste money on extra activities. He didn't allow me to do so and I was very unhappy, but I had no choice.

Joy's parents have never been to university, so they did not advise her about university education. Neither did she get much advice from her secondary teachers. Catching her friends' dream of university education, Joy praised the elite class streaming system, which socialised her with the culture of hard work and competition.

> Because of academic streaming, I was allocated to the elite class. Other classes played basketball or other things after lunch, but our class stayed to do homework or practice past papers. All my friends were academically focused. Our common goal was to get into university. That was very clear to us. We shared tips about how to get accepted into university. For example, which university would have an information day or open day – we would share the news among ourselves and go together. At the secondary level, teachers seldom give you help. They may have some information but not much. Hence, it is up to friends.

Joy is independent and self-reinforcing but is also prone to be influenced by classmates and friends.

> I was usually well-prepared for the exams, but, at the same time, I was very nervous about performing to the best of my abilities during the exams. I often feel inferior when I know other students live a better life than me. But then again, because of my low-income family root, I was determined to try my best to turn around my circumstances…

Interestingly, even though Joy encountered compulsory courses that she was not interested in, she could not stop appreciating her school's streaming system.

She was very interested in knowing the academic avenues and resources for achieving her PSE goals. There were many benefits to being enrolled in the elite class, and Joy had counted them one by one.

> First, being admitted to the elite class gave me a label. Second, the elite class is more resourceful than the other classes. Third, the teacher quality is better in the elite class. They are different from other ordinary classes. Unlike those teachers in regular classes who always joked and offered superficial lessons, teachers of elite classes were well-prepared, serious and skilful in teaching. They are also knowledgeable about their subject discipline to create a learning atmosphere and motivate students to learn. Every week we had 2-3 tests from different subjects. When there was no test, I would start to panic as if I had forgotten the dates.

Joy's secondary school held different kinds of career lectures to prepare students for their school exit. Apart from attending the talks delivered by professionals, alumni also shared their insights into PSE choices. Joy was inspired:

> I remember there was a sharing by an alumnus, saying that she took an Associate Degree programme when she was not admitted to the university, and after that she was able to enrol in university, which thrilled me a lot. That meant I too could have a chance.

This successful example of an alternate alternative path gave Joy hope that her effort would be recognised eventually, especially regarding the HKDSE. In the elite class, she was given better quality learning resources and study environments than ordinary classes. Joy felt that students need to learn how to face success or failure, deal with emotions, and make friends regardless of attending university. In hindsight, she wished her secondary school could have stressed the importance of further education and career planning more than they did. Also, successful alumni should be invited more to share their experiences and clear up some of the confusion some students have about their future. Senior secondary students should be exposed to different perspectives on education, career, and adult life when they transition to PSE.

Fiona received a full subsidy from the government when she was in secondary school. Living in a family of six members with both parents of basic education, Fiona was trained to be self-reliant in her studies. Recalling her preparation for HKDSE examinations, she maintained that:

> I often felt that I had very little time during my secondary education. S6 was highly packed, practicing past papers, going to tutorial classes after school. All my time was devoted to DSE. Super busy. No time for myself at all.

> I found the tutorial classes did not help boost my English language confidence. Moreover, because my foundation was weak, it was too late to catch up in S6.

The choice of university majors is directly linked with the HKDSE scores. Fiona did not have any knowledge of Psychology, but she ended up doing it.

> My current major was allocated by JUPAS. In fact, I placed Psychology at the bottom of my choice ranking. Anyway, it was somehow expected as my DSE scores were not high enough for me to be admitted to the top three universities in Hong Kong. I was somewhat puzzled about my future development when having a psychology degree. What job could I do?

Fiona enjoyed the university lifestyle and the study approach even though her university is far away from the city centre, and it is inconvenient to go out and have food.

> The first semester has been positive. The theories were interesting, and I believe I will continue to study Psychology. However, what happens beyond graduation is challenging to tell. My DSE electives were BAFS (Business, Accounting and Finance) and I planned to study Business. It is a pity that I could not study Business. It is very different from Psychology. I thought Business was the easiest subject to get into university. The requirements for doing Marketing were not high. But I guess I may also be able to join the Business field in the future.

> I am actually quite satisfied with my current major. I am not doing education; hence I have less homework and more free time. So I can participate in various activities. Still, I am somewhat stressed about my GPA, and I am pretty confused and uncertain about the future. I don't know what studying psychology may bring in the future, especially employment-wise.

Sunny (aged 19) is a single child. His father obtained a junior secondary education, and his mother finished her PSE. Growing up in public housing in a low SES community, Sunny did not compromise his dream for university education. His parents put a strong emphasis on higher education and encouraged him to pursue a degree. He graduated from a high banding English as EMI secondary school. Now his campus is far from home. Sunny makes multiple journeys to attend his university. On a typical school day, he has to spend three hours commuting between home and campus. He made a few comments about his campus life. The canteen food is not appetising but very expensive, and the library holdings are small.

Inspired by his Chinese History teacher, Sunny followed his teacher's footsteps by majoring in Chinese History.

> I've always liked History, and, my DSE results narrowed my institutional choice. I'm fine with it in terms of language as my secondary school was an EMI one. So English is not a problem for me. As for my future career, I am

still searching. Most likely, I will be a History teacher. But I'm also interested in working as a curator in a museum.

Sunny also likes making comparisons between his secondary school and his current university experience. For example, life may be more straightforward in secondary school, but it was more restrained than university.

Homework is easier in secondary school. Take group presentations as an example - students just copy the related information from the internet and relay it to the class. Test practices is more important, in any case. In university, presentations need to be supported by data and theory and substantiated by analyses and thesis points. Moreover, the university is stressful with all the credits and courses as well as activities in the university. It is also a challenge when the teacher teaches the A-level rather than the DSE method, making it difficult to absorb.

PSE programmes and school-based support

Senior secondary education is a highly focused springboard for university education in Hong Kong. Bourdieu's (1973) cultural capital and habitus concepts provide a critical lens by which to frame these students' educational experience, beliefs, motivation, and aspirations. The asymmetric distribution of wealth and sociocultural capital has caused inequality of opportunity in higher education and perpetuated social segregation and welfare dependence. However, the trajectories of the interviewed students show how they have overcome such barriers and demonstrated their strong motivation to succeed. They made frequent comparisons between personal habitus and the rule of the game in vertical social mobility. Being socialised in a highly competitive education system, they feel the pulse of the game and have demonstrated how self-agency works. They aspired for a better future and kept their hope to find a position for themselves. Within a meritocratic society, the effort is critical towards gaining a return. Against their backdrop, effort serves as a framework for these low SES mainstream youth to strive for their life ambitions. We may also discern their upbringing and parental values as fuelling their dedication to improving their disadvantaged situation. In addition, significant others, be it their parents, teachers, or peers, play a critical role in steering them towards the goal of pursuing higher education from an early stage.

In this regard, Corina and Harrison recognised that they must do well in secondary school to alleviate their disadvantaged situation. Winnie lamented the unfair treatment associated with the high-stake examination-oriented system, which discourages low-income students. As freshers navigating their PSE pathways, they strongly believe that the preparation programme should be broadened and balanced to cater to students with multiple talents.

Corina hopes one day to return to her alma mater middle school to be a teacher and then pursue a master's degree after one or two years of teaching.

Winnie wants to do nursing, and she wants to emigrate to Canada. Sunny may well become a Chinese History teacher. Harrison is "still exploring the future without much planning". Fiona is quite confused and uncertain about the future, not knowing "what studying Psychology may bring in the future, especially employment-wise". Teachers must listen to these inner voices of the students, especially their worries, confusions, obstacles, and struggles and learn to know their demands and offer suitable suggestions to help them.

Failing to attend university after the HKDSE, such students may choose to enrol for a two-year associate degree and afterward work for an opportunity to enrol in a university. Winnie is one such case. However, this pathway is not without some negativity. Associate degrees are regarded as the second-tier option for those who cannot enter university, and the fees for associate degrees are very high. It would then be natural for these youth to feel a sense of discontentment if they cannot go to university or struggle to find jobs with a college diploma.

Schools are key shapers in educational aspiration and use a commodity-based and examination-oriented approach to shaping parents' and communities' views on options for further education. Under neoliberalism, higher education expansion and competition are natural causes of marketisation and globalisation. The students have reiterated the importance of acquiring knowledge of future educational and career options. This must be made more available. Of course, a most critical step would be to increase PSE enrolment opportunities and instil the aspiration for university among low SES youth from both mainstream and non-mainstream backgrounds. To break the intergeneration poverty cycle, social mobility must be maintained so that members of society can reach their potential and ease social inequality. This would also mean that people from lower social classes would have the opportunity to traverse through classes via individual effort and improve their quality of life, reinforcing the spirit of hard work and enthusiasm (The Hong Kong Special Administrative Region, 2018). In addition, it may be a very effective way to improve vocational or technical education in helping young people to find jobs (Cooksey & Rindfuss, 2001). PSE programmes are an excellent way to provide youth with the opportunities and skills to equip themselves for the future.

However, the fact is that not all students are academic-oriented or wish to follow the conventional route in life. The EDB, schools, and industries should re-examine the possibility of revamping the senior secondary education, especially given that the importance of science and technology advancement has been restated. There is a need to incorporate career elements into learning experiences, which would allow students to know more and experience more. Alumni can be a useful resource in providing customised advice to students to apply to university and select majors. Corina's school is an example, and for that she is grateful. Joy praised her secondary school for the valuable experiences shared by prior graduates. Teachers stand at the frontline and spend time with the students to obtain first-hand knowledge of the characters of each student. Taking the students' perspective to a greater degree will allow them to offer more personalised suggestions that match these students' needs.

Teachers' expectations play an essential role in influencing the student learning process. These expectations vary greatly and are not all positive as with Joy, while the unreasonable expectations of others may also impact students negatively, such as with Winnie. Students with a low performance can develop a negative attitude and lose enthusiasm and confidence in learning because of their teachers' low expectations. Recalling one of the interviewees, Winnie complained, "The teachers for my secondary school always want to help us improve the grades, but some teachers may tell me directly that I could only get 2 for that subject, which shakes my confidence. They seldom encourage us". It is in this particular area, especially, that the communication between teachers and youth needs to be changed. Teachers ought to appropriate their expectations of youth and convey them effectively to generate a greater sense of encouragement.

Moreover, disadvantaged youth may fall into outstanding debt, as the tuition fee for associate degrees is very expensive. They may have difficulty in repaying the loan in that their income after graduation may not be very high. In recent years, many have expressed concerns about the affordability of associate degrees. To this end, some interested parties have monitored this issue and propose to optimise self-financed undergraduate programmes, expand the subsidised number of self-funded top-up undergraduate programmes, and attract "outstanding youth" towards enhancing their competitiveness and improving the employment environment by providing opportunities of internship, thus building the confidence of employers, and so on.

Hong Kong education has long been serving the socio-economic development of society. Parents, educators, and students understand that an individual's advancement can only be enhanced through formal education. Successful school life is defined by transferring one's academic achievements in generating good income, high social position, and recognition. The materialistic function of education has often been underscored and transmitted through media, school, and family socialisation. Within this Hong Kong cultural context, the capital habitus (Bourdieu, 1977) has to be sustained by schools. Put differently, schools are responsible for providing opportunities for students to transition from school to job seeking, vocational training, counselling, and lifelong learning (Lai & Chan, 2002). The qualities of friendships and networks influence the opportunity of youth to escape poverty more than just the number of friends a person has (Wong, 2006). It is vital for youth to be able to foster and keep good relationships with such persons in order to exchange skills to equip themselves, help in the preparation before interviews, share job information and work experiences, so as to gain more chances for the benefit of all concerned.

References

Appadurai, A. (2004). The capacity to aspire: Culture and the terms of recognition. *Culture and Public Action, 59*, 62–63.

Bourdieu, P. (1973). The three forms of theoretical knowledge. *Social Science Information, 12*(1), 53–80.

Bourdieu, P. (1977). *Structures and the habitus*. Cambridge University Press.
Cooksey, E. C., & Rindfuss, R. R. (2001). Patterns of work and schooling in young adulthood. *Sociological Forum*, *16*(4), 731–755. https://doi.org/10.1023/A:1012842230505.
Frenette, M. (2019). *Do Youth from lower- and higher-income families benefit equally from postsecondary education?* https://www150.statcan.gc.ca/n1/pub/11f0019m/11f0019m2019012-eng.htm
Ho, K. (2015). *The situation and resort of Hong Kong youths* (in Chinese). file:///D:/Desktop/Youth-Study-Presentation.pdf
Ho, S. C., Hung, S. K., Keung, P. C., & Sham, K. W. (2017). Apply PISA to study Hong Kong youths' expectation of higher education (in Chinese). *Education Journal*, *45*(1), 47–69.
Hong Kong Special Administrative Region. (2018). *Report on poverty in Hong Kong in 2018*. https://www.povertyrelief.gov.hk/chi/pdf/Hong_Kong_Poverty_Situation_Report_2018(2019.12.13).pdf
Lai, J. C. L., & Chan, R. K. H. (2002). The effects of job-search motives and coping on psychological health and re-employment: A study of unemployed Hong Kong Chinese. *The International Journal of Human Resource Management*, *13*(3), 465–483. https://doi.org/10.1080/09585190110111486.
Spires, R. W. (2016). Perceptions of disadvantaged youth on social and economic asymmetry: A case study in Hong Kong's new territories. *FIRE: Forum for International Research in Education*, *3*(3), 1–15. Lehigh University Library and Technology Services.
Wong, H. (2006). Human capital, social capital and social exclusion: Impacts on the opportunity of households with youth to leave poverty. *International Journal of Adolescent Medicine and Health*, *18*(3), 521–534. https://doi.org/10.1515/IJAMH.2006.18.3.521.
Wong, M. Y. H. (2016). "Welfare or politics? A comparative analysis on support for redistribution and political discontent in Hong Kong". *Final report*. Policy Innovation and Coordination Office.
Yuen, Y. M. C., Cheung, C. K. A., & Yuen, W. W. T. (2017). Spiritual health, school engagement and civic engagement of secondary students in Hong Kong (in Chinese). *Journal of Youth Studies*, *20*(1), 202–213.

10 Wellness of Underprivileged Youth Approaching Post-Secondary Education and Career in Hong Kong

On the exit of secondary education

As discussed in Chapter 1, students in late teens (10th–12th grades) are straddling the fence between education and work, with one foot in the world of adolescence and one foot in the world of adults. Approaching their exit of secondary education, senior secondary students become near-sighted about the prospect of gaining high-income employment upon PSE graduation rather than pursuing their dream jobs. Yet, these students have no first-hand experience in adult life and hence do not know what actions to take and what consequences those actions will bring. They negotiate a period of enormous uncertainty that leads to intense media use, identity seeking, and social recognition. This milestone challenges not only the students but also their parents and teachers. Research (Ma et al., 2018) shows that Asian parents hold high expectations on students' academic achievement, and which may alternatively lead to better results or low well-being. Developing a positive life goal is key to motivating people to strive for a meaningful and productive life (Emmons, 2005). Helping youth to make autonomous decisions about their future with adequate knowledge and experiences will develop their agentive in achieving their life goal. Hence the need for quality advice on education and career development can significantly contribute to their future planning.

Under the influence of neoliberalism and globalisation, the pressure is for education to become the means of meeting examination requirements and generating an economic gain. As a result, students are less concerned about the purpose of higher education than its market value (Brooks et al., 2020). Preparation for the labour market has been the prevalent trend in the higher education field. Pragmaticism dominates the school curriculum, and there has been a long trend to infuse career development with different educational systems (Organization for Economic Cooperation and Development, 2014). The increasing prevalence of higher education has stimulated the growth of self-funded fee-paying PSE programmes. However, the diversification of PSE programmes does not always align with the diversification of the labour market, and secondary school leavers are also often unclear about PSE programme offerings and are unprepared for the job market.

DOI: 10.4324/9780429439315-10

Alongside the pragmatic approach to education, in Hong Kong, a myriad of educational reforms was implemented from 2000 to further link senior secondary education with the preparation for lifelong planning and career development. The new secondary academic structure, which validates individual and group counselling on career choice and the curriculum reforms taken by the aims to integrate the work-related experience. The provision of the reforms offered increased human resources, additional grant allocation, community engagement, and allocating NGO collaboration with schools (Ho & Leung, 2016). However, despite these reforms, the accessibility of professional advice on PSE choices remains an issue. Underprivileged SES students still lack the necessary guidance for approaching further education or career choices (Yuen et al., 2021), and they have to struggle with obstacles such as severe competition, low language proficiency, and a lack of critical and high-order thinking skills. To resolve this long-standing need, empirical data and the views of young people on their actual life planning experiences can be a resource towards developing more positive outcomes for them.

Success and responsibilities

Most secondary students believe that obtaining a degree at university or pursuing PSE is their next life goal upon graduation from the HKDSE. Consistent with international studies (Brooks et al., 2020), the value of gaining socio-economic capital outweighs the value of making learning enjoyable and satisfactory. The societal context makes a difference in students' perception of life goals and PSE pursuit. To some extent, many students strive hard to get access to higher education to gain more social and economic capital to honour their parents, materialistically and non-materialistically. In a Confucian society like Hong Kong, filial piety is a major contributing factor for CIS and NCS students to hold such a belief. They tend to associate a university degree with a high-income and stable career. Those who are not high attaining and less ambitious about getting to the research-focused institutions target either vocation-focused or lower benchmarking institutions. This includes choosing alternative programmes and destinations, such as overseas universities with lower admission requirements or local sub-degree or associate degree programmes. Hong Kong education is a highly selective and performative system, and transition from senior secondary (grades 10th–12th) to PSE is a very stressful process associated with many detrimental effects. Drawing from the same data source of the last chapter, the interview data presented below were collected between 10/2020 and 3/2021. In the individual interviews, all participants were asked the following questions in addition to their basic demographic information. (1) How well was your school performance so far? (2) Do you have plans for PSE and beyond? (3) Are you aware of the requirements for different PSE programmes? (4) How likely will you enrol in PSE institutions? (5) How do your parents' educational level and occupations affect your PSE choice? Their responses were directly related to these questions.

Responsibility and financial factors are considerations for most students seeking to do a degree. Their aspirations for a high educational degree commonly derive from extrinsic motivations (Ryan & Deci, 2000), which are associated with income, social status, and recognition and expectation from others, including family members, teachers, or society as a whole. Some students are even prepared to sacrifice their interests for a higher income. For example, Reran's life aspiration is influenced by her real and imagined value ascribed to the PSE. She maintained:

> English is definitely my interest and something I enjoy. But business is definitely the career path that I really want to go with. It has a higher income. I try my best not to think a lot about living my life just for earning but at the same time money is almost everything if you really think about it. Without a single penny, you won't go anywhere, especially in Hong Kong. It's a well-developed city with a lot of keen competition.
>
> (Reran, NCS, S6)

Chang was approaching graduation, and he was burdened by sharing his family's financial needs. He was born and raised in the Mainland and moved to Hong Kong a few years ago. Having to make realistic decisions rather than aspirational dreams, Chang believed getting a university degree was a practical way to fulfil his responsibility.

> I think if I get a job, one thing I want the most is to be able to support [my parents'] living... to provide them with better living conditions. It is not out of filial piety, our relationship is not very close, but it is my basic family responsibility.
>
> (Chang, CIS, S6)

This is also true for Shaw:

> Because I am the eldest son of my family, I am obliged to take care of them [my parents], as our culture says that the eldest son must be responsible for raising the family.
>
> (Shaw, HKMS, S6)

Harrah's acceptance of family financial responsibilities is explicit too. Such awareness and burden become his extrinsic motivation to sustain his hard work in school.

> My parents make me work even harder because I've seen my mother and father go through so much not just financially but emotionally as well. We've gone through really rough times. That's why it motivates me to go to university and hopefully through education it will change my life.
>
> (Harrah, NCS, S6)

Senior secondary students are conscientious about their family responsibilities. They have widely recognised the pragmatic roles of higher education in their adult life. And the high income promised by a university degree makes it more desirable than ever as adult life becomes a closer reality. Yet, they are also aware that effort and hard work are the necessary prices for a promising future.

> If you work hard in Hong Kong, you can be successful. Hard work pays off. I am a positive-minded person. I believe I can get into UST, get a job with high-salary, and even do a master's degree. I think I can achieve all of these.
>
> (Monika, NCS, S6)

That is said, today's students do have different pursuits in life. For some students, studying is no longer their single or ultimate goal, but rather it is a stepping stone towards adulthood. Even though they may be occupied by preparing for HKDSE examinations, they have seeded doubts about this path. Apart from their responsibilities and the extrinsic benefits conferred by university degrees, they also want to discover and pursue their natural interests and intrinsic motivations in their study. And they are eager to have the freedom to do so.

> I don't think it is necessary to go to university, it is a shackle... Nobody says that you can only get a good job if you have studied in university. Even if you don't get into university, there are still many careers you can choose. I think being successful is achieving your dream.
>
> (Nicky, NCS, S6)

> I don't know what I'm doing and what I want to do really. I think I need recommendations to give me more advice on what the subject is that I could have fun in.
>
> (Kay, NCS, S6)

Engaging in intellectual struggle is part of growing up in adult life. Aside from being practical and realistic while navigating their future pathways, some participants had doubts about associating their motivations with their PSE. Some had begun to challenge convention and address the tension between economic gain and personal dreams. It was acknowledged that a well-paid career does not equate to success. Achieving their dreams and being able to do what they are genuinely interested in are seen as noble life goals. Thinking philosophically, being happy and true to oneself can represent major success in life. Getting into university is not necessarily for everyone, and different people have their own talents and weaknesses and should be allowed to have different aspirations and wants in their education and career. Moreover, some students could differentiate their need for money from their intrinsic interests, as Lucy said:

> Earning money is essential, but we don't need to earn a lot. Earning enough to make a living is good. Other than that, you may find your own interest… If I can earn a living and continue to take part in my interest at the same time, then this for me is the most successful life.
> (Lucy, CIS, S6)

Nei was the student union president in her school, and both her parents only had a few years of compulsory education.

> I aspired to be an actress and I participated in the drama stage play when I was in junior school. Being an extra in a TVB (Television Broadcasts Limited) drama and cooperating with my idol by acting in a film has changed my thinking about the future…I don't think university is the priority; sometimes, it can even be a burden for me. Even if you go to a university, you still have to work. No one has said that you can only get good jobs if you have a university degree. There are many types of work one can enjoy, not only sitting in the office.
> (Nei, CIS, S6)

Laments on the education system

The education system of Hong Kong is unbalanced and skewed towards examination requirements. Under the pressure of meritocracy and performativity, senior secondary education is being hijacked for serving the social selection system for higher education. The future of a generation of senior secondary students is hinged on one HKDSE examination. While drilling for HKDSE promotes the examination intelligence, it leaves training for critical thinking skills and social-emotional competence untouched. Life satisfaction and school engagement decline with grade level (Yuen & Cheung, 2018). The deprivation of extracurricular activities is a typical example. Even if they have exceptional performance in extracurricular activities or other non-academic subjects, those achievements are not valued by the education system or society, it seems. This skewed education orientation not only hinders students from achieving potentialities but also hurts their well-being. Leon laments on this system:

> DSE is a life barrier for me because, except for DSE, it seems that anything else is not counted… Society should not put all the emphasis just on the DSE results, and it is not fair only to consider the result of one DSE examination. The overall achievement of the students should be considered. For example, I was once in the top ten for the Harvard Book Prize Writing Competition.
> (Leon, HKMS, S6)

The common understanding is that studying is about preparing youth for the future job market, and education serves to raise students' examination performance. For Shaw, the competitive examination-oriented culture denies the potential of students with multiple intelligences. It also betrays the future of non-academic oriented students:

> I want to learn new things, but not only study for academic results. I want to learn, as learning can make my life better, but not just for examination, where afterward you will not remember anything you have learned… In Hong Kong, when you have good academic results, you are smart, while if you do not, you are stupid. But I think everyone has their different talents. I think the EDB is spreading a wrong mindset about education; teachers also shouldn't just focus on students' academic results; they should also understand students' dreams.
>
> (Shaw, HKMS, S6)

Schools are social communities and a part of the social system. Some students commented that they did not have sufficient electives and that knowledge acquired in class was superficial and focused on HKDSE. Immigrant and ethnic minority students are often pressured by the fear of failing examinations, committing themselves to endless revision and study, adapting to new learning environments as newcomers, all the time under the expectation and emphasis on PSE from teachers, schools, families, and peer pressure.

> All of my family members are successful. For example, my cousin is now studying in Oxford, and all of the children in my family are good at studying. It seems I am a burden for the whole family and it's unthinkable that I might not get into a university.
>
> (Wong, HKMS, S6)

Knowledge of future development and choices is critical for students to make informed decisions. Schools are the sole agent of information for most underprivileged students. Unfortunately, the students in this study felt ill-prepared for their advanced planning. They commented that teachers' guidance on life planning is fragmented or superficial.

> I won't say it [life planning] is a success so far. It is not out there for viewing, so there are not a lot of students aware of it.
>
> (Presa, NCS, S6)

> We can't say that these [life planning events] are bad. However, then again, the way of promoting them have not been efficient so far.
>
> (Neil, NCS, S6)

Chang expressed her disappointment at both academic guidance and career guidance:

> On the aspect of providing information about post-secondary information, the school has not done enough. Usually, my class teacher only mentions it briefly in class, and some talks have mentioned it before, but I only understand it very superficially… they mainly talk about how to fill in the choices for JUPAS, a few options, but I still don't know how to choose, so the information they provide is not that useful. I've asked for further education and career consultation, but this hasn't been much help… I hope that the school will help me find my interest, like holding some workshops or experiencing activities.
>
> (Chang, CIS, S6)

Construction of the PSE dream

The roles of financial prospect and family responsibilities in PSE choices have already been discussed, and the importance of career choices has been underscored (Kazi & Akhlaq, 2017). A career is a means of living that can change personalities, determine social status, predict expected earnings, determine social groups, and so on. And for students who are dedicated to academic dreams, their academic achievement is also a crucial factor for their university choices. In addition, culture is a further and influential factor for NCS students. Indian students, for example, are particularly prone in this regard to direct their studies towards medicine or law. Presa considers medicine only to meet her parents' expectations:

> I'm now taking Science; I may change to study Business if it's too hard. But my parents want me to be in the medical field because Medicine is relatively a higher achievement, and Indians like Medicine and Law, so they tend to push me to the medical field.
>
> (Presa, NCS, S6)

For some other ethnic minority girls, teaching, especially being an English teacher, is a highly desirable profession. One influence in this decision process is the often-exemplary role model of their teachers and their relatively high standard of English over Chinese.

Role of significant others

Although personal belief in effort plays a role in learning, peer influence is also shown to be vital in attaining academic achievement. NCS students appreciate their peers' encouragement. They often praised their friends during the interviews. They like to motivate and encourage each other, they speak highly of each other, they all want to help improve their family situation, and consequently, their motivation is often driven by financial enhancement. Such value is reflected in the observation that they appear more committed and motivated to study when there is an agreement between friends who are going to university.

Family is a known critical factor for student choice. Since most CIS and NCS parents would like them to have a university education, this generates obedience to parental expectations. In some NCS families, the girls are expected to marry at an earlier age, which can lead to a decrease in their dedication to studying. However, this situation often improves as parents communicate more with schools and interact with Hong Kong society.

Opportunity or opportunity cost

The attitudes and choices of CIS towards their future are strongly associated with their immigrant backgrounds. Some were involuntary immigrant students. They started new schooling in Hong Kong because of family decisions not to leave them behind in the Mainland. The uprooting process, however, is not without cost. Their experience can lead to a tendency towards wanting to relocate back to their hometown when the opportunity arises. In such a situation, engagement with society can become superficial, resulting in a lack of interest in Hong Kong and low motivation to connect with the city. Their understanding of Hong Kong becomes limited to their experience in school and interactions with their schoolmates, and so the picture they get is less than comprehensive.

> I don't have enough understanding of Hong Kong; I'm not interested in getting to know it. I watch the news but won't dig deep into it… Actually, I didn't want to come [to Hong Kong], I told my family I didn't want to come. At that time, my family was in Hong Kong already… and they thought it wasn't a good idea to leave me alone [in the Mainland], so they made me come here.
>
> (Chang, CIS, S6)

Opportunity costs. Comparatively, higher education choices in the Mainland seem to be more friendly and conducive to cultivating student dreams. First, the chance to get into Hong Kong universities is much lower. In 2020, only about one in seven students could obtain a place in the University Grants Committee funded universities (UGC, 2020). Though the chance to get into top universities in the Mainland runs to only a single digit, the enrolment ratio for higher education generally in the Mainland is more than 80% (Ministry of Education of the PRC, 2020). Failing to secure a place in a UGC-funded university will undoubtedly be a big disappointment to any DSE student irrespective of their cultural origin. The sense of agency in constructing a desirable future has been underlined in our interviews with CIS. With the Mainland's recent socio-economic development, especially in the Greater Bay Area, further studies in Chinese universities would have gained greater recognition among CIS than before.

As both Hong Kong and Mainland societies have evolved rapidly, young Mainland immigrants are also appropriating their aspirations for future development. After gaining first-hand experience in Hong Kong, they can often feel bleak about their future in the territory after graduation. Limited opportunities to obtain a PSE can defeat their confidence and reinforce self-prophecy fulfilment in that negative expectations can prevent them from improving their disadvantaged situation.

> When we were studying in the Mainland, we heard that Hong Kong was a well-developed society. When you (we) studied here, you (we) would get many opportunities…When you (we) have got here, you (we) found so many people in Hong Kong. But there are only (government funded) eight universities, you (we) have to compete with so many people for one degree. It may be up to thousands of people fighting for one degree, you (we) are not competent for that. And now, here [Hong Kong], the economic growth has peaked, like most are a customer service industry, but many other industries have not yet developed. Many industries have their factories in the Mainland because the land is too expensive here. If I can't get into university here, I will instead go back to the Mainland.
> (Zhang, CIS, S6)

> When I decided to come to Hong Kong, I thought the local education level would be high and more opportunities than in the Mainland. But after I got here, I realised the competition was very keen, many people fighting for a university place… Not much development potential for me. But back in the Mainland, some developing cities are now providing plenty of job opportunities. So, the job prospect is much better there than in Hong Kong.
>
> (Jin, CIS, S6)

In contrast to the CIS, and against the odds, evidence shows that NCS students motivated to achieve their life goals have successfully combated their disadvantaged social situation. The secret is how to remove their life obstacles and unleash their potentials. Pinky is an example. She is optimistic about higher education, with a more hopeful attitude towards their future.

> Hong Kong is a place that has given me a life worth living and education which I wouldn't have been given if I were in another country like Nepal. Education is not the most crucial thing there. But in places more developed like Hong Kong, you actually have a chance. Even if we are ethnic minorities, we still have a chance to make our future bright. My parents have never been to university. They really want me to work in a good environment, unlike them. They really also want me to have a really bright future. That really motivates me. They also told me about their past, which made me feel bad about it. That even motivates me to work harder… They are always on my mind 24/7 and they are the biggest inspiration for me.
> (Pinky, NCS, S6)

Educational inclusion

Both CIS and NCS students express that they lack chances or channels to mingle with local students in their educational process. Students are streamed from S4 to S6 classes according to their academic achievements, subject disciplines, language preference (English or Chinese medium), and ethnicity. In this way, CIS and NCS students interactions with elite HKMS only happen in occasional class meetings or school events. For the three busy senior secondary years, the academically oriented youth are fully occupied by HKDSE examination revision, while those less academically inclined may focus on part-time jobs. Meeting with local students just once or twice does not foster sustainable friendships among CIS, NCS students, and HKMS. Any meaningful and long-lasting relationships demand quality interaction and intentional actions.

Some have pointed out that because they lack the occasion to mingle with local students in an educational environment, due to limited exposure, their understanding of local culture is hindered, while at the same time, they feel not being understood by the locals.

> We just hang out with our own Mainland friends in this school. I think we don't have much interaction with other schools to know local students. I wish we would be given more chances to have exchange and interaction with students from other schools, but at the moment there isn't such an opportunity. From Project WeCan, I met some students from other schools, but we weren't in contact after that.
>
> (Celia, CIS, S6)

Co-ethnic socialisation cements the sense of in-group belonging, but, at the same time, it reduces outgroup interaction. Context is highly relevant to understanding educational inclusion and societal diversity. Quite a few students preferred to study in groups with someone sharing a similar cultural background.

> Maybe because there are many Mainland students with a similar background in my class, I feel easier to adapt to the local education. There are 23 students in my class, it's like only 4-5 of them are Hong Kong locals. But I don't know much about the local students
>
> (Liang, CIS, S6)

> Yes, feeling included. Because my school friends don't treat me like a person from another world.
>
> (Tamer, NCS, S6)

Either actively or passively, racial discrimination can be traced in public settings, such as public transportation. Tydor referred to an incident of his NCS friend.

> Sometimes when we are traveling at MTR, when some NCS people sit next to the Chinese people, they will stand up and move away, ignore us or stand away.
>
> (Tydor, NCS, S5)

> I think racial discrimination isn't that bad in my school. Personally, I don't experience anything like racial discrimination. The attitude is more like 'so-so'. For example, most of the people, the teachers and local Chinese students are really nice to me. But some of the people are bad.
>
> (Neil, NCS, S6)

Language is often the source of misunderstanding and is a recognised learning barrier.

> We are just not confident enough to express our tone. Chinese is really hard; it has eight tones, and you have to speak in the right tone so they can understand you. Especially we are learning traditional Chinese, so when we write, we have a lot of strokes to write. We can understand what people are saying, but we can't speak...Most of the teachers have alerted us to the importance of Chinese, but we have never been in a situation where we really need Chinese as we are in a school full of NCS students.
>
> (Pinky, NCS, S6)

Reality checks are always better appreciated in hindsight. But, perhaps, students need to have more systematic encouragement and advice to guide them to navigate their language as well as other subject learning in school to improve their learning effectiveness.

School support

Neoliberalism has shaped the nature of education in a market-driven and meritocratic society. Education has gained social recognition as a commodity, desirable for economic gains and vertical class mobility. In a way, it reinforces the social control of formal schooling. Students who can prove themselves capable in examination-focused schooling are rewarded, while those who fail to fit in the system are punished. Of course, the HKDSE examinations are critical portals for entering into university education. The university admission rate is an indicator for assessing the performance of teachers and schools, and the PSE student enrolment profile is public knowledge. Consequently, this governs the behaviour of teachers. Student-centred teaching has been substituted by assessment-task learning in senior secondary education. In this ethos, it comes as no surprise that senior secondary students are uncertain about their PSE.

From interviews with teachers from five secondary schools with a significant number of CIS and NCS students and low SES HKMS, career and higher education guidance is given some emphasis. Some schools even started the career guidance from the first year of secondary education.

> Our career guidance started from Secondary One. We began our aptitude test in the first year we met them, and the test was implemented in the

following years. We compared and monitored their changes to see whether their aptitudes were steady or changed a lot. Based on that, we gave students suggestions on their future careers.

(Tom, Panel Head of Career & Guidance Team)

Teachers asserted that they would give one-on-one tutorials and guidance to students and that a united effort was rendered by career teachers, the headmaster, and main subjects teachers of all senior grades to provide detailed and practical suggestions for students.

Students who aim at higher education would get more academic supports from teachers. They have their own study room, tutorials from excellent alumni, or mock interviews from native English speakers. Students who aim at vocational careers could also get support from multiple pathways, including applied learning, internships in social organizations or companies, and suggestions on vocational development.

(Teacher Choi, Career master)

As students vary in their plans, schools also have corresponding policies to help them. For example, one student wanted to make dessert, we suggested she explored Taiwan, another student wanted to be a chef, he went to Japan to further his dream. We provide many applied learning chances, for example, hotel management, fashion design, dancing, etc. We want the students to know that university is not the only way for them to fulfil their career dream. For example, if you (they) want to be an engineer, university is not the only path. Actually, there's a spectrum of pathways to choose from.

(Assistant Principal Stephen)

However, despite these claims, school principals acknowledged the limitations of schools in helping students work out their futures for different reasons. Some are systemic issues related to educational policy, and some are related to personal self-motivation.

I believe the government should do something for NCS students education. Why is their Chinese still not good enough after coming to Hong Kong for so many years? We want them to be more engaged in learning and help them get into universities, but it's a pity that they are barred just because of the Chinese issue. We know a lot of these NCS students who hadn't learned Chinese systematically from their primary school. There's not much we could do because they hadn't learned Chinese continuously for six years. It's complicated. Sometimes we have to see them go back to their home country for higher education.

(Assistant Principal Karl)

> They (NCS students) will complain that "if you want me to study your Chinese and Hong Kong culture, why don't you study something about my home country?" We need to understand their feelings why they are not that keen to learn Chinese.
>
> (Principal Crowford)

With the implementation of the mother tongue (Chinese) education policy, the Chinese Language standards for NCS students concentrated schools can be high. But the reality of this is that in order to meet the policy requirements and raise the standard of local-born NCS students, the Chinese Language standard in these schools is raised higher than their Chinese readiness. Even NCS students who graduated from local primary schools are found not to be up to the bar.

> The implementation of the policy of Chinese has created real problems for the school to educate the NCS students. We, on the one hand, have to uphold the Chinese standard. But, on the other hand, only a few NCS students can study mainstream Chinese. If NCS students have no decent capabilities in Chinese, they can't pass the exams and meet societal needs. They cannot have a good job serving the whole city.
>
> (Principal Crowford)

Some career teachers or principals opined that the Chinese criteria for ethnic minority students should be lowered to enhance their aspiration for higher education and acknowledge their potential in other subjects, citing the international students' situation as an example. These students are enrolled in local universities using a different channel. English is the medium of instruction at most universities. Therefore, the language policy for international students could also be applicable for ethnic minority students. And the fact is they can excel and actualise themselves in higher education if they are permitted to use English rather than Chinese. By contrast, those who have no plans to commit to high-end study are not interested in complicated Chinese reading or writing, which are not essential for manual work like driving, logistics, or canteen work.

As far as the CIS are concerned, teachers maintain that they have better foundations in Chinese and Mathematics than other subjects. Moreover, most of them treasure their opportunity to study in Hong Kong and accept their responsibility in making it to higher education. Their biggest challenge is, however, passing English.

> We know a lot of cases (CIS) who have high grades in other subjects but only can get a level 2 in English. Then they have to repeat S6, or else some will go back to Mainland China because they think they can't conquer the obstacles in English in Hong Kong.
>
> (Assistant Principal Karl)

Some teachers have observed an emerging trend of CIS considering the Mainland an alternative destination for higher education.

> A large proportion of students from Mainland China would choose to go back to the Mainland after leaving school. And the Chinese universities

they'll attend are pretty famous. Okay, they may not be able to study the disciplines they desire in Hong Kong, but they can fulfil their academic dream in Mainland China. We think it's a better choice for them.

(Assistant Principal Karl)

However, teachers stated that one of the concerns of CIS are their family structure and family support. As most of the parents of CIS are busy with work, students are deficient in their family's educational and emotional support. It is not uncommon for CIS to live with relatives in Hong Kong independent of their Mainland parents. As a result, they learn to be self-reliant in tackling their academic, emotional, and financial problems. Indeed, a large number of senior CIS are engaged in part-time jobs while managing their full-time secondary schooling.

I saw a student always sleeping in the class. I talked to her and she told me she has a part-time job in a convenience store after school till 11 pm every day to help her father pay some rent. Her father has no job, and they live in a subdivided flat near the school. I believe she is not the single case in our school. She plans to work full-time to support the family upon graduation rather than to go for further studying. Under such conditions, it is not easy for them to concentrate on learning at school.

(Teacher Wong, Career master)

As for mainstream students admitted to low attaining classes of low banding schools, teachers believe motivation is their biggest challenge.

Some students even ask us to stop persuading them to study. One student told me that he could claim his right to the village house as part of his inheritance. He indicated that he could rent out two layers of his village house for HK$30,000 each month. With that income, he doesn't have to work for a living. Education is clearly not his goal.

(Teacher Hui, Career master)

The real issues of motivation

Most of the teachers think that the crux of the educational problems for the NCS students lies outside financial needs because there are channels for applying for scholarships, grants, and loans from the government and NGOs should they wish to study further. Instead, the real issue of motivation is the lack of balanced senior secondary education pathways between vocational and educational, which obstructs their aspiration for self-actualisation. Teachers and principals opine that the government should have more specific programmes, funds, and personnel for new arrivals and low-income local teenagers, accounting for 40–50% in some schools. At the same time, the policies and funds are too broad for underprivileged students to consider their most desirable future education and development. Though the income may not be an obstacle for families, teachers face some difficulties cooperating with families. For example, some CIS families have minimal knowledge about the local society, and their goals are too high for their children. While for ethnic minority parents, language is a big problem as some parents do not understand English.

The interview data show that student choices are impacted by a multitude of factors, namely the highly selective education culture, family socio-economic capital, personal academic inclination, peers, gender, and teachers. Unfortunately, many of these factors are barriers to cultivating the full potentialities of CIS and NCS students. Language is critical for mental development and a necessary thinking tool for meaningful and practical learning.

Students from both mainstream and non-mainstream cultures are challenged by either Chinese, English, or both. It causes disaffections, leads to a self-fulfilling prophecy, and generates a loss of appetite for self-actualisation in the city. In addition, their aspirations for a desirable future are mediated by their own cultural background and level of acculturation (e.g., language). The interplay of all these forces has made decision-making for the future a complication for the students. However, as reflected by teachers and school leaders, student motivation matters. If education can fire up student motivation by showing a positive way forward, it will release their energy and be more devoted to the task. Unfortunately, the senior secondary school curriculum does not meet the diverse talents and aspirations of the students, higher education, and employers. Too few NCS students have adequate Chinese language skills, and too few CIS and low-income mainstream Chinese have adequate English skills to equip them for desirable future development. This long-standing issue needs to be fully addressed and is a crucial issue for the well-being of these youth.

References

Brooks, R., Gupta, A., Jayadeva, S., & Abrahams, J. (2020). Students' views about the purpose of higher education: A comparative analysis of six European countries. *Higher Education Research & Development*, 1–14. https://doi.org/10.1080/07294360.2020.1830039

Education Bureau. (2014). *Guideline on life planning education and career guidance for secondary school.* https://careerguidance.edb.hkedcity.net/edb/export/sites/default/lifeplanning/.pdf/about-careers-guidance/CLP-Guide_E_r3.pdf

Emmons, R. A. (2005). Striving for the sacred: Personal goals, life meaning, and religion. *Journal of Social Issues, 61*(4), 731–745. https://doi.org/10.1111/J.1540-4560.2005.00429.X.

Ho, Y. F., & Leung, S. M. A. (2016). Career guidance in Hong Kong: From policy ideal to school practice. *The Career Development Quarterly, 64*(3), 216–230. https://doi.org/10.1002/cdq.12056.

Kazi, A. S., & Akhlaq, A. (2017). Factors affecting students' career choice. *Journal of Research & Reflections in Education (JRRE), 11*(2), 187–196.

Ma, Y., Siu, A., & Tse, W. S. (2018). The role of high parental expectations in adolescents' academic performance and depression in Hong Kong. *Journal of Family Issues, 39*(9), 2505–2522. https://doi.org/10.1177%2F0192513X18755194.

Ministry of Education of the PRC. (2020). *Ignite the youth and age in 70 years*. http://www.moe.gov.cn/

Organization for Economic Cooperation and Development. (2014). *OECD reviews of vocational education and training: Skills beyond school*. http://www.oecd.org/education/innovation-education/skillsbeyondschool.htm

Ryan, R. M., & Deci, E. L. (2000). Intrinsic and extrinsic motivations: Classic definitions and new directions. *Contemporary Educational Psychology, 25*(1), 54–67. https://doi.org/10.1006/ceps.1999.1020.

University Grants Committee (UGC). (2020). *General statistics on UGC-funded institutions/programme*. https://cdcf.ugc.edu.hk/cdcf/searchUniv.action?lang=EN

Yuen, Y. M. C., & Cheung, A. (2018). Comparing school and civic engagement of Chinese and non-Chinese youth in Hong Kong (in Chinese). *Journal of Youth Studies, 21*(1), 150–164. https://search.ebscohost.com/login.aspx?direct=true&db=asn&AN=136266571&site=eds-live

Yuen, Y. M. C., Cheung, A. C. K., Leung, C. S. S., Tang, H. H. H., & Chan, L. C. H. (2021). The Success and obstacle factors in pursuing post-secondary education: The differences between Hong Kong mainstream and non-mainstream students (In Chinese). *Education Journal, 49*(2), 137–160.

11 Connecting Youth, Promoting Well-Being, and Facilitating Productive Engagement for Equitable Schooling

Tackling the risk of being double disadvantaged

The previous chapters have offered some rich empirical data and evidence suggesting how the quality of teaching and learning experience varies from school to school and classroom to classroom. Reflecting upon the student narratives, it would appear that immigrant or minority status is nearly always accompanied by socio-economic disadvantage. Such a disadvantage contributes to their educational impediments, frustration, under-performance, and a palpable lack in life planning. Consistent with international studies (Abatemarco et al., 2021; Francis et al., 2017), these disadvantaged youth struggle with poor academic inputs, poor teacher quality, and less resilience in combating the odds. Consequently, they often live under the stress of being excluded in the high-stake examination-oriented learning environment.

Chapter 1 has highlighted that youth are future pillars, a driving force, and valuable assets for building just and democratic societies and a sustainable world (United Nations, 2015). However, to this end, Hong Kong education has not responded adequately to the call for effectively nurturing youth as productive and responsible citizens for a better society. Data have unfolded that the 2019 social movement and prolonged pandemic has exacerbated the well-being and social connectedness of youth. Research (Zhu et al., 2021) has shown how an increased number of youth exhibit negative mindsets such as suicidal ideation, depression, loneliness, and social anxiety, especially during the COVID-19 pandemic social and physical distancing.

S6, the final year of secondary education, is certainly the most challenging year. Many S6 students felt uncertain and vulnerable about their future. The physical and social distancing has put them in an isolated and lonely condition, whilst the mental distancing from the education system has diminished their agency and aspirations for the future. The following few case examples give us a glimpse into their thoughts about their educational struggles with S6, running up to the HKDSE and beyond.

> During the Covid-19 class suspension, all DSE mock exams were cancelled. Without mock exams, we had no clue about our standards and could not

DOI: 10.4324/9780429439315-11

make any psychological preparation. Having said that, studying at home was better than studying at school. Because my classmates did not care much about their academic results, the classroom ethos did not help... The switch to online teaching was terrible, much worse than physical classes. Facing the screen without a real connection with the teacher was really inefficient.

After receiving my DSE results, I didn't have any communication exchanges with teachers or friends, as I scored poorly. So I chose to do the Foundation Diploma (an additional year of secondary education). My parents have no idea what PSE is about, so they let me choose. They encouraged me to seek opportunities in the Mainland as I am now doing the Found. Dip., I find it hard to catch up as everything is in English. My secondary school is CMI. I have to relearn everything in English once again.

I don't think my secondary school has given me an opportunity for future development. The school focused on elite students. The resources were skewed to the high attaining students – it is unfair. Motivated teachers were allocated to the elite class. For example, all of us failed in the DSE maths. Our maths teacher failed all of us.

(Wai, HKMCS, Foundation Diploma, Year 1)

Staying at home for independent studies was one challenge to Kwan during the class suspension period. With limited space and a limited attention span in revising, her DES results were compromised.

For a long time, since the 2019 social incident, we stopped physical classes. We stayed at home and received no support whatsoever from the school, just like sheep without a shepherd. We have to take care of our own studies...During the epidemic and before the DSE, I suffered from insomnia for one month. The condition persisted, and I could not overcome it. I tried to accept it until I finished DSE. Of course, I didn't do well in DSE, and I worried about my future. What path could I choose? I am now studying Data Science for Associate Degree, I found that I was totally unprepared. I had no prior knowledge of the programme for one thing. I like Maths and thought it was about Maths, but it is about computer stuff which I have never learned at school...moreover, I learned many more valuable things from outside organizations than from my secondary school.

My life goal is to get to university, no matter whether I failed once or twice. Anyway, I wish that eventually I could get there. If I really could, then I would apply for grants and loans from the government. And I will have to repay it within 20 years.

(Kwan, HKMCS, Year 1, Associate Degree)

Resilience does not come naturally. Sandy used to doubt her academic ability and despaired about the future. Fortunately, with the encouragement of teachers, she saw the light at the end of the tunnel.

> During my past years, I was really introverted. I had a lot of doubts about myself, so my confidence was low. When I was younger, maybe my first three years in secondary school, I only had a few friends. I didn't want to talk to anyone. Only when I started joining Maths duties in school and found that my strength was in language and all that did it gave me more confidence to do things.
>
> I was actually really lost. And then I talked to my teachers about further study. They were like, why don't you go for it and just try? I was scared because I doubted my ability as well. I was like, can I really do it? Can I really pursue it? Because one of my problems was a financial situation with my family. So, I was thinking about whether I should continue studying or not. My class teacher really pushed me because she thought that I could do it. She was saying, "Don't take a gap year. Just keep going. Think about the financial thing later because the university will help you, I was like 'okay'". So that's why I'm here.
>
> (Sandy, NCS, Year 1, B.A.)

Feeling unsure and confused are common among S6 students during the critical educational and life transition. Below is Amy's thought process about the future:

> A lot of us were really confused during our senior years from S1 to S6. Because teachers already started rushing us in S4 telling us that, "you need to know what to do and figure out what you want". I wasn't sure what I really wanted to do. But then I wanted to see if this or that was something I could do and I could pursue. I was still looking at different possibilities at that time. But this is the one I want to focus on right now. I won't say my former teachers were very bad, but they could have been better, and I wanted to be better than what they did. They really far off from each other.
>
> My family is very supportive of my studies. But my family income is not sufficient for my brother and me to study at university, so financial aid is very important for us.
>
> (Amy, NCS, Year 1, BEd)

Charlotte is an energetic and self-motivated Nepalese fresher who has started to pick up the speed to catch up with her university studies. However, when she learned how much she lagged behind the others, she wished that her senior secondary school teachers could have better prepared her for higher education.

> I don't think I received a lot of help from the school in general. Obviously, teachers were very motivating, but I definitely wouldn't say that the teachers' teaching was the factor that got me into HKU. I definitely will say that it was my own will ... Teachers were talking about DSE, but I didn't know about DSE because the education system in Nepal and in Hong Kong is so different. So, I didn't know what to expect. Until S4 I had no idea which university I wanted to go to or what course or what I wanted to do ... Not knowing what I had to expect in DSE was definitely very difficult ... my former teachers and school generally didn't prepare me for this study path.

> There were so many teachers that I could point at that didn't do anything for us. Telling us to work hard and do past papers is not helping. It's their job to teach us. So many of my classmates wanted to be physical trainers and didn't want to go to university. That was their choice which was okay, but the teachers made them think that it was not okay. Some students wanted to be a painter, and they went to VTC, which was okay too. They don't need to go to university to be successful. But the teachers told them that they had to go to university, the university is everything, and the university is the end game.
>
> (Charlotte, NCS, Year 1)

Gill is English, and her financial situation is no different from the other NCS students. With a score of 12, she could only seek a higher diploma outlet after her secondary education. Her experience was not that positive due to low teacher expectations.

> I think they did not expect us to score high marks in DSE. The NCS students, many of them come from the countries like the Philippines, Nepal, and Pakistan. I think there were 22-24 Pakistani students in my S6 class. But for my friend's school they have more than 30 Pakistani students. Among them, maybe only 5 continued to study after DSE. Most of them ended up working after they left school.

> So, we (our school) did not really talk much about PSE. Only one time did the Police come and say that we could join them, even if we did not do well in DSE. They can offer us training programmes and after a while, we can be police officers. But it is required to have certain Chinese proficiency, so the NCS students in my class were all excluded.
>
> (Gill, British, Year 1)

M. Gurung finished grade 7 in Nepal and arrived in Hong Kong without any Chinese proficiency. As a result, she had to repeat primary five, and her central problem was rooted in lacking the host language and self-confidence.

> The major problem for me has always been the language. So I studied really hard for Cantonese but the first year I was crying because it was so hard…it was about what I was going to do, it was pressurized, and I couldn't focus on my studies. I only had 1-2 years to catch up and I felt like I was rushed to think about what to study. Being an NCS student in Hong Kong, I don't think we NCS students have a bright future here. Even local students themselves think it's hard for them to get a good job. I thought to myself that no matter how hard I study, I am not going to have a future here anyway, so why would I study? So, I performed badly in my DSE because of that. I gave up on studying in S4…Secondary schools focus more on their own reputations than their students, especially band 1 & 2 schools.
>
> I want EMI kids to be able to receive the help they need and deserve. Providing help is necessary, but spreading awareness of the help available is vital. Being in Hong Kong, everyone has to be equal. There are other local kids whose parents can afford everything they need, while non-Chinese children like us struggle to study and work to support their families.
> (M. Gurung, Nepalese, Foundation Diploma, Year 1)

Despite the fact that Fung is local Hong Kong, he too has experienced tremendous stress before, during, and after his HKDSE education.

> During the DSE, I faced incredible pressure to the extent that I fell sick. Severe flu. I went to see the doctor three times in the first week of my DSE exams. I was on antibiotics for half a month. It was an extremely painful experience for me to go through DSE. I cried in the exam hall. Then I felt disappointed, stressed and lost. I don't know about the future. Because soon after I finished the exams, I knew I would have failed. Like during the English exam, I fell asleep because of the medicine. I got a "2" in English. Then I knew doing an Associate Degree was my fate. But I was so uncomfortable about this option. Every night I questioned myself why I had fallen sick during the exam period? I was so puzzled – I didn't know how to face the DSE results.
>
> In secondary school, everything was based on rote learning. It focused on our memory power on the date, facts and incidents. The DSE exam syllabi were just like many dictations. We joked about this kind of learning as "testing your writing speed" to recall the information we have memorized. As now I am doing an Associate Degree, we are required to have a deep understanding of the materials and provide a personal stance and reflections on them. Especially I study History, I need to understand why we Chinese

were being subject to the other in the Opium War. Critical thinking is very important.

(Fung, HKMCS, Associate Degree, Year 2)

The vivid memories of these students in going through the HKDSE hurdle invite us to consider the vitality of analysing the school ethos, teacher quality, the pedagogical and student support issues they experienced.

A call for teaching for a robust understanding

Socially disadvantaged students are concentrated in low-banding secondary schools, which are also under-resourced, and have less access to motivated and experienced teachers. Moreover, they are less likely to access quality support outside school. Research consistently shows that students from immigrant or low-income families tend to cluster in low streaming or disadvantaged schools, making for a double disadvantage (Bourdieu & Passeron, 1977; Coleman, 1990; Francis et al., 2017; Kennedy, 2012; Yuen et al., 2021). As reported by the students, this brings multiple challenges. First, the majority overlap with low family SES and struggle with quality home-work support. Second, they receive a low level of cognitive demand from teachers. In particular, they are engaged at a low level of subject learning and have fewer opportunities to go through productive intellectual struggles and sense-making. Third, they shared a common concern of insufficient content coverage compared to elite classes or high-attaining schools.

Students reiterated the detrimental impact of achievement groupings on student academic self-efficacy and learning quality. There is solid evident segmented participation in classroom learning. The formal curriculum is skewed to prepare the more able students for the public university entrance examination, HKDSE, through academic grouping. The core subjects, either English Language or Chinese Language, are not offered the same level of cognitive demand to all students. Neither are all students offered equitable access to content, agency, ownership, and identity. There is genuine concern over the decided lack of a conducive learning environment that nurtures productive habits for all learners. Consequently, teachers need to address the pedagogical content knowledge issue. The instructional strategies must be diversified to stimulate students' intellectual engagement and social interactions – providing a positive feedback loop for boosting self-confidence in learning. Such a strategy can increase the sense of ownership of all learners.

Our evidence has shown that tackling the Chinese Language learning of NCS students remains the most enduring challenge. First of all, the aims of the Chinese curriculum should promote the active engagement of all rather than the few. Likewise, the core content should allow all students to access the same opportunities to express correct and incorrect answers. The opportunity to learn is connected with the quality of the content. All students should be equipped to develop problem-solving skills, knowing the vital strategies in discerning the essential aspects. Secondly, teachers and school leaders are aware of narrowing the attainment gap and stopping the increase of under-achievers. However, schools fail to provide the same quality of Chinese Language teaching to all students. Neither do teachers possess the same level of expectations for Chinese and NCS students. It is unequal. Third, the pedagogy varies from high-attaining to low-attaining schools. Pedagogy for easy Chinese is widely perceived to be tolerant and relaxed, spoon-feeding, with fewer opportunities for independent studies. The ongoing stereotyping and low expectations for students from diverse, disadvantaged backgrounds have caused low self-esteem, poor agency, and low aspirations for life. Finally, the wealth gap between rich and poor continues to worsen. Ongoing capital inequality means unequal access to advice and guidance, potential disengagement, a lack of practice support, less advice on curriculum choices and career pathways, etc. Labelling impacts such as engaging and disengaging students from different backgrounds must be taken seriously, and proper talent management administered.

School culture

The previous chapters have unfolded the situations that secondary school students have to face. Student voices are valuable evidence for diagnosing the educational needs in transforming senior secondary education into more relevant and effective talent cultivation. This helps foster the positive engagement, well-being, and connectedness of students towards attaining their desired future. School curriculum is a social construction reflecting the core values of society (Lawton, 1973). As such, the notion of normality is not a natural phenomenon. Culture is similar to values in that it is a social construction and it is connected with a set of social norms, principles, and rules. Therefore, culture must be analysed within the social context.

Hong Kong schools are entrusted with the task of improving social mobility and cohesion. Education and social change mirror each other. Bernstein (2018) argues that the realisation of formal educational knowledge necessitates three systems: curriculum, pedagogy, and evaluation to validate knowledge in its transmission. The socialisation of school knowledge is to frame students into a specific type of experience to serve multiple societal needs. Hong Kong education has been shaped by its core economic and industrialising values of free-market competition. Under the impact of Confucianism, respect, obedience, and work ethics values are emphasised in the formal school curriculum and pedagogical practice. When considering the relevance of education for preparing the youth for a desirable future, attention is drawn to appreciate the unique sociopolitical fabric of Hong Kong society as it shapes the direction of education. In particular, Hong Kong society is now entering a new transition with a strong emphasis on harmonising its development with Guangdong and

Macao, collectively known as the Greater Bay Area (Greater Bay Area, 2019). The Hong Kong core values are revitalising to suit and support the new phase of development and have a new bearing on the school curriculum and youth development.

The assimilated and exclusive school culture

Student narratives expose the cultural and academic assimilation of the education system through the implementation of the standardised curriculum and assessment practices. The student voices demonstrate that secondary schools are inhibited in responding to student diversity with regard to the depth of learning (Skerrett & Hargreaves, 2008). Immigrant and ethnic minority students are disadvantaged by mono-cultural schooling that does not recognise student diversity or connect their cultural identities and expressions with academic pursuits (Banks, 2015). Those who struggle to fit into the super-utilitarian education system remain in a state of vulnerability and battle with self-doubt, frustrations, unproductive beliefs, low self-esteem, and, in some cases, self-victimisation.

Student voices are strong evidence to prove that intergroup relations among ethnic Han Chinese groups and between the Chinese and ethnic minority South/Southeast Asian groups are disconnected. Students adhere to their co-ethnic groups and seldom step out of their comfort zone to reach out to other cultural groups. The minimalist approach to friendship building only reinforces cultural stereotypes and discrimination towards one another. This is a significant impediment to meaningful educational inclusion in Hong Kong classrooms.

As solutions to the hegemonic education and social system, the bottom-up student voices must be acknowledged. Furthermore, all school campuses must have an inclusive policy, cultivating an ethos of diversity to promote intergroup relations and collaboration. Native Hong Kong students cannot be ignorant of their non-native friends and vice versa, as today's society is highly interconnected and contextualised. But placing students in intercultural contexts without proper instructional guidance may lead them to develop feelings of superiority or inferiority, which can be counter-productive (Hurtado et al., 2002). Therefore, schools should provide clear guidelines on teaching classes of ethnically diverse students as an integral aspect of good practice (e.g., Arkoudis et al., 2013).

Preparation for PSE and development

Echoing Chapter one, PSE consists of complex institutional hierarchies that perpetuate racial and class inequalities (Kim, 2014; Urdan & Bruchmann, 2018). Following the mass of PSE in Hong Kong, there is a stratified pattern of privileged and underprivileged student groups across the PSIs (Kember, 2010). The need for developing diversity strategies for helping students to complete their studies successfully has come under renewed public attention (Nutt & Hardman, 2019).

The common barriers for PSE choices and planning are language, social networks, and financial assistance. Like elsewhere (Sadowski, 2013), immigrant-origin students who graduated from the mainstream secondary education system usually target second-tier or even foundational level PSE. Educational interventions are concentrated on boosting their academic English Language proficiency. Aside from addressing the language issue, it is still the necessary means for them to turn around their challenging social circumstances.

Due to family financial needs and familial roles, the majority of underprivileged students have expressed their eagerness to share the family financial burden after their education. Some have strong motivation to carry on academic success or future work, especially students who have determined interests in a career (Chapter 10). But for students who are in the middle ground, it would be challenging to encourage them to get involved in secondary and post-secondary planning as they have low impetus and inspiration. This problem cannot be easily handled, and no one should replace the students themselves to make their most meaningful decisions because autonomy is a priority for future success (Gutiérrez & Tomás, 2019). Whereas from the teachers' perspective and experience, it is the responsibility of school and society to provide real-world information to broaden student horizons and provide support and suggestions for them. As motivation is never unitary (Ryan & Deci, 2000), it may be more profound for schools to respect students' autonomy and help to foster students' competence and their sense of relatedness with the society in the process of whole-person education. Schools must then consider the inclusion of whole-person development in the implementation of curriculum changes.

Focus on significant others

Internationally, parental care and teacher support not only boost students' competence, self-efficacy, and self-concept beliefs (Bouchey & Harter, 2005; Wang & Neihart, 2015), but they also help them with education planning and choices (Holland, 2011; Sjaastad, 2012). They are significant in influencing the self-concept and attitude of students toward PSE. In Hong Kong, the CIS and NCS students rated significant others higher than HKMS (Yuen et al., 2021). The previous chapters reveal the significant factor of agency and parental expectation in the pursuit of higher education. Significant others (especially mothers) are influential persons who substantially impact the PSE choices and planning. Parents are both valuable and underdeveloped resources for schools. Engaging parents in whole education promote home-school collaboration.

Despite strong evidence proving that family SES backgrounds and heritage capital link with school performance and satisfaction, the parental factor has also been highlighted as a positive mitigating factor for raising the confidence and resilience of immigrant students, especially in terms of giving encouragement, financial assistance, and trust in their academic ability (Orupabo et al.,

2020; Sandoval-Hernández & Białowolski, 2016; Stanton-Salazar, 2001). Apple (2006) argues that social capital is not a zero-sum game between the upper and the lower classes (p. 458).

Successful alumni are potential role models and sources of inspiration for ethnic minorities to raise hopes of being successful in a competitive society (Chapters 7, 8, and 10). Alumni, family influence, and the successful career of relatives all convey family expectations on students, and parental respect for a student's interest in choosing PSE subjects is appreciated.

Higher parental expectations entail higher educational aspirations (Gale & Parker, 2015; Nicholas-Omoregbe, 2010). The pursuit of PSE has become a significant educational concern for all youth irrespective of their cultural backgrounds. Even though some students did not have a clear goal and direction in PSE, they felt it necessary to seek PSE opportunities and is a desirable goal for every student. However, talks on PSE information and the desire for PSE information or information on practical in-job experiences and diverse PSE pathways are not given due priority. Student feedback confirms the comment of Ladd (2012) on the negligence of the needs of the disadvantaged students resulting in the ineffectiveness of educational implementation plans, which cannot be attained without first targeting the needs of disadvantaged students to increase their attainment or diminish the inequality existing between the advantaged and disadvantaged students. Getting students ready for PSE and connecting them with successful pathways deserves much more deliberate attention.

Curricular implications: Promoting well-being and educating the mind and the soul

Well-being and inner strengths are vital to combat negativity and to thrive and achieve. Resilience is defined as good outcomes in spite of serious threats to adaptation or development (Yeager & Dweck, 2012; p. 303). Chapter 3 has underscored that the role of spiritual health in youth well-being. Academic achievement, by contrast, does not directly impact youth well-being, even though it is a desirable goal to pursue. Student narratives (Chapter 4) have shown that religious youth are resilient, positive, and can handle aversive life events better. Finding the meaning in life renews their spirit and endorses their purpose of doing. In contrast, the HKDSE induces excessive stress in students and causes them to be sick and unable to perform in the actual examinations. Many students have experienced severe reactions during the HKDSE season caused by biological, physiological, psychological, and mental issues (Lo, 2020).

It is a high calling to provide an education for holistic development, cultivating self-agency and resilience. Rotter (1966) regards locus of control as a vital resilience factor. The highly motivated CIS and NCS students and low-income HKMS are also highly aspired for PSE. They believe that diligence and frugality are imperative attributes to academic success and can change disadvantageous life circumstances. Their parents have demonstrated how a positive attitude towards adversity can overcome adversity (Chapter 10). Like international studies (Devlin,

2010), Hong Kong youth struggle with their multiple roles in cultural, economic, and family dimensions and often sacrifice their student role or work part-time to support their schooling or future PSE aspirations (Chapters 5, 8, and 10).

Curricular implications: Teaching for social-emotional competence

Much has been discussed about the challenges facing students. They are described as digital natives, although some are not necessarily literate. Hong Kong youth live under a highly stressful global and mental health crisis and learn to adjust to the new normal ways of school operation. During the unprecedented COVID-19 epidemic, physical class learning or face-to-face learning was replaced by online virtual learning, requiring students to observe the social distancing and be self-disciplined to attend the examinations. This was a totally unprepared for and critical incident that required schools to transform pedagogical issues to accommodate diverse student needs, especially during the critical HKDSE examination season. Low-income CIS and NCS students were further disadvantaged by the lack of quality teacher inputs or a proper environment to get ready for the HKDSE. Although some schools implemented blended learning in which students could choose what particular modalities of learning they prefer, it cannot be denied that teachers and students found it hard to cope with the sudden change in society. This has revealed all too clearly both the difficulty and the need for better preparation to manage the teaching reality in a world city like Hong Kong.

The school curriculum faces a tough challenge to improve its status and cater to whole-person development of diverse students. This challenge is particularly critical for those directly involved in school guidance and curriculum planning and who are responsible for promoting students' capacity for resilience, developing a friendly approach to enhance their well-being, and building connections for their personal development. The interplay of all these elements determines the pathways of the students. When they navigate the upward educational pathways, they will encounter adversity, challenges, disappointment, and feel vulnerable or disillusioned about their future (Yeager & Dweck, 2012). However, as reflected by teachers and school administrative personnel interviews, one major impediment senior secondary students have to face is their determination or rather lack of it. Hence the school curriculum should be balanced and should aim to cultivate positive mindsets of self-confidence and nurture inner strengths in facing a challenging future by addressing their unproductive beliefs and values.

Curricular implications: Fostering academic success and resilience

Academic resilience has a special place in student life. It is a source of self-confidence, assurance, recognition, and a sense of self-control over academic success and failure (Perez et al., 2009). As shown in the previous chapters, academic resilience does not happen for most underprivileged students. Only a minority of them are armed with resilience to navigate this process successfully. When they do not do well in HKDSE examinations, lack sufficient language proficiency, or encounter unprecedented social incidents and pandemics, this can easily confuse their life planning and future aspirations.

Academic transitions have impacts on self-belief, identity and well-being, and learning. Students who encounter multiple academic and life transitions are vulnerable and run a greater risk of unproductive mindsets. By contrast, positive academic self-efficacy and meaning of life are protective factors for academic engagement and coping with aversive life circumstances. Self-belief is an essential construct to understand the mechanism behind academic motivation and performance (Schunk & Pajares, 2002). In terms of self-efficacy belief, it is an indication of personal abilities in handling learning commitments. It can boost individuals' confidence in personal capabilities in making decisions, being courageous in new initiatives, and overcoming adverse life instances and emotions (Bandura, 1977, 1986, 1997).

The glass ceiling effect is prevalent in many CIS and NCS student thoughts. Most parents have little knowledge of the education and examination systems and cannot afford extra tuition. They become accustomed to having low test scores on their examinations, especially in English Language and/or Chinese Language. Moreover, these students somehow accept that they will not have good results in the HKDSE because their schools are under-resourced. Therefore, the chances to enter university are much slimmer than those in better-resourced schools. Jackson et al. (2014) highlight that the glass ceiling effect is closely related to impacts of intersectionality. Chowdry et al. (2013) accentuate that the glass ceiling effect exists among students from low SES backgrounds and suggests that PSEIs, through outreach programmes, increase PSE aspirations of these students from secondary school for a higher participation rate of low SES students in higher education. Likewise, Williams (2014) opines that glass ceiling effects in PSE can be diminished or eliminated by transforming PSE institutional culture through efforts to overcome hidden racial prejudice and discrimination and the lack of accountability and devise infrastructures of diversity.

Indeed, immigrant students can have strong PSE aspirations and self-efficacy and high expectations for their new education. Resilient immigrant students outperform their native peers despite being placed in a socially disadvantaged situation (Sandoval-Hernández & Białowolski, 2016). Linking the notion of success with the drive of individual students to battle against the odds deserves deliberated attention. Moreover, ethnicity can be a strong base for mobilising resources inside each ethnic HKMS, CBS, CIS, and NCS group. For example, successful alumni and resilient members can be role models and support for younger students to learn about the education system.

Curricular implications: Developing a career identity

In Hong Kong, as a Chinese society, success in examinations links with personal pride, well-being, life planning, and future career advancement. Hence, the competitive educational ethos can be detrimental to low SES and immigrant students, especially if they are not academic-oriented or lack academic agency. Student choices are impacted by multiple elements, including family factors (family of NCS, parents' expectation, siblings), school factors (teacher expectation), academic achievement, peers (friends and role senior graduate students), gender, culture, schools, and teachers (Yuen et al., 2021). For CIS and NCS students, their choices for the future are also impacted by their perceived opportunities, personal capabilities, financial aid, parental expectation, and acculturation (e.g., language) in Hong Kong society.

The EDB (2014) issued the *Guide on Life Planning Education and Career Guidance for Secondary Schools* (1st edition). Senior secondary students often feel very confused and vulnerable about career and life development upon graduation. Cadaret and Hartung (2021) argue that adolescents with marginalised identities are particularly in need of early-career intervention. The student narratives have indicated that the current career intervention programmes are not effective. When students fail in the academic assessments, mainly the HKDSE, they will fall into the thought guilt trap that they are not as worthy as the others, that teachers reject them, and they have no place in society.

All in all, school preparation programmes have not yielded the intended results for equipping the HKDSE graduates for their desired futures (Yuen et al., 2021). They have no clue what to do as they lack the essential professional preparation, knowledge, and advice. There is an urgent call to review the senior secondary curriculum and diversify their attention away from drilling students just for the HKDSE examination towards equipping them more for the workplace. The school curriculum should adopt a broader spectrum of vocational and career education in articulation with the professional education and training (VPET) to equip students with the relevant knowledge, skills, and attitudes for developing their future career self-efficacy and identity. Achieving this, the school curriculum has to be strengthened and streamlined to establish students' higher career self-esteem instead of just organising a few field visits to industry and organisations (Savickas et al., 2009). This will help to alleviate educational failure as low SES, immigrant, and minority students have a greater likelihood of joining the labour market straight after secondary education.

Curricular implications: Teaching for active civic engagement and sustainable citizenship

Cultivating youth for sustainable global development is a global initiative. Youth, irrespective of their sociocultural and political backgrounds and characteristics, are recognised as a driving force and valuable assets for building just and democratic societies and a sustainable world. Each society is responsible for providing the optimal conditions to nurture their talents and future leaders for their social and economic development. School curriculum is often charged with this critical social obligation to systematically prepare students for their future role in social development and building a transparent and effective society. Second, because of the significant role of youth engagement, teaching for active youth participation in the sociocultural, political, pandemic, gender, social inequality issues has been underscored.

Chapter 5 presents teachers' perspectives on the civic engagement of the CIS and NCS students and concludes that deliberate research attention and educational strategies are needed to nurture their connectedness and civic-mindedness. Despite the fact that many of these students desire to build a home in Hong Kong, their behavioural civic engagement has been restricted due to various reasons (Chapters 6 and 8). This is particularly true in Hong Kong since the two recent major social incidents supported by mainstream students in 2014 and in 2019 have raised serious concerns about youth engagement, well-being, connectedness, and their capability in life planning (Ng, 2020; Shek, 2020; Yuen, 2018).

More importantly, the teaching of morality, value-formation, and whole-person education has received renewed attention from the EDB in response to the mental health and well-being issues following the social incidents and the enactment of the National Security Law (Government of the HKSAR, 2021). To unpack the notion of morality and whole-person education within the national security framework, students will need to learn how to internalise the aspirations, values, and standards of the national macro-culture. Education for good citizenship is being revamped to align with the government's expectations and fulfil its social and educational duties. For example, regarding cultivating good law-abiding citizens, as stated in paragraph 10, EDB Circular No. 3/2021, school management, teaching and non-teaching staff and students (irrespective of their ethnicity and nationality) are required to adopt a correct and objective understanding and appreciation of the concept of national security and the National Security Law. In particular, schools of all sectors are charged with the duty to cultivate a law-abiding spirit among their students. Educators and school personnel should address these centralised school curriculum issues with the corresponding pedagogical and assessment strategies.

Creating equitable pedagogical practices

Equitable access is the precondition for education for all. The life narratives of the mainstream poor, CBS, CIS, and NCS students call for a review of pedagogical strategies in senior secondary schools. Too many students have drifted away from pursuing further education when they could have done so precisely because their secondary education was not so rewarding. Gradually, they believed that higher education was only for the elite or the privileged and so they have to look elsewhere to PSE or compromise with second best. The culture of early student stratification or social stratification in the selective education system defeats the spirit of educational agency and may lead to academic disengagement.

There is a shared sentiment and lamentation about the market-driven and exclusive school cultures in senior secondary education among the socially disadvantaged and immigrant youth in Hong Kong. They have expressed dissatisfaction with the HKDSE assessment mechanism, which focuses on superficial knowledge taught. Consequently, they have felt discriminated against in the system, are demotivated to learn, and have been failed by their teachers and school curriculum. The standardised curriculum issue calls for urgent attention towards diversifying the curriculum and engaging the mind and hearts of students to curb educational failures and improve PSE attainment (Devlin & McKay, 2018).

Teachers must address the intersectionality of students' family SES, cultural capital, self-agency, and emotion gaps. Teacher intercultural competence is crucial since they have to acknowledge the sociocultural incongruities of multicultural and multilingual students who have to make frequent switches between heritage and host languages to interpret the correct meaning (Devlin & McKay, 2018). As facilitators and cultural bridges, teachers must be armed with positive attributes in communicating expectations to students from effective learning (Devlin & O'Shea, 2011). Multicultural classrooms require teachers to put extra patience into accommodating linguistic diversity by acknowledging ethnic-cultural differences and assisting students both academically and emotionally. Implications for teacher education will be further elaborated in the next chapter.

References

Abatemarco, A., Cavallo, M., Marino, I., & Russo, G. (2021). *Age effects in education: A double disadvantage for second-generation immigrant children* (No. 761). GLO Discussion Paper. https://www.econstor.eu/bitstream/10419/228707/1/GLO-DP-0761.pdf

Apple, M. W. (2006). Review of class practices: How parents help their children get good jobs. *Educational Policy, 20*, 455–462.

Arkoudis, S., Watty, K., Baik, C., Yu, X., Borland, H., Chang, S., & Pearce, A. (2013). Finding common ground: Enhancing interaction between domestic and international students in higher education. *Teaching in Higher Education, 18*(3), 222–235. https://doi.org/10.1080/13562517.2012.719156.

Bandura, A. (1977). Self-efficacy: Toward a unifying theory of behavioral change. *Psychological Review, 84*(2), 191–215. https://doi.org/10.1037/0033-295x.84.2.191.

Bandura, A. (1986). *Social foundations of thought and action: A social cognitive theory* (1st ed.). Prentice Hall.

Bandura, A. (1997). *Self-efficacy: The exercise of control* (1st ed.). W. H. Freeman.

Banks, J. A. (2015). *Cultural diversity and education: Foundations, curriculum, and teaching*. Routledge.

Bernstein, B. (2018). On the classification and framing of educational knowledge. In R. Brown (Ed.), *Knowledge, education, and cultural change* (pp. 365–392). Routledge.

Bouchey, H. A., & Harter, S. (2005). Reflected appraisals, academic self-perceptions, and math/science performance during early adolescence. *Journal of Educational Psychology, 97*(4), 673–686. https://doi.org/10.1037/0022-0663.97.4.673.

Bourdieu, P., & Passeron, J. C. (1977). *Reproduction in education, culture and society*. SAGE.

Bowles, A., Fisher, R., Mcphail, R., Rosenstreich, D., & Dobson, A. (2014). Staying the distance: Students' perceptions of enablers of transition to higher education. *Higher*

Education Research & Development, 33(2), 212–225. https://doi.org/10.1080/07294360.2013.832157.

Cadaret, M. C., & Hartung, P. J. (2021). Efficacy of a group career construction intervention with urban youth of colour. *British Journal of Guidance & Counselling, 49*(2), 187–199. https://doi.org/10.1080/03069885.2020.1782347.

Chowdry, H., Crawford, C., Dearden, L., Goodman, A., & Vignoles, A. (2013). Widening participation in higher education: Analysis using linked administrative data. *Journal of the Royal Statistical Society: Series A (Statistics in Society), 176*(2), 431–57. https://doi.org/10.1111/j.1467-985X.2012.01043.x.

Coleman, J. S. (1990). *Foundations of social capital.* Belknap.

Devlin, B. M. (2010). *Effects of students' multiple intelligences on participation rate of course components in a blended secondary family and consumer sciences course* (Doctoral Dissertation). Iowa State University.

Devlin, M., & McKay, M. (2018). Facilitating the success of students from low SES backgrounds at regional universities through course design, teaching, and staff attributes. In M. Shah, & J. McKay (Eds.), *Achieving equity and quality in higher education: Global perspectives in an era of widening participation* (pp. 73–95). Palgrave Macmillan.

Devlin, M., & O'Shea, H. (2011). *Teaching students from low socioeconomic backgrounds: A brief guide for University teaching staff.* http://www.lowses.edu.au/assets/advice-teachers.pdf

Education Bureau. (2014). *Guide on life planning education and career guidance for secondary schools.* https://lifeplanning.edb.gov.hk/uploads/page/attachments/CLP-Guide_E_r3.pdf

Francis, B., Connolly, P., Archer, L., Hodgen, J., Mazenod, A., Pepper, D., & Travers, M. C. (2017). Attainment grouping as self-fulfilling prophesy? A mixed methods exploration of self-confidence and set level among Year 7 students. *International Journal of Educational Research, 86,* 96–108. https://doi.org/10.1016/j.ijer.2017.09.001

Gale, T., & Parker, S. (2015). Calculating student aspiration: Bourdieu, spatiality and the politics of recognition. *Cambridge Journal of Education, 45*(1), 81–96. https://doi.org/10.1080/0305764X.2014.988685.

Government of the HKSAR. (2021). *Education Bureau Circular No.2/2021. National security: Maintaining a safe learning environment, nurturing good citizens.* https://applications.edb.gov.hk/circular/upload/EDBC/EDBC21003E.pd

Greater Bay Area. (2019). *Outline Development Plan for the Guangdong-Hong Kong-Macao Greater Bay Area.* https://www.bayarea.gov.hk/filemanager/en/share/pdf/Outline_Development_Plan.pdf

Gutiérrez, M., & Tomás, J. M. (2019). The role of perceived autonomy support in predicting university students' academic success mediated by academic self-efficacy and school engagement. *Educational Psychology, 39*(6), 729–748. https://doi.org/10.1080/01443410.2019.1566519.

Holland, N. E. (2011). The power of peers: Influences on postsecondary education planning and experiences of African American students. *Urban Education, 46*(5), 1029–1055. https://doi.org/10.1177%2F0042085911400339.

Hurtado, S., Engberg, M. E., Ponjuan, L., & Landreman, L. (2002). Students' precollege preparation for participation in a diverse democracy. *Research in Higher Education, 43*(2), 163–186. https://www.jstor.org/stable/40196884.

Jackson, J., O'Callaghan, E., & Adserias, R. (2014). Approximating glass ceiling effects using cross-sectional data. In J. Jackson, E. O'Callaghan, & R. Leon (Eds.), *Measuring glass ceiling effects in higher education: Opportunities and challenges.* John Wiley & Sons.

Kember, D. (2010). Opening up the road to nowhere: Problems with the path to mass higher education in Hong Kong. *High Education, 59*(2), 167–179. https://doi.org/10.1007/s10734-009-9241-x.
Kennedy, K. J. (2012). The 'no loser' principle in Hong Kong's education reform: Does it apply to ethnic minority students. *Hong Kong Teachers' Centre Journal, 11*(23), 1–23.
Kim, E. Y. (2014). When social class meets ethnicity: College-going experiences of Chinese and Korean immigrant students. *The Review of Higher Education, 37*(3), 321–348. http://doi.org/10.1353/rhe.2014.0015.
Ladd, H. F. (2012). Education and poverty: Confronting the evidence. *Journal of Policy Analysis and Management, 31*(2), 203–227. https://doi.org/10.1002/pam.21615.
Lawton, S. B. (1973). Distribution of instructional resources in Detroit. *The Journal of Negro Education, 42*(2), 134–141. https://doi.org/10.2307/2967009.
Lo, H. (2020, March 31). *The DSE: Hong Kong's high pressure exams inflict long-term harm on survivors*. Hong Kong Free Press. https://hongkongfp.com/2018/03/24/dse-hong-kongs-high-pressure-exams-inflict-long-term-harm-survivors/
Ng, R. (2020). Mental Health Crisis in Hong Kong. *Psychiatric Times*. https://www.psychiatrictimes.com/view/mental-health-crisis-hong-kong
Nicholas-Omoregbe, O. S. (2010). The effect of parental education attainment on school outcomes. *IFE PsychologIA: An International Journal, 18*(1), 176–182. https://hdl.handle.net/10520/EJC38791
Nutt, L., & Hardman, L. (2019). *Complete the agenda in higher education*. Rowman & Littlefield.
Orupabo, J., Drange, I., & Abrahamsen, B. (2020). Multiple frames of success: How second-generation immigrants experience educational support and belonging in higher education. *Higher Education, 79*(5), 921–937. https://doi.org/10.1007/s10734-019-00447-8.
Perez, W., Espinoza, R., Ramos, K., Coronado, H. M., & Cortes, R. (2009). Academic resilience among undocumented Latino students. *Hispanic Journal of Behavioral Sciences, 31*(2), 149–181. https://doi.org/10.1177%2F0739986309333020.
Rotter, J. (1966). Generalized expectancies for internal versus external control of reinforcement. *Psychological Monographs, 80*(1), 1–28.
Ryan, R. M., & Deci, E. L. (2000). Self-determination theory and the facilitation of intrinsic motivation, social development, and well-being. *American Psychologist, 55*(1), 68. http://doi.org/10.1037110003-066X.55.1.68.
Sadowski, M. (2013). *Portraits of promise: Voices of successful immigrant students*. Harvard Education Press.
Sandoval-Hernández, A., & Białowolski, P. (2016). Factors and conditions promoting academic resilience: A TIMSS-based analysis of five Asian education systems. *Asia Pacific Education Review, 17*(3), 511–520. https://doi.org/10.1007/s12564-016-9447-4.
Savickas, M. L., Nota, L., Rossier, J., Dauwalder, J. P., Duarte, M. E., Guichard, J., Soresi, S., Esbroeck, V. R., & Van Vianen, A. E. (2009). Life designing: A paradigm for career construction in the 21st century. *Journal of Vocational Behavior, 75*(3), 239–250. https://doi.org/10.1016/j.jvb.2009.04.004.
Schunk, D. H., & Pajares, F. (2002). The development of academic self-efficacy. In A. Wigfield, & J. S. Eccles (Eds.), *Development of achievement motivation* (pp. 15–32). Academic Press.
Shek, D. T. (2020). Protests in Hong Kong (2019–2020): A perspective based on quality of life and well-being. *Applied Research in Quality of Life*, 1–17. https://dx.doi.org/10.1007%2Fs11482-020-09825-2

Sjaastad, J. (2012). Sources of inspiration: The role of significant persons in young people's choice of science in higher education. *International Journal of Science Education*, *34*(10), 1615–1636. https://doi.org/10.1080/09500693.2011.590543.

Skerrett, A., & Hargreaves, A. (2008). Student diversity and secondary school change in a context of increasingly standardized reform. *American Educational Research Journal*, *45*(4), 913–945. https://doi.org/10.3102%2F0002831208320243.

Stanton-Salazar, R. D. (2001). Subtractive schooling: US-Mexican youth and the politics of caring. *Contemporary Sociology*, *30*(2), 210. http://dx.doi.org/10.2307/2655442.

United Nations. (2015). *Transforming our world: the 2030 Agenda for Sustainable Development*. https://sustainabledevelopment.un.org/?menu=1300

Urdan, T., & Bruchmann, K. (2018). Examining the academic motivation of a diverse student population: A consideration of methodology. *Educational Psychologist*, *53*(2), 114–130. https://doi.org/10.1080/00461520.2018.1440234.

Wang, C. W., & Neihart, M. (2015). How do supports from parents, teachers, and peers influence academic achievement of twice-exceptional students. *Gifted Child Today*, *38*(3), 148–159. https://doi.org/10.1177%2F1076217515583742.

Williams, D. (2014). Organizational learning as a framework for overcoming glass ceiling effects in higher education. In J. Jackson, E. O'Callaghan, & R. Leon (Eds.), *Measuring glass ceiling effects in higher education: Opportunities and challenges*. John Wiley & Sons.

Yeager, D. S., & Dweck, C. S. (2012). Mindsets that promote resilience: When students believe that personal characteristics can be developed. *Educational Psychologist*, *47*(4), 302–314. https://doi.org/10.1080/00461520.2012.722805.

Yuen, Y. M. C. (2018). Perceptions of social justice among the South Asian and Chinese immigrant youth in Hong Kong. *Peabody Journal of Education*, *93*(3), 332–344. http://doi.org/10.1080/0161956X.2018.1449928.

Yuen, Y. M. C., Cheung, A. C. K., Leung, C. S. S., Tang, H. H. H., & Chan, L. C. H. (2021). The success and obstacle factors in pursuing post-secondary education: The differences between Hong Kong mainstream and non-mainstream students. *Education Journal*, *49*(2), 137–160.

Zhu, S., Zhuang, Y., Lee, P., & Ching, W. W. (2021). The changes of suicidal ideation status among young people in Hong Kong during COVID-19: A longitudinal survey. *PsyArXiv. June*, *1*.

12 Educating Teaching Professionals for Cultural Inclusion and Connectedness

Fostering educational equity

Internationally, the recognition of the need for teaching equity and equity in education is widespread, and reforms concerning teacher education, especially at initial teacher education (ITE) levels, are being advocated. (Darling-Hammond, 2017; Grossman & McDonald, 2008; Kerr & Andreotti, 2019). The interface between globalisation and localisation of teacher education must be reframed concerning the global agenda of access, equity, and success for all, as advocated by UNESCO. Due to the accelerated changing student demographics, the ITE programmes are coming under public scrutiny. Teacher standards and their competence to mesh with the conceptualisation of "practice for equity" need also to be redefined (Cochran-Smith et al., 2016, p. 67).

Researchers are aware that learning and teaching are interactive by nature, and ITE has a history of adopting a theory-practice integrated approach to enhance professional standards and capacity-building (Ball & Forzani, 2009; Darling-Hammond, 2017). To achieve the intended learning outcomes, teachers must diagnose the learning needs and subsequently apply the theories of pedagogy to match the learners' styles. One of the characteristics of Hong Kong society is a boundary-crossing population. The diaspora of ethnic groups suffering from multiple forms of inequality and inequity in education represents a serious barrier against the formation of an equitable society. OECD (2010) noted the following characteristics of immigrant and ethnic minority students: They have a lower education performance than native students; the tendency to early drop out or leave school early is greater; students with a second-generation immigrant background outperform first-generation ones but both are still behind their native peers; they have weaker family support with limited access to learning opportunities outside the compulsory education period. Due to an ethnocentric approach to multicultural teaching, teachers are generally under-prepared for educating learner diversity in multiple settings (Ball & Forzani, 2009; Darling-Hammond, 2010; Sleeter, 2008). Hong Kong teachers fall short of intercultural learning and teaching, and the clinical side of teacher education is thus underscored to better prepare teachers to learn from expert

DOI: 10.4324/9780429439315-12

colleagues and gain insights from student realities (Darling-Hammond, 2016). Workplace practice has received increased attention in teacher preparation institutions to provide prospective teachers with richer and deeper hands-on, real-life teaching experience. Internationally, a range of affirmative actions have been launched, such as strengthening university-school partnerships and providing induction support to better prepare future teachers to enact the policies of eliminating social inequities at multiple levels.

The demographic factors of diverse learners are linked with their educational performance and success issues (OECD, 2008). Teachers are charged with the responsibility to enact equity and quality in education. Grossman and McDonald (2008) argue that teaching practice should consider the students' ethnicity, socio-economic status, and linguistic diversity. Failure to do so only leads to the reproduction of educational inequality because immigrant and ethnic minority students mainly come from underprivileged and under-resourced homes. There is a shared understanding of the teaching framework that teachers should be prepared to educate the whole child rather than just for content pedagogy. Effective teachers must apply "know-how" practice and declarative knowledge to engage the learner intellectually, socially, and emotionally (Ball & Forzani, 2009).

Teaching for equity

The heart of teaching is to enable the success of every learner throughout their journey, from getting ready towards full completion then to pursuing their dreams and actualising their talents (Lachat, 1999). Hong Kong, as an international metropolis, is well connected with global societies. Teachers are called to prepare future-ready students with the right mindset and skillset to accept the challenge for future success. Intercultural competence is needed to recognise cultural diversity in the community. It must begin with teacher education. Intercultural teacher education focuses specifically on preparing teachers to support the needs of culturally, linguistically, and socio-economically diverse populations (Wassell et al., 2018). In the face of cultural diversity in classrooms, teachers are expected to be effective in empowering students to be productive citizens who are adaptable to a changing society and able to handle intergroup relations regardless of racial, ethnic, ability, or cultural diversity.

In practical terms, teachers have to demonstrate an awareness of non-mainstream Cantonese culture and make a difference in their daily interaction with students. They need to learn and relearn essential knowledge and skills in intercultural teaching and learning. The communication styles of CIS, CBS, and NCS students do not fit in the conventional way of behaviour in Hong Kong schools. Reaching out to other cultures is the first step to recognising and experiencing how social variables such as ethnicity, values, religious beliefs, dialects, traditional customs, and upbringing contribute to the behaviour, attitudes, aspiration, and interactional styles of mainstream and non-mainstream Hong Kong students. Most of all, these factors define teacher-student distance, trust, and connection.

The standard-based education focuses on raising the expectation of teachers for all students. Discussion of intercultural ethnic-based issues has only been dealt with indirectly or through small components in the teacher preparation programme. As noted by Gaudart (1998), teacher preparation programmes lagged behind the rapid change of social and student changes. In this Hong Kong is no exception. This calls for a paradigm shift in teacher education to pave the way and attract interracial preservice teacher groups to collaborate in action research projects. In an interconnected and interdependent global age, education should celebrate inclusive practice rather than exclusive practice. Education is a means to promote intercultural understanding, and it should start from teacher preparation programmes offered by higher education institutions. This includes fostering a deep understanding of the heterogeneity of cultures among students and the teaching communities. Taking the medium of instruction with regard to English and Chinese (Cantonese and/or Putonghua) as an example, this has been a key educational issue in creating subcultures and subgroups between the haves and have-nots and between the high and low social and cultural capital of different student groups. Linguistic diversity is a known factor. Chinese, immigrant Chinese, and ethnic minority NCS student groups with various dialectal mother tongues are characterised by their own values and subcultures. Religion, cultural heritage, and legacies are all mediators among these student groups. Even though students may be affiliated with Islam, for instance, some may believe in active social engagement, while others may prefer religious participation. Likewise, the diversity among Christian, Buddhist, Taoist, and non-religious Chinese immigrant groups gives rise to a range of associations within and without their clans and organisations, support groups, and clubs.

The beliefs of teachers have a direct bearing upon their perspectives on equity in education and their sensitivity to the structure of power and knowledge. Because of such perspectives, many teachers, for instance, are committed to affirmative action to equalise the uneven situation facing disadvantaged student groups. A teacher preparation programme represents a primary foundation for shaping teachers' thinking and understanding of the reality of unequal teaching. They need to become more reflective and analytical in their own beliefs and practice. Addressing this deep-seated problem, we must begin by treating the root cause – the structural inequality in a local society underpinned by the education system itself under the influence of neoliberalism. The free-market economy celebrates the spirit of survival of the fittest. Only those who respond well to the high-stake testing system can excel. Education is reduced to serving society's human capital rather than diversifying social development according to the diversified talents of the young generation. Precisely for this reason social inequality is like a fortress that cannot be overcome, self-perpetuating a generation of failures through the educational process of exclusion. Such is not in the best interest of society.

Teachers' perceptions of equity education

Understanding the perspectives of preservice teachers on the issues of equity and equity in education provides insight into the effectiveness and responsiveness of (ITE). Their perspectives on equity and equity in education will directly impact their pedagogical practices and educational effectiveness. However, very few research studies have interrogated preservice teachers' understanding of equity in education, especially in connection to the changing student demography in schools in Hong Kong. Framed within the discourse of equity and quality in education, attention now turns to case studies on the development of preservice teachers' understanding and perception of equity education in relation to their teacher education programmes.

Dialogues with preservice teachers

All the student teachers are Han Chinese, and their names are pseudonyms. Cantonese was used for the Hong Kong mainstream, and Putonghua was used for those from Mainland China. We used a small pool of initial informants to nominate through social networks other participants who were majoring in Bachelor of Education (B.Ed.) and who could potentially contribute to this specific study. Semi-structured individual interviews were conducted from 2017 to 2018 with 30-course participants from the Full-time B.Ed. programme at one local university with a focus on teacher education. Each interview lasted from 45 to 60 minutes. Among the 30 participants, there were 20 Years 1–3 students and 10 Years 4–5 students. All participants were invited to share their opinions on the following topics: (1) perspectives on equity education; (2) experience in addressing student diversity; and (3) teacher education programmes in terms of equipping them for equity learning. They were invited to transcribe their own audio-recorded interview to assure the confidentiality and accuracy of the data. This also allowed them to modify or confirm their responses after the interview if they so wished.

Theorising equity in education

Participants expressed their views on equity in education mainly from their course learning and/or their exposure to classroom teaching. Moon, a second-year student majoring in Early Childhood Education (ECE), asserted that "the attitudes and teaching methods to students must be totally the same, regardless of their race, country, gender, personality and learning ability". This view was echoed by Lam (Year 1, ICT) that "everyone should receive the same education service".

From a different perspective, Violet and Sana interpreted the essence of equity as catering for individual needs in teaching.

> Equity is like being fair. It is different from equality in a way that you actually see the needs of the students. If you give the students what they really need, it's equity.
>
> (Violet, Year 1, English)

Equity means giving people what they exactly want... It's a good practice for the teacher to give the disabled girl half an hour to finish her work or maybe give her some different materials. So she does understand, and she learns.

(Sana, Year 1, English)

To Hong, the key to getting every student to meet the standard was to provide appropriate learning support rather than differentiating the pedagogy and the outcomes. "Equity is not equality" (Year 2, Chinese). Hong believes that:

...for teachers, equity means they devote the same time and energy to each student and expect them to achieve the same learning outcomes. Therefore, we cannot arrange for lazy, new or bad teachers to teach the so-called "low ability" students.

For Chan (Year 3, Mathematics), equity was about "students having equal access to education, regardless of their ability and cultural backgrounds". Yue, however, offered a slightly complex understanding of equity in education. Teachers should be non-discriminatory in terms of attitude but should be willing to make differentiation in their teaching.

Equity, I think, means treating people in the same way with the same attitudes. For example, equity in education is not discriminating nor having a prejudice against the students.

(Yue, Year 2, Business, Accounting & Finance)

Yin elaborated this point further by acknowledging the different meanings of equity associated with different people.

To students, equity means equal access to knowledge. To teachers, equity means to treat every student the same without discrimination. To parents, equity means they should not compare their kids with other children but acknowledge every child for his/her strengths.

(Yin, Year 2, English Language Education)

It is significant that the notion of treating everyone the same was widely shared by these Year 1–3 participants. In their belief, this meant having a "non-discriminatory" attitude towards students in delivering lessons, although some did accentuate the role of differentiation in instruction.

Senior year participants place a greater emphasis on respecting individual differences, and many of them made particular reference to the challenge of learning a new language encountered by the non-mainstream students:

Equity is about respect... Both South Asian and CIS don't speak Cantonese so we should provide English and Putonghua explanations for them to understand the lessons.

(Leung, Year 5, ECE)

> Equity rejects uniform teaching. If my Maths class has Pakistani and the Filipino students, I will provide individualized support for them. I think they will have many learning obstacles due to language and thinking problems.
> (Grace, Year 5, Mathematics Education)

> To me equity is to give more time to students with special needs. But my field experience tells me that it is easier said than done. The student diversity within one class is too big to be catered for.
> (Tang, Year 5, Chinese Language Education)

> I tried out some strategies to increase the motivation of South Asians in learning Chinese. I know they struggled with it and often disengaged in the class.
> (Jesse, Year 5, Chinese Language Education)

Without much exposure to real-world teaching as professional teachers, participants from Years 1–3 offered vague conceptions of educational equity. Sharing a Confucian heritage, the notion of "sameness" was stressed as having the same attitudes for all students in order to avoid labelling or discrimination (Moon, Lam, Hong, So & Yue). Sana and Hong further highlighted the differences or deficiencies of the students and additional efforts needed to facilitate learning. Interestingly, the common perception was to bury the differences among individual learners. For example, according to Yue, this would help minimise adverse effects in the teacher-pupil interaction process rather than lead to ignored learner needs. Perhaps this is how they try to be culturally sensitive, especially given they are not equipped to address student diversity and individual differences. This in itself is a call for a deeper critical reflection upon preservice teachers' personal beliefs to avoid discriminatory attitudes led by their unintentional insensitivity.

The differences among the participants of the study can also be attributed to their exposure to real-world teaching. As far as the final-year participants were concerned, after two blocks of field experience exercises, they exhibited some awareness of the complexity of addressing equity in actual teaching. Interestingly, having gained some hands-on experience in managing the dimension of student diversity in teaching, they were more cautious about their confidence in responding to equity issues in teaching. They understood that some structural obstacles must first be resolved before they could actualise their wish of providing individualised teaching to all. Student diversity appeared too great to handle by one teacher in a class with a very demanding and tight schedule.

How programme offerings are addressing equity issues

When asked how their programmes prepared them for equity teaching and learning, the participants underlined how their knowledge came from courses rather than hands-on experience. For example, Tung recalled that:

The Psychology course informs us how to understand students' mental readiness by observing their words, expressions, etc., and then manage the whole class well to facilitate equity in education.

(Tung, Year 2, Business, Accounting & Finance)

Ming referred to how a Sociolinguistics course "made us know something about diversification, but did not tell us how to deal with student ability difference".

(Ming, Year 2, English Language Education)

Kit, in his final year, believed that the pedagogy course was most helpful.

Some courses like Chinese Education Pedagogy One to Three and Learning Difference taught me that teachers should employ different methods to address different students' learning needs, which indirectly prepared me for education for equity.

(Kit, Year 5, Chinese Language Education)

ITE has a solid connection to professional development. The programme structures are increasingly practice-based. The findings show that both subject content pedagogy and professional pedagogy were of greater relevance to these preservice teachers in response to fostering equity in education.

Suggestions for ITE programme improvement

The interviews prompted the participants to reflect on their programme offering and learning. Again, practical experiences were recognised as key (Sun, Year 2, Liberal Studies). "We need more class observation to know how students react in class and how teachers are supposed to deal with sudden incidences".

Fiona offered the following recommendations:

The university should advocate for learning equity. Some elective courses involving equity issues could be changed into compulsory courses. More opportunities for teaching practice are needed.

(Year 5, Visual Arts)

Irene argued for change, believing the ITE programme offerings were too theoretical to be helpful for real-world teaching.

We need more courses that specifically tell us how to teach students, what pedagogy we can learn, and what instructional strategies we can use when dealing with specific student problems.

(Year 5, Music Education)

According to Cheung, more real-life case studies on responding to gender equity and racial equity in classrooms would be desirable.

> I do not know what to do when incidents relating to student diversity happen. So more case studies are needed, like what kind of problems can happen to students with SEN and how to cater for those. Examples will help me master the knowledge more easily.
>
> (Year 5, Music Education)

The participants have reiterated the importance of experiential learning and site-based teaching practices to master the core knowledge and skills in responding to equity and diversity in the ITE programme. The formation of equity in education is founded on-field experience, coursework, and other non-formal learning activities. Non-formal learning activities, such as Project Aspire to offer training for students with Asperger or Autism, the Co-curricular Course such as Intercultural Sensitivity and Provision of Community Service, voluntary work, and exchange programmes in foreign countries, provided complementary learning experiences for preservice teachers in their full-time structured programme. Additionally, the participants were unanimous in highlighting how courses related to counselling, student diversity, educational psychology, and pedagogy were conducive to their understanding of student learning needs and individual diversity.

Discussion and recommendations for ITE

According to the interview data, there appears to be some inconsistency in the perceptions of participants regarding equity in education. While final year participants tended to make sense of equity in education according to their field experience and exposure to real classroom scenarios, participants in their first three years of study understood the concept vaguely, exhibiting only rudimentary knowledge. In a nutshell, there is a strong correlation between the perception and understanding of equity in education and the ability to address the issue in classroom settings. The formidable challenge to actualise equity in education in Hong Kong is very real, and it is clear that the well-roundedness of preservice teachers, with a robust readiness to promote equity in the classroom, will yield a profound impact on the lives of every student in Hong Kong.

At the early stages of their professional education, most preservice teachers address the issues of offering an equal amount of resources to all and teaching without discrimination against individual differences. As the interview data of Moon, Lam, and Hong unfolded, differentiation of educational services was often understood as allocating the same amount of learning resources to every student. Key to note that educational justice consists of equalising opportunities for achieving essential educational outcomes. This fundamental difference needs to be recognised more fully to foster quality in education and appropriate learning for diverse and individual needs.

Inclusive education policy: Creating the right learning conditions for all

Fennes and Hapgood (1997) argue that teacher education programme should take the lead to integrate intercultural learning in the school curriculum. Intercultural learning can be a framework for teacher education to prepare intercultural facilitators. As stated in Chapter 1, both mainstream and non-mainstream cultural students are full members of the schools and the society enjoying the same entitlement for equal and quality education in the society. In the absence of the necessary support structure, only a tiny portion of disadvantaged students could excel against the odd, and the majority fell into their self-fulfilling prophecy of losing and failing. To alleviate the problem, teacher education must begin with an inclusive education policy to make intercultural learning a new pedagogy to be applied by the teaching community. This is to enhance the practical field-based teacher education to better align with the cultural diversity within the society to overcome cultural bias. Institutional deliberations in creating the right conditions for learning for all across educational sectors and institutions are advocated (Thomas, 2013). Unless students with diverse cultural backgrounds are treasured as assets to enrich the mono-cultural outlook of the school culture, the teaching community will only see them as a hindrance to the curriculum and pedagogical practices outside the prevailing high-stake testing-score system. The relevance of the current definition of inclusive education in the local society has to be reconsidered. Its current assumption is rooted in the historical categorical approach to view all "outliers" as having SEN. As such, the putative solutions offered by the Three-Tired Support Model of Inclusion are no longer adequate for teacher preparation and professional development (Education Bureau, 2008). There is an apparent omission of official and professional policy response to the culturally insensitive framework in understanding inclusivity in education within the ever-changing student diversity across all educational sectors in Hong Kong from early years' education to PSE. Catering for individual differences remains the sole responsibility of the delegated teachers rather than a shared school vision and mission. This policy fallacy needs urgent rectification.

Implications for initial teacher education

While acknowledging the fact that we cannot prepare teachers for teaching any specific culture given the dimension of diversity among the current student population, there are key principles and approaches to shift the perspectives of teachers and educators on teaching equity and enabling success for all. From the narratives, we learn that language defines success and failure in academic and career advancement. Raising English proficiency is the key to the academic success of mainstream low-income and CIS. Mastering the Chinese Language has been reiterated as one key factor for promoting functional and meaningful integration of ethnic minority students in

Hong Kong (Loh & Hung, 2020; Oxfam Hong Kong, 2019). Unlike elsewhere, such as New South Wales, Australia, and British Columbia, preservice language teachers in Hong Kong are not required to be qualified in second language teaching (Loh & Hung, 2020). This is a significant barrier for them to provide the necessary learning support to the NCS students in multilingual classrooms.

Moreover, there is no hint of parallel curriculum tailoring initiatives in the classroom to engage students in learning. A study of achievement of fairness, justice, and impartiality in education underlines the need for equal access for student success. Simply put, what is needed is to ensure every student has an equal opportunity to participate in all aspects of the educational process inside and outside the school curriculum regardless of their socio-economic and cultural backgrounds. The highest performing education systems combine equity with quality (OECD, 2012) as proposed by the OECD Report, No More Failures. Equity in education consists of fairness and inclusion dimensions, while the quality of teachers makes a difference in student outcomes, especially in equalising the students from minority and/or low socio-economic backgrounds (Simon et al., 2007). Drawing from the findings, below outlines how the future Hong Kong teacher education may look like in order to increase teacher intercultural competence in a diverse society (Table 12.1).

Table 12.1 Aspiring intercultural teacher education for a diverse Hong Kong society

	\multicolumn{2}{c}{*The teacher education policy context*}	
	Present	*Future*
Teacher standards	T-standard for teachers and teacher education providers	Building intercultural competence in the T-standard and making it mandatory for all teachers Teacher education should embrace interculturalism/multiculturalism in the teacher education curriculum
Teacher registration and licensure	– Teacher licensure is for life – Registered teacher possessing Qualified Teacher Status (QTS) – Except for promotion, professional development is voluntary	Envisioning intercultural teacher education from early years to secondary education Teacher professional registration and licensure have to be renewed after a certain period. There should be clear professional development pathways for all teachers to upkeep with the latest education policy and landscape
Initial teacher education (ITE)	All teachers must get registered and licensure from the Education Bureau The Quality Assurance Council serves as the quality assurance body for teacher education	Building a university-school partnership approach to ITE and strengthening the clinical part of teacher education Establishing a regulatory mechanism to uphold the professional practice and teacher education

Educational inclusion – towards social equity

At the heart of multiculturalism, there must be equity and equal opportunities throughout the learning process of admission, placement, exit, and post-exit stages. Education for socially and culturally diverse students means a differentiation in curriculum, pedagogy, and assessment. As most teachers in public schools are Han Chinese, their own culture and values are adopted to benchmark student behaviours and achievements in mainstream schooling. In order to shift this ethnocentric view on "success" or "standard", the first task is to make teachers aware of the difference between their own and their students' cultural upbringing and worldviews. Put differently, deliberation must be done to help the teachers realise the inequality between power and education in the hierarchical structure between the privileged and the underprivileged. For the voices of the underprivileged to be heard, teachers have to shift their perspectives on pedagogy from Hong Kong-centric to student-centric. The multiple narratives of low-income mainstream, Chinese immigrant, South Asian youth clearly show that Hong Kong classrooms are rich in cultural and learning diversity and vulnerabilities. Facilitating equity and quality education, we need to scaffold new and experienced teachers. To develop such skill, one must first listen to the voices of these individuals who have felt excluded from the mainstream for one reason or another – either because of outright, overt racism, or subtle, institutional racism, general ignorance, subtle pressures, or genuine dislike.

To engage in intercultural communication, preservice and serving teachers should be informed or led to understand what kind of classrooms and what student needs they need to address upon their graduation (Goodwin, 2017). Many of them are oblivious to their own role as culture-bearers and may ignore or downplay the experience of students socially subordinated or targeted (Adams et al., 2007). As argued by Goodwin (2017), preparing teachers for today's classrooms, we must re-orientate our teacher education concerning the drastic changes occurring in student demographics in terms of linguistics, ethnicity, religious faith, values, and in-group interaction. From my interaction with preservice teachers in the past decade, it is clear to me that NCS students such as Pakistanis, Nepalese, and Indians have posed new challenges to the policymakers and school personnel. On the one hand, these immigrant and minority students usually come to school under-prepared as their families are under-resourced. Additional efforts are therefore essential for assisting them in adapting to the public school culture and meeting the expectation to pace themselves accordingly. On the other hand, it is human nature to identify oneself with certain cultural bubbles to create a sense of belonging and connectedness. These bubbles both protect and exclude people who do not share the same cultural frames or language. Under such circumstances, teachers usually find themselves at a crossroads or feel inadequate in dealing with learner diversity in their teaching practicum. As Hong Kong-born teachers are educated in a Cantonese-oriented cultural context, it is important to shift their worldview from Hong Kong ethnocentricity to an ethnorelative orientation in understanding cultural diversity.

Intercultural knowledge towards ethnorelativism

Intercultural sensitivity refers to our subjective experience of cultural difference, and it is learned as opposed to being an integral aspect of our past (Bennett, 1993; p. 22). Broadening the definition of culture is a necessary step for discerning its objective and subjective components. Cultural universalism focuses on the similarities among cultures and burying the differences to maintain cognitive consonance or maintain cognitive harmony. This is characterised by ethnocentrism locating one's own cultural norms, values, and expectations in the centre of everything and assigning students culturally and linguistically to different categories. Teachers' perceptions, beliefs, and attitudes towards non-mainstream students have led to stereotypes and negative labelling. Without multicultural awareness and competence, the mainstream Chinese teachers tend to assign their expectations, attitudes, motives, or potential to the students solely based on explicit behaviours, the big "C", which is featured by the tangible ethnic heritage of a particular group such as CIS. This is reflected in some of the vignettes presented in Chapter 4 concerning teachers' perceptions of the civic-mindedness and engagement of Chinese immigrant and South Asian students.

A clinical approach to teacher education and professional development can help address issues of multicultural insensitivity and eliminate adverse labelling effects on culturally and linguistically diverse student populations. Multicultural events focusing mainly on the big "C", cuisine, music, and dance, may be impressive and attractive to the participants. However, they are not able to make any impact on improving intercultural competence. Professional attention should be given to the intent behind the observed behaviours and to understand the whole person from the invisible aspect of culture – the little "c" or the beliefs and values of the specific group. What we see can be different from what we do not see behind explicit behaviours. Undoubtedly, the impact of cultural values on student behaviours and emotions is far-reaching and subtle. Hence, teachers must be equipped with an intercultural competence framework that enables them to fully understand the linkage between student worldviews from a specific culture and their responses to reality (Hook, 2000). Being competent in dealing with sophisticated intercultural differences and recognising their diverse cultural needs, teachers have to wear a cultural lens to understand the distinct experience of different groups when working with diverse student populations. The goal of intercultural training is to raise the self-awareness of personal cultural perspectives, especially on issues relating to catering for the diverse learner needs in multicultural classrooms. Prerequisites for teaching towards ethnorelativism include teachers' awareness of other ethnic cultures, a flexible attitude towards difference, and the ability to communicate and interact with persons having different assumptions. Simulation exercises and clinical practices are critical tools to unravel the cultural blindness of preservice teachers. Adopting a critical reflection approach, they need to be encouraged to review and identify their own intentional or unintentional stereotyping towards the worldviews of their students.

Field-based approach to preparing teachers for intercultural context

To increase preservice teachers' sensitivity to student diversity in contemporary classrooms, they require rich hands-on experience interacting with diverse student groups. The case of American teachers can be an example (Cushner, 1994). A major obstacle in cultivating the intercultural competence of preservice teachers is how best to address issues of equity and excellence within the learner diversity context. Hong Kong is not alone in this problem. Immigrant and ethnic minority students are often educated in schools or classes with a high concentration of co-ethnic peers and cultural homogeneity. This may help them to cultivate a sense of belonging in the class, but the separation approach offers minimal interaction between the mainstream (dominant) and non-mainstream (weak) groups and this leads to unequal access to the quality of education from admission to completion stages. This leaves students with diminished understanding and experience in the host society (Fennes & Hapgood, 1997).

Recognising that preservice teachers and serving teachers have hesitations and no little anxiety in encountering students from foreign cultures, field experience is imperative to expose them to multicultural and multilingual classrooms. By communicating and interacting with students from diverse cultures, they will gradually become aware of personal values and recognise the conflict, fears, and prejudices towards language minority students within intercultural environments. In doing so, they will become more aware of their personal judgments on each student group and consequently will gradually develop a language for understanding their intercultural interactions. In the day-to-day teaching and evaluation of interactions with students, teachers formulate their understanding and evaluation of students' performance and classify them according to ability and/or multicultural groups. It is not uncommon to hear mainstream Chinese teachers making the same comments on the learning behaviours of minority students such as "laid back", "lazy", "noisy", or "doesn't care much academically". Teachers often hold a very dim view of the parents of CIS or mainstream underprivileged students, thinking they lack parental support for academic work. Unless these categories are challenged and verified, it will only lead to labelling effects. Classroom exposure is another word for active learning and observing. Teachers are expected to employ a basket of pedagogical strategies in addressing a vast array of learning challenges in which students with diverse cultural backgrounds engage in meaningful and quality learning. In achievement of this, preservice teachers must know a great deal about the learners and establish a good rapport. Building trust and mutual understanding is key to minimising intercultural miscommunication and creating a conducive environment for learning. The initial steps for professional development and personal growth begin with tackling personal bias, stereotypes, and acknowledging personal limitations in interacting with diverse student groups. A team approach will better enable the teachers to report, discuss, and resolve the critical issues encountered in the field exercises. It is also an effective way for them to engage in active reflection on teaching self-beliefs.

Teachers are leaders in effecting change for equitable learning

Equity and equitable education must be accompanied by a change in school leadership style to recognise and develop leadership among teachers. Davies and Davies (2011) argue that schools are open systems facing a multitude of challenges both from within and outside, especially in uncertain and unusual times. Following the social unrest in mid-2019 and school suspension due to the COVID-19 pandemic situation in 2020 and the Omicron variant surge in 2022, Hong Kong society has faced numerous and unprecedented challenges and disruption. In addition, natural phenomena like storms can also disrupt the proceedings and in Hong Kong do so regularly. No single leader can adequately address the ever-changing and diversified student demographics in a globalised society. This requires a principal plus approach to stretch out the influence of leadership among the teachers. Creating a professional community of practice is one way to link ideas and energy among novice and experienced school personnel to acknowledge learner diversity. Inclusive and multicultural education is rooted in a shared vision and commitment, which requires collaborative team building. Shared or distributed leadership brings synergy, builds vision, and accelerates the process of pedagogical change in promoting an inclusive school climate and provide what is needed for the new educational environments. The key is to create the right conditions for formal and informal leaders to work together. This leads to the development of teacher mentors.

An action-research approach to formulate a professional learning community (PLC)

Multicultural pedagogy is an action-oriented approach relating to the beliefs, values, and cultural expectations of mainstream society. Shifting teachers' pedagogy from Hong Kong-centric (ethnocentric) to Hong Kong-plus (ethnorelative) must begin with shifting teachers' beliefs and values in teaching for equity and social justice. This is rooted in experiential learning and through constant dialogic conservations among professional teachers within a given school context in which the formation of a PLC is proposed. As indicated previously, today's teacher education must focus on cultivating future leaders in leading change in turbulent times. Although, with the increase of diverse student populations, there will be an increase of international colleagues with pluralistic values and perspectives, intergroup conflicts, exclusion, and rejection of one another are inevitable if we only focus on the present without preparing the teaching community for the future.

Creating a PLC in schools must begin with appropriating the leadership pace and direction. While school leaders must generate consensus in leading the team to accept multiple unprecedented educational challenges, teachers of different professional stages should be empowered to respond to new waves of development. Making teaching and learning an intentional business will yield the intended pedagogical outcomes. A PLC is a community of intellectual professionals dedicated to improving the quality of inclusive practice in their school-wide community and is based on evidence. Therefore, an action research approach is advocated to engage every teacher in classroom-based observations and try out various pedagogical strategies to accommodate diverse learners. It is especially imperative for preservice teachers to link theories with practice in their teaching practice or field exercises. When teachers are empowered to participate in the decision-making process, sharing their observations and analysis of learner needs, this will encourage them to own their teaching and commit to further professional development and enhancement Azorín et al., (2020). They should be encouraged to share their intellectual thinking actively.

Envisioning educational inclusion

Vision is all about the idea, and it ascribes meaning and directs action for future development and improvement. It is about acknowledging the potential of teachers in taking new initiatives in promoting inclusive and equitable education in their specialty. It also includes changing the traditional mentality that teachers are merely followers of school leadership and policy. Building a vision for an equitable, accessible, and inclusive society, it is vital to empower preservice teachers to explore their version of equity and equitable education in their future teaching careers. Some teachers may only have vague ideas about students from other cultures or be equipped with limited knowledge in dealing with students with SEN. A deficit approach to viewing student diversity is relatively common among teachers. Disadvantages of having diverse culture and individual differences are perceived as value-laden constructs shaped by the cultural norm of ability, especially within teaching for examination practice. Unless preservice teachers have developed a sense of personal commitment to an actual value of diversity in their teaching, it will take double effort to become alert to prevailing practice. We have underscored how the concept of disadvantage is socially constructed and is a kind of social control. Consequently, pluralism in teaching is particularly urgent and relevant to classrooms in Hong Kong due to the Hong Kong-centric curriculum and rapidly changing sociocultural circumstances.

In order to translate ethnorelativism into classroom practice, preservice teachers must be equipped with a framework that assists them in repackaging content and pedagogical knowledge for a deeply integrated approach to address learner diversity (Lancaster & Bain, 2019). Preservice teachers need more deliberated training attention and exposure to immerse themselves in the real-world context, first-hand experience in mastering pedagogical and content knowledge, and to develop evidence-based pedagogies of inclusion. In a nutshell, changing pedagogy to be culturally relevant is key to enabling both mainstream and non-mainstream students gain the essential knowledge, skills, and attitudes necessary for them to become full member of our pluralistic society and lead competent adult lives irrespective of racial, ethnic, gender, and cultural diversity.

References

Adams, M. E., Bell, L. A. E., & Griffin, P. E. (2007). *Teaching for diversity and social justice*. Routledge/Taylor & Francis Group.

Azorín, C., Harris, A., & Jones, M. (2020). Taking a distributed perspective on leading professional learning networks. School Leadership & Management, 40(2-3), 111–127.

Ball, D., & Forzani, F. M. (2009). The work of teaching and the challenge for teacher education. *Journal of Teacher Education*, 60(5), 497–511. https://doi.org/10.1177%2F0022487109348479.

Bennett, M. J. (1993). Toward ethnocentrism: A developmental approach to training for intercultural sensitivity. In R. M. Paige (Ed.), *Education for the intercultural experience* (pp. 1–71). Intercultural Press.

Cochran-Smith, M., Stern, R., Sánchez, J. G., Miller, A., Keefe, E. S., Fernández, M. B., Chang, W., Carney, C. W., Burton, S., & Baker, M. (2016). Holding teacher preparation accountable: A review of claims and evidence. *National Education Policy Center*. http://nepc.colorado.edu/publication/teacher-prep

Cushner, K. (1994). Preparing teachers for an intercultural context. In W. R. Brislin, & T. Yoshida (Eds.), *Improving intercultural interactions* (pp. 109–128). Sage.

Darling-Hammond, L. (2017). Teacher education around the world: What can we learn from international practice? *European Journal of Teacher Education*, 40(3), 291–309. https://doi.org/10.1080/02619768.2017.1315399.

Davies, B., & Davies, B. J. (2011). The nature and dimensions of strategic leadership. In N. Preedy, N. Bennett, & C. Wise (Eds.), *Educational leadership: Context, strategy and collaboration* (pp. 83–95). Sage.

Education Bureau. (2008). *Catering for student differences – Index for inclusion*. https://www.edb.gov.hk/attachment/en/edu-system/special/policy-and-initiatives/indicators-082008_e.pdf

Fennes, H., & Hapgood, K. (1997). *Intercultural learning in the classroom*. Cassell.

Gaudart, H. (1998). Interculturalism in education: A Malaysian perspective. In K. Cushner (Ed.), *International perspectives on intercultural education* (pp. 71–89). Routledge.

Goodwin, A. L. (2017). Who is in the classroom now? Teacher preparation and the education of immigrant children. *Educational Studies*, 53(5), 433–449. https://doi.org/10.1080/00131946.2016.1261028.

Grossman, P., & McDonald, M. (2008). Back to the future: Directions for research in teaching and teacher education. *American Educational Research Journal*, 45(1), 184–205. https://doi.org/10.3102%2F0002831207312906.

Hook, V. C. W. (2000). *Preparing teachers for the diverse classroom: A developmental model of intercultural sensitivity*. https://eric.ed.gov/?id=ED470878

Kerr, J., & Andreotti, V. (2019). Crossing borders in initial teacher education: Mapping dispositions to diversity and inequity. *Race Ethnicity and Education*, 22(5), 647–665. http://doi.org/10.1080/13613324.2017.1395326.

Lachat, M. A. (1999). *What policymakers and school administrators need to know about assessment reform for English language learners*. Northeast and Island Regional Educational Laboratory at Brown University.

Lancaster, J., & Bain, A. (2019). Designing university courses to improve preservice teachers' pedagogical content knowledge of evidence-based inclusive practice. *Australian Journal of Teacher Education, 44*(2). http://dx.doi.org/10.14221/ajte.2018v44n2.4

Loh, K. Y., & Hung, O. Y. (2020). *A study on the challenges faced by mainstream schools in educating ethnic minorities in Hong Kong*. https://www.eoc.org.hk/en/policy-advocacy-and-research/research-reports/2020-4

OECD. (2008). *Policy brief: Ten steps to equity in education*. http://www.oecd.org/education/school/39989494.pdf

Organisation for Economic Co-operation and Development. (2010). OECD Reviews of Migrant Education Closing the Gap for Immigrant Students: Policies, Practice and Performance. OECD Publication.

OECD. (2012). *No more failures: Ten steps to equity in education*. https://www.oecd.org/education/school/45179151.pdf

Oxfam Hong Kong. (2019). *The research report on the non-Chinese speaking kindergarteners learning Chinese in Hong Kong: Situation and support measures*. https://www.oxfam.org.hk/tc/f/news_and_publication/44611/%28English%29%20Report%20-%20teachers%20survey%20-Summary.pdf

Simon, F., Małgorzata, K., & Beatriz, P. O. N. T. (2007). *Education and training policy no more failures ten steps to equity in education: Ten steps to equity in education*. OECD Publishing.

Sleeter, C. (2008). Equity, democracy, and neoliberal assaults on teacher education. *Teaching and Teacher Education, 24*(8), 1947–1957. https://doi.org/10.1016/j.tate.2008.04.003.

Thomas, G. (2013). A review of thinking and research about inclusive education policy, with suggestions for a new kind of inclusive thinking. *British Educational Research Journal, 39*(3), 473–490. https://doi.org/10.1080/01411926.2011.652070.

Wassell, B. A., Kerrigan, M. R., & Hawrylak, M. F. (2018). Teacher educators in a changing Spain: Examining beliefs about diversity in teacher preparation. *Teaching and Teacher Education, 69*, 223–233. https://doi.org/10.1016/j.tate.2017.10.004

13 Conclusion

In an equitable society, policies for educational equity and social inclusion should be prioritised to promote internal wellness and positive engagement of young people in Hong Kong in the face of the changing student demographic landscape. Drawing on the voices of secondary students, both Hong Kong-born and foreign-born, Chinese and non-Chinese, we offer a window into their struggles, aspirations, and pathways towards engagement with schooling, community, and society. The low-income Chinese immigrant and ethnic minority South/Southeast Asian adolescents represent the major marginalised and silenced groups in society. Their voices are usually ignored or played down by mainstream teachers within the highly regimented education system with its focus on test-scores. Yet, this book has amplified their voices, examining their perspectives on both barriers to and the enablers of process that increase their wellness, connectedness, and academic success at individual, systemic, and societal levels. Inclusion and equity of education are universal values celebrated and addressed by all educational institutions. The question is, how can this be realised in the local school context? Reflection on their educational trajectories results in an alarming awareness that a generation of human capital will be wasted if the talents of these multicultural youth are under-cultivated by school personnel and policymakers. There is a need to raise public awareness, as they deserve a greater public space to let their voices be heard. The power of their voices can stimulate affirmative education measures, challenge the status quo, and transform education.

The call to make Hong Kong schools responsive to equity in terms of both policy and practice, as well as student diversity, has received renewed attention. With the ever-growing number of ethnic Chinese and ethnic minority students from diverse cultural backgrounds and the changing societal values in recognising human diversity and talent development, more people are aware of the issues of multiculturalism in the local education system. So far, the voices mainly come from NGOs such as Hong Kong Unison, Oxfam Hong Kong, and a few researchers from ethnic minority backgrounds. Teachers are charged with marginalising them in their teaching by ignoring their unmet learning needs. When teachers fail to relate to students from a different culture or family heritage, they naturally adopt an assimilation approach to make all students one with those in

DOI: 10.4324/9780429439315-13

the mainstream. Such a tendency is reinforced by a standard-oriented education system and a Hong Kong-centric teaching mentality. Discrimination is a shared experience of both the Chinese immigrant and ethnic minority students live in the society they called home, only to a varying degree. This is a disturbing fact, and it reflects the perception of the oppressed as they make frequent references to the discriminative and segregated nature of society. Even schooling has often curbed their ambition to excel. This brings to the question of how talent development and promoting an equitable and inclusive society can bear for people from all walks of life. To build a society of fairness, equity, and harmony in a post-conflict society, deliberated efforts are desired to enable students from diverse cultural, linguistic, and religious backgrounds to be successful in the education system. It is against this background that this book was initiated to respond to the disappointing situation. It is research-based, grounded in spiritual well-being and engagement theories, to address the connectedness and global well-being of young people of diverse backgrounds in the city, and more widely, following the 2019 social unrest and the unprecedented spread of the novel coronavirus (COVID-19) epidemic. It has not been a small task to compose this book, and there are limitations. While it is easy to discuss the deficits in the senior secondary education system and recommend what teachers and educators can do better by improving the system, the value-added dimension of education deserves more attention (Mfume, 2019).

Looking ahead – anchoring students from diverse cultural backgrounds

There are clear policy implications drawn from the empirical cases in this book. Financial assistance and support can make a remarkable difference to offset the socio-economic inequalities in secondary and PSE. All these findings underscore an urgent need for closing the equity gaps in PSE and indicate a requirement for holistic and collaborative institutional research that draws upon the synergies of different investigators to generate a big dataset and a comprehensive understanding of the current situation in local higher education.

A school is a place to cultivate every student's potential and aspiration for life. In undertaking this task, teachers must make classroom teaching beneficial for all and avoid a learning process that promotes only the elite few. Teaching for social justice is of paramount concern in education across the globe. At the time of writing this concluding chapter, the HKSAR is taking a historic step forward in accelerating its amalgamation with the cities of the Greater Bay Area of China (Guo, 2021). The vision of driving the Greater Bay Area as a global innovation and technology hub and exciting opportunities for innovation in the Greater Bay Area hinges on strategic talent development and management across all Chinese cities. Such societal and political development gives new meaning and scope to education and, especially, to multicultural teacher education. There is a greater need than ever for current and future teachers to further enhance an inclusive, multicultural, and equitable society for microcultural Chinese and multicultural NCS student groups within the Chinese national macroculture. At the very least, schooling should aim to optimise the educational opportunities for both privileged and underprivileged students throughout the whole process of formal education.

References

Guo, S. (2021). *Guangdong-Hong Kong-Macao Greater Bay Area: Planning and global positioning*. World Scientific.

Mfume, T. B. (2019). *The college completion glass – Half-full or half-empty?* Rowan & Littlefield.

Index

Note: Page numbers in **bold** represent tables; page numbers in *italics* represent figures

academic achievement/success 66, 176, 177–178
academic transitions 178
acculturation 25–26, 63, 65; challenge of CIS 76–77; strategies 119
adolescents: self-identity construction 28; spiritual health 38
Adserias, R. 178
agency: and CIS and NCS civic participation 74–75; and knowledge gap 75–76
Álvarez-Rivadulla, M. J. 121
anti-China sentiments 90
Appadurai, A. 106
aspiration 1, 2, 5, 24, 45–46, 56, 96–97, 106, 109, 118, 120–121, 132–133, 137–149, 153, 165, 176, 178
assimilation, of education system 174

Baroutsis, A. 29
Basic Law Article 23 81
Bates, G. 36
Belmont, M. J. 71
belongingness: CBS 114–115; defined 5; education and 5–6
Bennett, J. 26, 27, 28
bicultural constructivists 27
bicultural identity 26
Bigatti, S. M. 36
biliteracy 6
Blumenfeld, P. C. 46
Bourdieu, P. 9, 101, 147
Bowles, A. 11
Briones, E. 25

Cadaret, M. C. 179
Cantonese 9–10, 21, 53, 72

career identity 178–179
Census and Statistics Department 13, 19, 20, 21, 22, 24–25, 120
Cheuk, M. 119
child labour 4
child poverty 25
Chinese Hong Konger 89
Chinese immigrants 19, 20, **20**; youth in North America 45
Chinese immigrant students (CIS) 6–9, 20–21, **20**, 27–28, 39, 53; acculturation challenge of 76–77; attitudes and choices of 158–159; career identity 179; civic engagement of 70–72; civic identity construction 92–93; civic knowledge among 75–76; civic participation 73–75; educational inclusion 160–161; ethnic identities, inclusion and rejection 97–99; home and identity construction among 88–89; Hong Kong identity 89; hybrid identity 90–91; immigration process for 66; impacts of home values 77–79; narratives 61–65; parents of 87; political participation 95–96; portraits of 87–99; real issues of motivation 164–165; in schools and beyond 66; and school support 161–164; stereotyped perceptions of 80; transformative citizenship education 81–82
Chinese Language 6–7, 8, 119–120, 163; competence in 9; framework for NCS students 12–13; learning 121, 125; medium of instruction 10
Chinese Language Curriculum Second Language Learning Framework 12

Chinese national identity 71
Chineseness 90–91
Chowdry, H. 178
citizenship 69–70; sustainable 179–180; transformative education 81–82
civic engagement 69, 129–131; active, teaching for 179–180; of CIS/NCS students 70–72; high expected 93–96; school engagement and 71
civic participation 69, 73
Clayton, J. 121
co-ethnic socialisation 160
collective family culture 72–73
collectivism 72–73
competitive examination-oriented culture 156
comprehensive social security assistance (CSSA) scheme 19
Confucianism 173
connectedness 1, 8, 24, 25, 27, 29, 30, 36, 37, 47, 73, 98, 120, 173, 180, 195, 203
Corredor, J. 121
COVID-19 pandemic 9, 167, 198; Hong Kong Diploma of Secondary Education during 167–168
Crawford, C. 178
cross-boundary students (CBS) 22–23, 27, 65, 71; aspiring *vs.* disillusion 110–111; belongings 114–115; cases of 106; disconnectedness 111–112; education 101–103; families 103, 105–106; immigrant paradox and resilience in 108–110; as outperformers 106; portraits of 103, **104**; as school lovers 106–108; self-identity 112–114
Crozier, G. 121
cultural identity: construction of 25–26; Hong Kong context of 27–28
Cultural Revolution (1966–1967) 81
culture: collective family 72–73; defined 196; as hurdle for NCS students 118; school 173–174
curriculum, school 177–180

Davis, R. F. III 128
Dearden, L. 178
digital learning 9
Diploma of Secondary Education (DSE) *see* Hong Kong Diploma of Secondary Education (HKDSE) examination
disconnectedness, cross-boundary students 111–112, 114–115

Dobson, A. 11
doubly non-permanent residents (DNR) CBS 22–23

education 9, 53–54; and belongingness 5–6; civic 70; for cross-boundary students 101–103; equity in *see* equity, in education; exclusion 118; higher, aspirations for 120–121; investment in 6; and life chances 5; and life satisfaction 44–47; post-secondary, expansion of 10–11; secondary *see* secondary education; system 155–157; for underprivileged students 24–25; and well-being 5–6
educational equity *see* equity, in education
educational gaps 13–14
educational inclusion 118, 195
Education Bureau (EDB) 9, 13, 120, 148, 152
Education 2030 Framework for Action 3
e-Learning 9
Elmore, G. M. 71
empowerment, students 30
English as the MOI (EMI) 10, 146
English Language 21
equality in educational practice 4–5
equitable access 180–181
equity, in education 4–5; fostering 185–186; global popularisation of 3–4; inclusion towards 195; issues 190–192; language and 6–9; teachers' perceptions of 188; teaching for 186–187; theorising 188–190
Esquivel, G. B. 38
ethnic Chinese 70
ethnic identity 80, 81–82, 86–87, 97–99
ethnic minorities 19–20, 21, 23, 24–25, 27, 28, 29, 30, 44, 46, 54, 61, 70, 71, 73, 81, 118, 119, 120, 125, 129, 130, 131, 133, 157, 163, 165, 174, 176, 193–194, 202, 203
ethnic minority students 24, 174; challenges in schooling for 120–121; characteristics of 185; profiles of 20
ethnorelativism 196
exclusion, education 118

fairness 4
family 54; capital, and language 9; collective family culture 72–73; cross-boundary students 103, 105–106

Fennes, H. 193
Finn, J. D. 71
Fisher, J. W. 36
Fisher, R. 11
Fong, B. C. 72
Fredricks, J. A. 46
fresher students, in tertiary education 138–147
friendship 53–54

Gaudart, H. 187
gender difference 43
General Certificate of Education (GCE) 13, 120
General Certificate of Secondary Education (GCSE) 13
glass ceiling effect 178
globalisation 2, 70, 151
Gomez, R. 36
Goodman, A. 178
Goodwin, A. L. 195
Gove, M. 9
Greater Bay Area (GBA) 99, 158, 174, 203
Grossman, P. 186
Guide on Life Planning Education and Career Guidance for Secondary Schools (Education Bureau) 179

Han Chinese 81
Hapgood, K. 193
Hartung, P. J. 179
high-stakes examination 96, 147, 167, 187
higher education, aspirations for 120–121
home factors, as source of inequality 4–5
home values 77–79
Hong Kong: context of cultural identity 27–28; demographics 19–20, **20**
Hong Kong Diploma of Secondary Education (HKDSE) examination 6, 13, 125, 137–138, 167–168
Hong Kong identity 58, 72, 86, 89, 130
Hong Kong mainstream students (HKMS) 13, 39, 109
Hong Kong Racial Discrimination Ordinance, 2008 6
Hong Kong Special Administrative Region (HKSAR) 9, 19, 22–23, 86–87, 99, 101, 105, 108, 114, 203
Hong Konger 19, 58, 70, 72, 75, 76, 86, 88, 89, 90, 91, 97, 103, 112, 113, 131

host society 26, 72, 77, 80, 82, 91, 92, 119, 128, 129, 130, 131–133
Huang, G. H. 9
Huebner, E. S. 71
hybrid identity 90–92

identity: bicultural 26; construction among CIS 88–89; construction of 25–26; ethnic 80, 81–82, 86–87; hybrid 90–92; religious 27, 131–132; self-identity 28–30
immigrant paradox 108–110
immigrants 53, 174; characteristics of 185; Chinese 19, 20, **20** *see also* Chinese immigrant students (CIS); and socio-economic disadvantage 167–172; youth 25–26
"in-between" identity 80
inclusion 4, 92–96; educational 118, 195
inclusive education policy 193
inequality: in educational outcomes 4–5; home factors as source of 4–5; social 4
initial teacher education (ITE) 185; discussion and recommendations for 192; implications for 193–194, **194**
intercultural competence, of teachers 197–198
intercultural sensitivity 196
International General Certificate of Secondary Education (IGCSE) 13, 120

Jackson, J. 178
Japan 97
Joint University Programmes Admissions System (JUPAS) 121
justice 4

Kahu, E. R. 6
Kelley, B. S. 38
Kiang, L. 128
Kim, S. 38
Kliewer, W. 37
knowledge gap, agency and 75–76
Kwan, Y. K. 54

language: competence in 9–10; and equity 6–9; family capital and 9; standards for admission 12–13
Lareau, A 4, 88
law, spirituality and 64
leaders, teachers as 198
Legislative Council 23, 73, 75
Liberal Studies (LS) 72, 92, 98, 109

life chances, education and 5
life experiences, of fresher students 138–147
life satisfaction, spirituality and 37–38, 44–47
localism 72
Ludden, A. B. 37
Lundy, L. 29

Marginson, S 91
Mainland China 7, 86, 97, 98
Maldonado-Carreño, C. 121
marginalisation 80
McDonald, M. 186
McGregor, G. 29
Mcphail, R. 11
medium of instruction (MOI) 7; Chinese 10; English as 10
Miller, L. 38
Mills, M. 29
Milot, A. S. 37
monocultural defenders 27
Montgomery, M. J. 25
mother-tongue 9–10
motivation, student 8
Mplus (version 7) 40
multidimensional school engagement framework 46

narratives 53–57, 61–65, 138–147, 174, 176, 179, 180, 193
Nelson, K. 6
neoliberalism 148, 151, 161
No More Failures (OECD Report) 194
non-academic oriented students 156
Non-Chinese speaking (NCS) students 6–9, 10, 19–20, **20**, 21–23, 39, 53; adaptation in host society 131–133; attitudes and choices of 159; career identity 179; challenges in schooling 119–120; Chinese language framework for 12–13; Chinese language standards for 163; civic engagement 129–131; civic engagement of 70–72; civic knowledge among 75–76; civic participation 73–75; educational inclusion 160–161; ethnic culture as hurdle for 118; impacts of home values 77–79; involvement in school activities 128–129; parents as primary sources of support and inspiration 126–127; profiles, struggled with Chinese language proficiency 121, **122–124**; real issues of motivation 164–165; religious identity 131–132; school attendance rate 21; in schools and beyond 66; and school support 161–164; self-identification 129–131; teacher support 127–128; transformative citizenship education 81–82

O'Callaghan, E. 178
One Country, Two Systems rule 1, 6
One-Way Permit (OWP) 86–87
opportunity costs 158–159
Organization of Economic Cooperation and Development (OECD) 44
outperformers, cross-boundary students as 106
over-age placement 21

parents/parenting 45–46, 54–55; primary sources of NCS support and inspiration 126–127
Paris, A. H. 46
Park, G. C. 37
pedagogy 8, 23, 173, 185, 186, 189, 191, 193, 195, 198
personal identity 25
political participation 95–96
post-secondary education (PSE) 7, 10–11; construction of dream 157; earnings premiums associated with 138; language standards for admission to 12–13; pathways 125–126; preparation for 174–175; and school-based support 147–149; underprivileged youth approaching 151–165
post-secondary institutions (PSIs) 11
poverty **24**, 24–25, 137; child 25
prayer frequency 41–43, **42**
preparation for PSE 174–175
preservice teachers: dialogues with 188; suggested programme improvement for 191–192
Probit Regression 40
professional learning community (PLC) 198–199
Putonghua 7

Raftopoulos, M. 36
Reay, D. 121
Reichert, F. 70
rejection 76, 88, 90, 92–93, 95–96, 97–99
religion 39; engagement in 38

religious activities frequency 42, **42**
religious identity 27, 131–132
religiousness 37
resilience 96–97, 108–110, 169, 176, 177–178
Reutter, K. K. 36
Rosenstreich, D. 11
Rotter, J. 176

Sadowski, M. 108
schooling 53
schools: activities, NCS students involvement in 128–129; on boundary towns 101–103; culture 173–174; engagement 37, 71; and immigrant students 46–47; inclusion inside/outside 93–96; support 161–164
Schwartz, S. J. 25
SDG4 agenda 4, 6
secondary education: on exit of 151–152; senior 147–149; students, success and responsibilities of 152–155
self-belief 178
self-concept, student voices and 30
self-efficacy 7, 63
self-esteem 44–45; student voice and 30
self-formation 25
self-identity 28–30, 112–114, 129–131
self-motivation 162
self-reflective narratives, of fresher students 138–147
senior secondary education 3, 138, 142, 147, 148, 155, 164, 173, 180, 203
senior secondary students 1, 5, 96, 151, 154, 155, 161, 177, 179
sense of belonging 5, 47
significant others 175–176
Singapore 70
Skinner, E. A. 71
social-emotional competence 177
social inequality 4
socially disadvantaged students: risk of being double disadvantaged 167–172; teaching for robust understanding 172–173
socio-economic status (SES) 23; of South and Southeast Asians 25
South/Southeast Asians students (SAS) 21–22; CIS students 39; cultural identity of 27; NCS students 39, 80; religious 43; socio-economic status of 25; spiritual health and life satisfaction 37; working poverty 24, **24**

Special Administrative Region (SAR) 6, 8, 19, 72, 86
special educational needs (SEN) students 11, 193
Spires, R. W. 137
Spiritual Health and Life Orientation Measure (SHALOM) 36, 39
spirituality 36–38, 39, 46, 57–61; defined 36; impact of 36; as internal experiences 37; and law 64; and life satisfaction 37–38, 44–47; questions regarding 67
spiritual well-being 38–43
S6 students 167, 169
student empowerment 30
student engagement 5
student motivation 8
student voices 28–30, 173, 174
successful school life 149
Superstition 64
Sustainable Development Goals (SDGs) 4

Taiwan 97
teachers: initial teacher education *see* initial teacher education (ITE); intercultural competence 197–198; as leaders in change for equitable learning 198; perceptions of equity 188; support, to NCS students 127–128
tertiary education 6, 57, 58, 106, 115, 137, 138–147
Three-Tired Support Model of Inclusion 193
Torney-Purta, J. 70, 96
transcendental well-being (TWB) 38, 39–43; indirect effect of prayer frequency on 42, **42**; path analysis on factors affecting 40; regression coefficients on **41**
transformative citizenship education 81–82
transition barriers 11–13
trilingualism 6

Umbrella Movement 81
underprivileged students, education for 24–25
United Nations Convention on the Rights of the Child 3, 29
University Grant Commission (UGC) 12, 120, 125, 158
UNESCO 2, 3, 12, 185

Vignoles, A. 178
vision, for educational inclusion 199–200
Voelkl, K. 5

Waterman, A. S. 129
well-being 5–6, 36, 46–47; promoting 176–177; questions regarding 66–67; spiritual 38–43, 47
wellness 36–38, 44, 151–165
Williams, D. 178
Wright, A. W. 37

Xu, C. L. 102, 108

Yendork, J. S. 37
youth: challenges of 137–138; identity construction 25–26; impacts of spirituality 36–38; importance of 2–3; perception of TWB 42; and sustainable global development 179–180; underprivileged, approaching post-secondary education and career 151–165; wellness 36
Yuen, Y. M. C. 118